GREAT
AMERICAN
DOCUMENTS

GREAT
AMERICAN
DOCUMENTS

Quercus

Contents

Introduction

Significant documents form part of the heritage of many states but those of the United States of America have a peculiarly strong historical, cultural, and emotional appeal. The documents that record the creation of the nation, and its earliest constitutional decisions—the Declaration of Independence, the Constitution, and the Bill of Rights—stand at the very core of what it is to be American, and seem destined always to do so.

These iconic documents are collected here with a wide variety of others that chronicle the growth and development of modern America. Legislative acts and amendments to the Constitution are naturally prominent, but there are many less solemn yet no less important documents that demand inclusion.

Some of the documents in this book do not have the gravity of signed, sealed parchment, yet provide evidence of some of the most important events in U.S. history. The Great Seal, a newspaper headline recording the shock of the Wall Street crash of 1929, audio tapes from the White House about the Watergate scandal, a missing persons notice board following the atrocities of 9/11—none of these is a document in the strictest sense of the word, yet each in its own way captures events, concepts, and feelings that are now deeply embedded in the American psyche.

In fact, to "document" the full scope and diversity of the American experience we have to go beyond conventional definitions of the term. The United States is still a young country and its history sometimes appears to be on fast-forward, coinciding as it does with the most rapid phase of human technological development ever seen. In less than 280 years, the documentary evidence of our nation has progressed from signing the death warrant of a woman accused of witchcraft to devising a plaque to be placed on the Moon. What better way to illustrate such progress than with a telegram, a headline, a manufacturer's blueprint, or an astronaut's calling card left on another world?

This collection gives the reader the rare opportunity to scrutinize original source material. Wherever practicable, the documents are reproduced in their entirety with facsimile photographs of the original. How many of us have actually read the whole text of the Constitution? How many of us know exactly what it was Nixon said to Haldeman that became the "smoking gun" leading to his downfall? History is often presented to the general reader through the filter of the historian, summarized, analyzed, and even occasionally sanitized. Here, with a commentary that places each document in context, readers can consider the critical words or images for themselves.

This is the story of the United States documented through a variety of media, recounting political and social watersheds, economic and environmental landmarks, and events both tragic and triumphant. They narrate America's story like a series of stills taken from a motion picture capturing the nation's extraordinarily rapid development from vulnerable trading colony to global superpower.

CHRISTOPHER COLUMBUS (1451–1506), NAVIGATOR AND
EXPLORER, AT THE COURT OF FERDINAND AND ISABELLA

Letter from

CHRISTOPHER COLUMBUS

to Ferdinand and Isabella of Spain

CONCERNING THE COLONIZATION AND
COMMERCE OF HISPANIOLA

MARCH 14, 1493

CHRISTOPHER COLUMBUS was a man with strong self-belief. For years he sought the patronage of the king and queen of Spain to embark on his voyage of exploration—and when he at last received it, he insisted that he be appointed viceroy of any new lands he discovered. He also demanded ten percent of all the gold, spices, and trade he found. When he made landfall in the West Indies, Columbus was convinced that he had reached Asia—his planned destination. Columbus remained unaware of the real significance of his discovery: it was the precious metals of the New World that fueled the rise of European capitalism—and the gradual shifting of political and economic power from the Mediterranean to the lands fronting the Atlantic.

■ *Christopher Columbus first went to sea as a boy of ten. He made four separate voyages to the New World between 1492 and 1502, staying some years on the islands he discovered, and surviving shipwreck and rebellion. He was later reprimanded for the harshness of his conduct as "Governor of the Indies" and removed from office.*

Although Christopher Columbus died believing that by voyaging westwards from Spain he had reached Japan and China, he had actually come across the West Indies and South and Central America. Before his voyage, it was thought that the ocean between Europe and Asia was uninterrupted, and that the world was made up of three continents: Europe, Asia, and Africa. In this letter of 1493 to his patrons, Ferdinand and Isabella of Spain, Columbus makes suggestions that were later to become Spanish colonial policy for exploiting the New World (as the previously unknown continent was called, despite already being inhabited by indigenous peoples).

Born in 1451, the son of an Italian weaver, Columbus began his seafaring career at the age of 14. In 1476, while sailing from the Mediterranean to the Atlantic Ocean, he was shipwrecked off the Portuguese coast and only survived by clinging to wreckage and swimming ashore. He settled in Lisbon, at that time a magnet for explorers, merchants, and adventurers. Unusual vegetation was frequently washed ashore, and Columbus concluded that it must come from Asia. Having studied widely, he believed that it would be possible to find a nautical route between Europe and the spice-rich islands of the East Indies, the archipelago now known as Indonesia, off the southeastern shores of Asia.

Unable to persuade the king of Portugal to support his plans, Columbus also failed to convince the rulers of England and France. He was received at court by Isabella and Ferdinand of Spain in 1486, but they were preoccupied with reconquering the Moorish kingdom of Granada, the last remaining Muslim stronghold in Spain. Eventually Granada was regained, and Ferdinand and Isabella, keen to convert native populations to Christianity and tempted by the promise of untold wealth, offered Columbus three small ships – the *Niña*, the *Pinta*, and the *Santa Maria*. So, finally, with a crew of 90, Columbus left Palos in southwest Spain on August 3, 1492.

COLUMBUS DAY

Columbus Day is celebrated on October 12 every year by many countries in the Americas, commemorating Columbus's arrival in the New World on that date in 1492. In 1937 it was established as a national holiday in the United States by President Franklin D. Roosevelt. However, the state of Minnesota does not observe Columbus Day. Minnesotans, many of whom are of Scandinavian descent, emphasize that the Vikings established a settlement in Newfoundland around 500 years before Columbus arrived in the New World. Other groups oppose Columbus Day because of the treatment of the Native American peoples by Spanish conquistadors.

After more than a month at sea and with no sight of land, Columbus's crews became mutinous. However, disaster was averted by landfall at a small island in what is now the Bahamas. With the help of a local Arawak guide, Columbus explored nearby islands. He believed that he had found Japan—in fact, he had found Cuba and Hispaniola. He left 39 men at the settlement of La Navidad on Hispaniola (which he called Española, or "little Spain"). After a very dangerous return journey, Columbus returned in triumph to Spain.

On his second voyage the following year, Columbus surveyed almost the entire Caribbean archipelago. The colony at La Navidad had been destroyed, so Columbus set up a new colony, which he named Isabella, on the north coast of Hispaniola.

On a third voyage, starting in 1498, Columbus reached the South American mainland before returning in disgrace because of rebellions against his rule in Hispaniola. He did not actually see mainland North America during any of his voyages.

Columbus gradually lost royal favor, and after his fourth voyage (1502–04), during which he sailed along the Central American coast, he returned to Spain, where he spent his last lonely years. When he died in 1506 he still stubbornly believed that he had found a new route to the East. What he had in fact done was to lay the foundations for something with far greater implications: the Spanish empire in the Americas.

Columbus's letter to Ferdinand and Isabella of Spain, written in 1493 and describing his discoveries in the New World, provides a fascinating record of the early inhabitants of the Bahamas, Cuba, Haiti, and the Dominican Republic. The letter was widely published across Western Europe: there were over 16 different editions produced between 1493 and 1497, of which 80 copies have survived to this day.

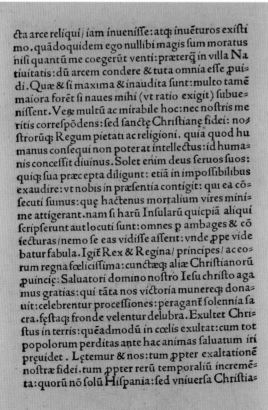

Within a few decades of Columbus's death, the Spanish conquistador Hernán Cortés had destroyed the Aztecs of Mexico, Francisco Pizarro had done the same to the Incas of Peru, and Spain had established a vast empire in the Americas that was to last for 300 years. The Spanish used enslaved native people to work in their mines and farms, and when supplies of native slaves became exhausted they looked further afield. Thus Columbus's discovery led to the growth of the European slave trade, in which millions of Africans were transported across the Atlantic to work in the plantations of the New World. The first shipload of African slaves landed in the West Indies before Columbus's last voyage, and this dreadful trade would continue for 350 years.

Transcript of COLUMBUS'S LETTER TO FERDINAND AND ISABELLA

'This island is to be desired and is very desirable, and not to be despised; in which, although as I have said, I solemnly took possession of all the others for our most invincible king, and their government is entirely committed to the said king, yet I especially took possession of a certain large town, in a very convenient location, and adapted to all kinds of gain and commerce, to which we give the name of our Lord of the Nativity. And I commanded a fort to be built there forthwith, which must be completed by this time; in which I left as many men as seemed necessary, with all kinds of arms, and plenty of food for more than a year. Likewise one caravel, and for the construction of others men skilled in this trade and in other professions; and also the extraordinary good will and friendship of the king of this island toward us. For those people are very amiable and kind, to such a degree that the said king gloried in calling me his brother. And if they should change their minds, and should wish to hurt those who remained in the fort, they would not be able, because they lack weapons, they go naked, and are too cowardly . . .

"I found no monstrosities among them, as very many supposed, but men of great reverence, and friendly. Nor are they black like the Ethiopians."

In all these islands, as I have understood, each man is content with only one wife, except the princes or kings, who are permitted to have 20. The women appear to work more than the men. I was not able to find out surely whether they have individual property, for I saw that one man had the duty of distributing to the others, especially refreshments, food, and things of that kind. I found no monstrosities among them, as very many supposed, but men of great reverence, and friendly. Nor are they black like the Ethiopians. They have straight hair, hanging down. They do not remain where the solar rays send out the heat, for the strength of the sun is very great here, because it is distant from the equinoctial line, as it seems, only 26 degrees . . .

Finally, that I may compress in a few words the brief account of our departure and quick return, and the gain, I promise this, that if I am supported by our most invincible sovereigns with a little of their help, as much gold can be supplied as they will need, indeed as much of spices, of cotton, of mastic gum (which is only found in Chios), also as much of aloes wood, and as many slaves for the navy, as their Majesties will wish to demand. Likewise rhubarb and other kinds of spices, which I suppose these men whom I left in the said fort have already found, and will continue to find; since I remained in no place longer than the winds forced me, except in the town of the Nativity, while I provided for the building of the fort, and for the safety of all. Which things, although they are very great and remarkable, yet they would have been much greater, if I had been aided by as many ships as the occasion required.

Truly great and wonderful is this, and not corresponding to our merits, but to the holy Christian religion, and to the piety and religion of our sovereigns, because what the human understanding could not attain, that the divine will has granted to human efforts. For God is wont to listen to his servants who love his precepts, even in impossibilities, as has happened to us on the present occasion, who have attained that which hitherto mortal men have never reached. For if anyone has written or said anything about these islands, it was all with obscurities and conjectures; no one claims that he had seen them; from which they seemed like fables. Therefore let the king and queen, the princes and their most fortunate kingdoms, and all other countries of Christendom give thanks to our Lord and Savior Jesus Christ, who has bestowed upon us so great a victory and gift. Let religious processions be solemnized; let sacred festivals be given; let the churches be covered with festive garlands. Let Christ rejoice on earth, as he rejoices in heaven, when he foresees coming to salvation so many souls of people hitherto lost. Let us be glad also, as well on account of the exaltation of our faith, as on account of the increase of our temporal affairs, of which not only Spain, but universal Christendom will be partaker. These things that have been done are thus briefly related. Farewell.

Lisbon, the day before the Ides of March.
Christopher Columbus, Admiral of the Ocean Fleet.

> "I promise this, that if I am supported by our most invincible sovereigns with a little of their help, as much gold can be supplied as they will need."

The Signing of the Mayflower Compact,
by Edward Percy Moran (1862–1935)

The

MAYFLOWER COMPACT

FIRST GOVERNING DOCUMENT OF THE
PLYMOUTH COLONY, MASSACHUSETTS

NOVEMBER 21, 1620

ALTHOUGH BACKED by the London Company, which had been granted permission by King James I of England to settle in Virginia, the pilgrims on the *Mayflower* were forced off course by bad weather and actually dropped anchor at Cape Cod, Massachusetts, outside the Company's jurisdiction. The majority of voyagers were religious dissenters known as Separatists. All on board were aware that previous settlements had failed through weak leadership. Before landing, the leaders drew up the Mayflower Compact to counter fears that, once landed, the non-Separatists in the group would not adhere to the law in this ungoverned area of the New World. The Compact was the first of several similar agreements used by religious groups settling in New England, and remained the Plymouth Colony's basis for government until 1691, when the colony was subsumed into Massachusetts.

The Mayflower Compact was signed aboard the Mayflower *on November 21, 1620 by the ship's 41 free adult men. Edward Percy Moran (1862–1935), an artist who specialized in colonial and historical subjects, recreated the scene in a famous painting (1900), which now hangs in the Plymouth Museum.*

Unlike some Puritan groups, Separatists had irreconcilable differences with the Church of England, and wanted their worship to be governed at the congregational level, rather then by a central church authority. The Mayflower Compact, in style very similar to a Separatist church covenant, aimed to establish a governing authority of majority rule. The 41 signatories formed a "civil body politic," pledging to obey its laws and vowing allegiance to the King. Later patents, granted in 1621 and 1630, gave the pilgrims proper legal status.

The Plymouth Colony was to become the first permanent colonial settlement in New England, but this seemed far from likely during its first winter. Half of the settlers died from disease, malnutrition, and lack of effective shelter. The colonists do not appear to have been adequately prepared for life in a new land: one pilgrim brought to the New World 126 pairs of shoes and 13 pairs of boots, but it seems that no one thought to bring a plow, horse, cow, or even a fishing line.

The hardships of the *Mayflower's* voyage and the settlers' first winter were vividly described in the *History of Plymouth Plantation, 1620–47* by William Bradford, one of the group's leaders. Bradford, a zealous Puritan from the age of 12, helped organize the journey, and was one of the signatories of the Compact. In 1621 he became the second governor of the settlement, and was re-elected 30 times. He discouraged sectarianism, welcoming all Separatist groups to New England, and found ways of involving non-believers in the life of the colony.

Among the many other signatories who went on to play significant roles in the new colony were John Carver, Myles Standish, and a crewmember, John Alden, who decided to remain with the settlers rather than return when the *Mayflower* left for England in April 1621. John Carver became the first governor of the colony, and before his death in 1621, he negotiated a treaty with local Native Americans that helped maintain peace for many years. Myles Standish

BRAVE NEW WORLD

The voyage and first months of settlement took their toll on the pilgrims. A crewmember and passenger died at sea, although one child was born on the journey. However, by March 1621, only 50 of the original 102 pilgrims, and half the Mayflower's *crew, had survived their first winter in the New World.*

joined the settlers as military adviser, learned the local language, led an expedition to protect a neighboring settlement from a Native American attack, and co-founded the town of Duxbury. Alden and Standish became known as arbitrators of disputes between Native Americans and settlers.

Gradually the settlers learned to farm the land and to trap beavers, thanks in part to the help of a Native American interpreter and guide, Squanto, who had lived in England after escaping from slavery in Spain and then returned to New England in 1619. Speaking fluent English, Squanto was used as an emissary by Governor William Bradford, and acted as an interpreter for Edward Winslow (another future governor) during negotiations with other Native American groups. Help provided by Native Americans was critical in ensuring that the pilgrims survived the first difficult years. Ironically, this friendly contact brought dire consequences, as large numbers of Native Americans died of diseases brought by the Europeans, such as smallpox.

Although mainly motivated by a desire to establish a godly society, the pilgrims also needed to trade in order to repay the London Company for funding the establishment of the colony. Lacking good harbors or large amounts of fertile land, the colonists eventually moved away from their original ethos of communal labor, and established instead a system of small private holdings.

Finally, in 1627, eight pilgrim leaders, including John Alden, took on the settlement's obligations to their investors in return for a six-year monopoly of the fur trade and offshore fishing. In time, the Plymouth plantation was overshadowed by a later Puritan influx into Massachusetts in the 1630s under John Winthrop. In 1643 the Plymouth plantation joined the New England Confederation, and was subsumed into Massachusetts in 1691.

Although ultimately the pilgrims were not especially significant in the later history of New England, they became a hugely potent symbol, and it is the Plymouth settlers' first harvest in 1621 that is remembered today in the annual feast of Thanksgiving.

The Mayflower Compact—signed in November 1620 on board the ship that brought the Pilgrim Fathers from Plymouth, England, to the New World—provided a social contract whereby the settlers, for the sake of survival, agreed to observe the laws set down by the colony's government. In return, the government derived its power from the consent of the settlers.

Transcript of THE MAYFLOWER COMPACT

‘In yᵉ name of God Amen· We whose names are vnderwriten,
the loyall subjects of our dread soueraigne Lord King James
by yᵉ grace of God, of great Britaine, franc, & Ireland king,
defender of yᵉ faith, &c
Haueing vndertaken, for yᵉ glorie of God, and aduancemente
of yᵉ christian faith and honour of our king & countrie, a voyage to
plant yᵉ first colonie in yᵉ Northerne parts of Virginia· doe
by these presents solemnly & mutualy in yᵉ presence of God, and
one of another, couenant, & combine our selues togeather into a
ciuill body politick; for our better ordering, & preseruation & furtherance of yᵉ ends aforesaid; and by vertue hearof, to enacte,
constitute, and frame shuch just & equall lawes, ordinances,
Acts, constitutions, & offices, from time to time, as shall be thought
most meete & conuenient for yᵉ generall good of yᵉ colonie: vnto
which we promise all due submission and obedience. In witnes
wherof we haue herevnder subscribed our names at Cap-
Codd yᵉ ·11· of Nouember, in yᵉ year of yᵉ raigne of our soueraigne
Lord king James of England, france, & Ireland yᵉ eighteenth
and of Scotland yᵉ fiftie fourth. Anᵒ: Dom ·1620·

∽◦⌇

In modern English:

In the name of God, amen. We whose names are underwritten, the loyal subjects of our dread sovereign lord King James, by the grace of God of Great Britain, France, and Ireland king, defender of the faith, etc.

Having undertaken, for the glory of God, and advancement of the Christian faith and honor of our king and country, a voyage to plant the first colony in the northern parts of Virginia, do by these presents solemnly and mutually in the presence of God, and one of another, covenant and combine ourselves together into a civil body politic, for our better ordering and preservation and furtherance of the ends aforesaid; and by virtue hereof to enact, constitute, and frame such just and equal laws, ordinances, acts, constitutions, and offices, from time to time, as shall be thought most meet and convenient for the general good of the colony, unto which we promise all due submission and obedience. In witness whereof we have hereunder subscribed our names at Cape Cod the 11th of November, in the year of the reign of our sovereign lord King James, of England, France, and Ireland the eighteenth, and of Scotland the fifty-fourth. Anno domini 1620.’

PORTRAIT OF JOHN WINTHROP (1587/8–1649),
BY CHARLES OSGOOD (1809–90)

A Model of

CHRISTIAN
CHARITY

SERMON GIVEN TO COLONISTS ON THEIR
DEPARTURE TO THE NEW WORLD

APRIL, 1630

THE SUCCESS of the Massachusetts Colony in New England—in contrast to other shorter-lived colonies of the time—owes much to the strong leadership of John Winthrop and his emphasis on group discipline. The son of a wealthy gentleman, and raised on a large country estate in Suffolk, England, Winthrop was born to lead. At 15 he studied law at Cambridge University, serving afterwards as a local magistrate and holding government office. For 20 years he lived a comfortable life as an English country squire, and had no interest in overseas colonization. His future was changed by an economic slump in the 1620s, and by the anti-Puritan policies instituted by King Charles I.

John Winthrop— puritan, lawyer and governor of the Massachusetts Bay Colony—married four times and fathered 16 children. His sons became successful traders rather than religious leaders, reflecting the changing nature of the Massachusetts Bay community.

As a result, Winthrop faced reduced income from his land, and lost his government position. A devout Puritan, he was also dismayed by reforms to the Church of England that he feared would lead to the restoration of Catholicism and invite divine retribution. He began to ally himself with other Puritans keen to leave England and establish a godly community in the New World.

In 1629 the Massachusetts Bay Company was granted a royal charter to plant a colony in New England. Winthrop joined the company and was soon elected its governor. By April 1630 a group of over 700 Puritans was ready to set sail, fortified by the belief that their new community was ordained by God. During their journey, Winthrop wrote and delivered his now-famous sermon, "A Model of Christian Charity," in which he described the colonization as a covenant with God, under which the new community would set an example to the world.

The fleet of 11 ships in which Winthrop and his followers sailed was the largest ever assembled to take English settlers abroad, and the enterprise was carefully planned and funded. However, during the voyage 200 passengers died, and soon after arrival on June 12, 1630, 100 decided to return to England. Of the remaining settlers, 400 stayed in Salem—the place where the fleet first arrived—while others moved on to Boston or other settlements.

Winthrop was re-elected governor a further 12 times, and was instrumental in establishing a network of small towns, each with their own church. He himself settled on a modest farm in Boston, much smaller than the estate he had owned in England.

By the early 1630s Winthrop was meeting opposition from some settlers who had begun to trade very profitably and were less committed to the good of the whole community. Religious disputes broke out and Winthrop struggled in his role as custodian of Puritan orthodoxy. Although widely respected, in 1634 he was criticized for opposing the formation of a

AN ABIDING IMAGE
Ronald Reagan, fortieth President of the United States, recalled Winthrop ("an early freedom man") and his "city on a hill" in his leaving address in 1989: "In my mind it was a tall, proud city built on rocks stronger than oceans, wind-swept, God-blessed, and teeming with people of all kinds living in harmony and peace, a city with free ports that hummed with commerce and creativity, and if there had to be city walls, the walls had doors and the doors were open to anyone with the will and the heart to get here. That's how I saw it and see it still."

representative assembly. Eventually, an accusation that Winthrop had exceeded his authority as a magistrate led to his impeachment, although he was acquitted after a three-month dispute about the charges. Despite this, Winthrop was for the most part held in high esteem until his death from natural causes aged 61.

The populations of the Massachusetts Bay Colony and its successors in Boston and Salem had great economic power, and grew to dominate the New England region. The Province of Massachusetts Bay was named for this community, when it subsumed Plymouth and other neighboring colonies in 1691–2.

John Winthrop's famous "city on a hill" sermon was delivered to more than 700 English Puritans before they crossed the Atlantic to colonize Massachusetts Bay. Using imagery from the Sermon on the Mount in St. Matthew's Gospel in the New Testament, it aimed to inspire its listeners to build a godly community as an example to the world.

Transcript of A MODEL OF CHRISTIAN CHARITY

'Now if the Lord shall please to hear us, and bring us in peace to the place we desire, then hath He ratified this covenant and sealed our commission, and will expect a strict performance of the articles contained in it; but if we shall neglect the observation of these articles which are the ends we have propounded, and, dissembling with our God, shall fall to embrace this present world and prosecute our carnal intentions, seeking great things for ourselves and our posterity, the Lord will surely break out in wrath against us, and be revenged of such a people, and make us know the price of the breach of such a covenant.

Now the only way to avoid this shipwreck, and to provide for our posterity, is to follow the counsel of Micah, to do justly, to love mercy, to walk humbly with our God. For this end, we must be knit together, in this work, as one man. We must entertain each other in brotherly affection. We must be willing to abridge ourselves of our superfluities, for the supply of others' necessities. We must uphold a familiar commerce together in all meekness, gentleness, patience and liberality. We must delight in each other; make others' conditions our own; rejoice together, mourn together, labor and suffer together, always having before our eyes our commission and community in the work, as members of the same body. So shall we keep the unity of the spirit in the bond of peace. The Lord will be our God, and delight to dwell among us, as His own people, and will command a blessing upon us in all our ways, so that we shall see much more of His wisdom, power, goodness and truth, than formerly we have been acquainted with. We shall find that the God of Israel is among us, when ten of us shall be able to resist a thousand of our enemies; when He shall make us a praise and glory that men shall say of succeeding plantations, "may the Lord make it like that of New England." For we must consider that we shall be as a city upon a hill. The eyes of all people are upon us. So that if we shall deal falsely with our God in this work we have undertaken, and so cause Him to withdraw His present help from us, we shall be made a story and a by-word through the world . . .

> "For we must consider that we shall be as a city upon a hill. The eyes of all people are upon us."

And to shut this discourse with that exhortation of Moses, that faithful servant of the Lord, in his last farewell to Israel, Deuteronomy 30: "Beloved, there is now set before us life and death, good and evil," in that we are commanded this day to love the Lord our God, and to love one another, to walk in his ways and to keep his Commandments and his ordinance and his laws, and the articles of our Covenant with Him, that we may live and be multiplied, and that the Lord our God may bless us in the land whither we go to possess it . . .

Therefore let us choose life, that we and our seed may live, by obeying His voice and cleaving to Him, for He is our life and our prosperity.'

EXAMINATION OF A WITCH BY TOMPKINS HARRISON MATTESON
(1813–84)

Death warrant of Bridget Bishop

The

SALEM WITCH TRIALS

MARCH–JUNE, 1692

By 1692 the growth of the Puritan community in the Massachusetts Bay Colony was leading to land disputes with both neighboring settlements and Native Americans. In January of that year, Wabanaki warriors carried out a brutal massacre of settlers in York, a coastal town in the north of the colony (now in Maine). Other factors contributed to a climate of general uncertainty: the colony had no charter or governor, and England was only beginning to settle down after the revolution of 1688, when the Catholic King James II had been overthrown by the Protestant William of Orange. Salem itself, soon to be in the grip of witchcraft hysteria, was torn by internal divisions over the choice of Samuel Parris as its first ordained minister.

Matteson's dramatic depiction of the examination of a witch for "the Devil's mark" was painted in 1853, a time that saw a resurgence of interest in the Salem Witch Trials.

Salem was a typical small town in the Massachusetts Bay Colony—a place where few secrets could be kept and gossip about neighbors was regarded as fact. Women and girls led restricted, domestic lives, subordinate to the men of the community. This was accepted as normal: women were not allowed to preach, and they were considered to have innately lustful natures. For the Puritans, the invisible world was as real as the visible world, which they constantly scanned for signs of God's favor or disfavor, as well as evidence of the Devil's power.

In the sixteenth and seventeenth centuries, European hysteria about witchcraft had led to thousands being executed as witches. The superstition had been carried to colonial America, and the Salem episode was its worst manifestation in the New World. The incident began when three young girls in the household of the Reverend Samuel Parris began to behave very strangely, throwing objects and making odd sounds, seemingly tormented by unseen weapons and voices. The girls were found to have attended meetings at which attempts had been made to foretell the future. After examination by a doctor, ministers, and magistrates, it was decided they had been bewitched.

In March 1692 Parris's black slave, Tituba, and two frail and eccentric older women who did not attend church, were accused of having bewitched the girls and were imprisoned. During April there were many arrests, and by the middle of May more than 60 people were awaiting trial for suspected witchcraft in prisons in Salem, Ipswich, Charlestown, Cambridge, and Boston.

None of these cases was heard until late May when the new royal Governor, Sir William Phipps, arrived and set up a court to try the prisoners. The jurors were all church members, and the defendants had no counsel to represent them. The main evidence presented was so-called "spectral evidence."

POSSESSION OR HYSTERIA?
Various explanations have been advanced for the symptoms shown by the three young girls whose strange behavior triggered the witchcraft obsession in Salem. Theories include mental illness, or hallucinations caused by eating mouldy rye bread, or Huntington's chorea, or a bird-borne form of encephalitis. However, the rapid end of the episode after Sir William Phipps's arrival, and the fact that the symptoms of illness were so contained, suggest a socio-psychological rather than physical cause.

If someone claiming to have been bewitched had a dream in which they saw the apparition or shape of the accused person, this was taken as admissible evidence, based on the theological argument that the Devil could not use a person's shape without permission. In these circumstances, defense was virtually impossible.

The accused could be found guilty of the charge of "afflicting with witchcraft" or "making an unlawful covenant with the Devil." In June, Bridget Bishop became the first person to be found guilty: she was executed by hanging. By September, there had been 19 more hangings. Convicted women were given temporary reprieves if they were pregnant, but the jails were still full of people awaiting trial, and accusations had been made against another 200.

Gradually, after the governor's own wife was accused, the hysteria began to subside. Public opinion changed. The influential preacher Increase Mather, who had initially supported the trials, criticized the admission of spectral evidence, maintaining, "It were better that ten suspected witches should escape, than that one innocent person should be condemned." The governor dissolved the courts and freed those in jail. Later, the Massachusetts House of Representatives passed a bill disallowing spectral evidence.

In the lengthy aftermath, jurors, witnesses, and judges publicly admitted error and responsibility, and in 1711 the Massachusetts General Court awarded damages to many of the accused and their families.

However, the events cast a long shadow. Even as late as 1957 descendants of those convicted at the time were still demanding that the court clear the names of their family members. It was not until October 2001 that a resolution was passed by the Massachusetts House of Representatives proclaiming the innocence of all named individuals who had been convicted and executed.

The warrant drawn up for the execution of Bridget Bishop, one of those accused of witchcraft in Salem, Massachusetts, in 1692. The outbreak of witch hysteria in Salem lasted little more than a year, but led to the hanging of 20 men and women and the imprisonment of many more.

Transcript of THE DEATH WARRANT
OF BRIDGET BISHOP

'To George Corwin Gent'm high Sherriffe of the County of Essex

Greeting

Whereas Bridgett Bishop als Olliver the wife of Edward Bishop of [Salem] in the County of Essex Sawyer at a speciall Court of Oyer and Termin[er held at] Salem the second Day of this instant month of June for the Countyes of Esse[x] Middlesex and Suffolk before William Stoughton Esq'r and his Associates J[ustices] of the said Court was Indicted and arraigned upon five severall [Seal]I[ndictments] for useing practiseing and exercisein[g] [on the Nyneteenth day of April] last past and divers other dayes and times [before and after certain acts of] Witchcraft in and upon the bodyes of Abigail Williams, Ann Puttnam J[un'r] Mercy Lewis, Mary Walcott and Elizabeth Hubbard of Salem village singlewomen, whereby their bodyes were hurt, afflicted pined, consu[med] Wasted and tormented contrary to the forme of the Statute in that Case [made and] provided To which Indictm'ts the said Bridgett Bishop pleaded no[t guilty] and for Tryall thereof put her selfe upon God and her Country, where[upon] she was found guilty of the felonyes and Witchcrafts whereof she stood Indicted and sentence of Death accordingly passed ag't her as the Law directs, Execution whereof yet remaines to be done These are theref[ore] in the Name of their Maj'ties William and Mary now King & Queen [over] England &c to will and Comand you That upon fryday next being the Tenth day of this instant month of June between the houres of Eight and twelve in the afternoon of the same day You safely conduct the s'd Bridgett Bishop als Olliver from their Maj'ties Gaol in Salem afores'd to the place of Execution and there cause her to be hanged by the neck untill she be de[ad] and of your doings herein make returne to the Clerk of the s'd Court and pr'cept And hereof you are not to faile at your peril And this shall be [your] Sufficient Warrant Given under my hand & Seal at Boston. the Eig[hth day] of June in the fourth Year of the Reigne of our Sovereigne Lord and [Lady] William & Mary now King & Queen over England &c Annoq'e Dm 1692;

Wm Stoughton
June 10th 1692 ,

> "...You safely conduct the s'd Bridgett Bishop als Olliver from their Maj'ties Gaol in Salem afores'd to the place of Execution and there cause her to be hanged by the neck untill she be de[ad] ..."

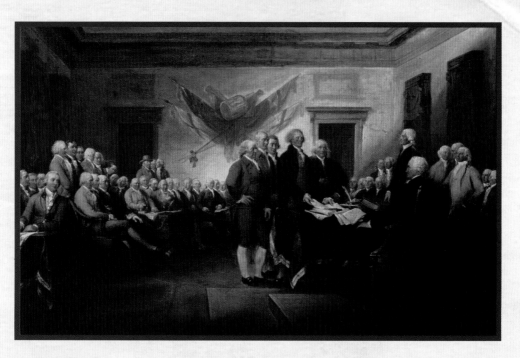

Thomas Jefferson (with Benjamin Franklin on his left) presents the Declaration of Independence to John Hancock, as depicted by John Trumbull (1756–1843)

The

DECLARATION

OF

INDEPENDENCE

Philadelphia, Pennsylvania

July 4, 1776

THE DECLARATION OF Independence was written to influence public opinion in America and abroad, particularly France, which was providing America with military aid against the British. The document's author, Thomas Jefferson, wrote of it later: "Neither aiming at originality of principle or sentiment, nor yet copied from any particular and previous writing, it was intended to be an expression of the American mind." King George III was very unwilling to accept that the "American mind" could differ from the minds of the British who ruled the colonies. His reluctance to recognize the colonists' viewpoint led to the outbreak of the Revolutionary War in 1775.

■ *Two future Presidents, Thomas Jefferson and John Adams, signed the Declaration of Independence. An indication of Jefferson's pride in his participation is given in the epitaph on his gravestone, which he wrote himself: "Here was buried Thomas Jefferson, author of the Declaration of Independence, of the statute of Virginia for religious freedom, and father of the University of Virginia." He omitted to mention his two terms as President.*

From the establishment of Virginia as a trading colony in 1607, and the later settlement of New England, the British presence in North America grew until, by 1770, they were ultimate rulers of 13 American colonies. However, France had also established territories in North America, and the two countries clashed over the boundaries of their colonial possessions during the French and Indian War (1754–63).

After 1763, when the war ended, the British continued to maintain an army in America to safeguard their colonies. However, in order to cover the costs of this defensive force, the British imposed a succession of taxes on the colonists—on sugar and imports of lead, paint, paper, and tea, as well as a stamp tax on all legal documents and newspapers. Colonists strongly resented this, arguing that they should not be taxed by the British Parliament since they were not represented in it.

"No taxation without representation" became a rallying cry as dissatisfaction increased. There were a number of violent outbursts. In 1765 an American mob destroyed the British governor's house in Boston, and in 1770 British soldiers, having been stoned by a mob, fired at and killed five Americans in the so-called Boston Massacre. In 1773, 100 colonists disguised as Native Americans staged the famous Boston Tea Party, boarding three British ships in Boston Harbor and throwing their cargo of tea into the sea in protest against a British import duty on tea. Small-scale rebellion steadily escalated into full-scale war.

Against this background, lawyer and Virginian landowner Thomas Jefferson and four others were deputed to draft the Declaration of Independence by the Continental Congress, a representative assembly of all 13 colonies formed in 1774.

Jefferson argued that civil resistance to a government is justified when that government's policies are unmistakably tyrannical—this is why the Declaration details King George III's actions so closely.

A PROTOTYPE OF DEMOCRACY
The Declaration has been used as a model for many political statements, including the Declaration of the Rights of Man and of the Citizen, which marked the start of the French Revolution in 1789. Thomas Jefferson wrote to John Adams in 1821: "The flames kindled on the fourth of July, 1776, have spread over too much of the globe to be extinguished by the feeble engines of despotism; on the contrary, they will consume these engines and all who work them."

Signed by leaders of the 13 American colonies, the Declaration of Independence lists in detail America's grievances against Britain's King George III. As well as justifying why America wanted independence from Britain, the document also identifies principles by which the signatories wanted their country to be governed.

As well as trying to establish a clear justification for the rebellion, the Declaration was also intended to unite the members of the Continental Congress, most of whom knew that signing the Declaration might be their death warrant if the revolution failed. As Benjamin Franklin commented, "We must all hang together, or we will all surely hang separately."

Jefferson's initial draft was amended by fellow committee members, Benjamin Franklin and John Adams. On July 4, 1776, the Declaration was signed, read out publicly, and copies given to most colonists, although the names of the signatories were originally kept secret for fear of British reprisals in the event of an American defeat. On July 9, George Washington ordered the Declaration to be read before the American army in New York.

The Declaration marked the birth date of the United States of America, a republic born in revolution and war.

Transcript of THE DECLARATION OF INDEPENDENCE

' The unanimous Declaration of the thirteen United States of America,

When in the Course of human events, it becomes necessary for one people to dissolve the political bands which have connected them with another, and to assume among the powers of the earth, the separate and equal station to which the Laws of Nature and of Nature's God entitle them, a decent respect to the opinions of mankind requires that they should declare the causes which impel them to the separation.

> "We hold these truths to be self-evident, that all men are created equal, that they are endowed by their Creator with certain unalienable Rights, that among these are Life, Liberty and the pursuit of Happiness."

We hold these truths to be self-evident, that all men are created equal, that they are endowed by their Creator with certain unalienable Rights, that among these are Life, Liberty and the pursuit of Happiness.—That to secure these rights, Governments are instituted among Men, deriving their just powers from the consent of the governed,—That whenever any Form of Government becomes destructive of these ends, it is the Right of the People to alter or to abolish it, and to institute new Government, laying its foundation on such principles and organizing its powers in such form, as to them shall seem most likely to effect their Safety and Happiness. Prudence, indeed, will dictate that Governments long established should not be changed for light and transient causes; and accordingly all experience hath shewn, that mankind are more disposed to suffer, while evils are sufferable, than to right themselves by abolishing the forms to which they are accustomed. But when a long train of abuses and usurpations, pursuing invariably the same Object evinces a design to reduce them under absolute Despotism, it is their right, it is their duty, to throw off such Government, and to provide new Guards for their future security.—Such has been the patient sufferance of these Colonies; and such is now the necessity which constrains them to alter their former Systems of Government. The history of the present King of Great Britain is a history of repeated injuries and usurpations, all having in direct object the establishment of an absolute Tyranny over these States. To prove this, let Facts be submitted to a candid world.

> "The history of the present King of Great Britain is a history of repeated injuries and usurpations . . . "

He has refused his Assent to Laws, the most wholesome and necessary for the public good. He has forbidden his Governors to pass Laws of immediate and pressing importance, unless suspended in their operation till his Assent should be obtained; and when so suspended, he has utterly neglected to attend to them. He has refused to pass other Laws for the accommodation of large districts of people, unless those people would relinquish the right of Representation in the Legislature, a right inestimable to them and formidable to tyrants only. He has called together legislative bodies at places unusual, uncomfortable, and distant from the depository of their public Records, for the sole purpose of fatiguing them into compliance with his measures. He has dissolved Representative Houses repeatedly, for opposing with manly firmness his invasions on the rights of the people. He has refused for a long time, after such dissolutions, to cause others to be elected; whereby the Legislative powers, incapable of Annihilation, have returned to the People at large for their exercise; the State remaining in the mean time exposed to all the dangers of invasion from without, and convulsions within. He has endeavoured to prevent the population of these States; for that purpose obstructing the Laws for Naturalization of Foreigners; refusing to pass others to encourage their migrations hither, and raising the conditions of new Appropriations of Lands. He has obstructed the Administration of Justice, by refusing his Assent to Laws for establishing Judiciary powers. He has made Judges dependent on his Will alone, for the tenure of their offices, and the amount and payment of their salaries. He has erected a multitude of New Offices, and sent hither swarms of Officers to harrass our people, and eat out their substance.

He has kept among us, in times of peace, Standing Armies without the Consent of our legislatures. He has affected to render the Military independent of and superior to the Civil power. He has combined with others to subject us to a jurisdiction foreign to our constitution, and unacknowledged by our laws; giving his Assent to their Acts of pretended Legislation: For Quartering large bodies of armed troops among us: For protecting them, by a mock Trial, from punishment for any Murders which they should commit on the Inhabitants of these States: For cutting off our Trade with all parts of the world: For imposing Taxes on us without our Consent: For depriving us in many cases, of the benefits of Trial by Jury: For transporting us beyond Seas to be tried for pretended offences: For abolishing the free System of English Laws in a neighbouring Province, establishing therein an Arbitrary government, and enlarging its Boundaries so as to render it at once an example and fit instrument for introducing the same absolute rule into these Colonies: For taking away our Charters, abolishing our most valuable Laws, and altering fundamentally the Forms of our Governments: For suspending our own Legislatures, and declaring themselves invested with power to legislate for us in all cases whatsoever.

He has abdicated Government here, by declaring us out of his Protection and waging War against us. He has plundered our seas, ravaged our Coasts, burnt our towns, and destroyed the lives of our people. He is at this time transporting large Armies of foreign Mercenaries to compleat the works of death, desolation and tyranny, already begun with circumstances of Cruelty & perfidy scarcely paralleled in the most barbarous ages, and totally unworthy the Head of a civilized nation. He has constrained our fellow Citizens taken Captive on the high Seas to bear Arms against their Country, to become the executioners of their friends and Brethren, or to fall themselves by their Hands. He has excited domestic insurrections amongst us, and has endeavoured to bring on the inhabitants of our frontiers, the merciless Indian Savages, whose known rule of warfare, is an undistinguished destruction of all ages, sexes and conditions.

In every stage of these Oppressions We have Petitioned for Redress in the most humble terms: Our repeated Petitions have been answered only by repeated injury. A Prince whose character is thus marked by every act which may define a Tyrant, is unfit to be the ruler of a free people.

"We . . . solemnly . . . declare, That these United Colonies are, and of Right ought to be Free and Independent States."

Nor have We been wanting in attentions to our British brethren. We have warned them from time to time of attempts by their legislature to extend an unwarrantable jurisdiction over us. We have reminded them of the circumstances of our emigration and settlement here. We have appealed to their native justice and magnanimity, and we have conjured them by the ties of our common kindred to disavow these usurpations, which would inevitably interrupt our connections and correspondence. They too have been deaf to the voice of justice and of consanguinity. We must, therefore, acquiesce in the necessity, which denounces our Separation, and hold them, as we hold the rest of mankind, Enemies in War, in Peace Friends.

We, therefore, the Representatives of the United States of America, in General Congress, Assembled, appealing to the Supreme Judge of the world for the rectitude of our intentions, do, in the Name, and by Authority of the good People of these Colonies, solemnly publish and declare, That these United Colonies are, and of Right ought to be Free and Independent States; that they are Absolved from all Allegiance to the British Crown, and that all political connection between them and the State of Great Britain, is and ought to be totally dissolved; and that as Free and Independent States, they have full Power to levy War, conclude Peace, contract Alliances, establish Commerce, and to do all other Acts and Things which Independent States may of right do. And for the support of this Declaration, with a firm reliance on the protection of divine Providence, we mutually pledge to each other our Lives, our Fortunes and our sacred Honor.

The Great Seal of the
United States of America, 1782

THE GREAT
SEAL

of the
United States of America

ACCEPTED ON

JUNE 20, 1782

ON THE DAY THE DECLARATION OF INDEPENDENCE was issued, the Continental Congress established a committee to create a seal for the United States of America, to act as a symbol of the newly independent nation. Achieving this to everyone's satisfaction was not easy. Four amended versions were submitted before the design met Congress's approval. The seal has an obverse (the main side) and a reverse. The obverse still appears on all official documents verifying the President's signature, as well as doubling as the U.S.A.'s national coat of arms—it appears on the buttons of military uniforms, and over the entrance to all U.S. embassies around the world.

■ *The Great Seal die, counter, and press, and the cabinet in which they are housed, are held inside a locked glass enclosure in the Exhibit Hall of the Department of State in Washington D.C.*

The original Great Seal was not a picture at all but a written document (a blazon), couched in the language of heraldry and describing in intricate detail the imagery to be used. This was then used to create an illustration and accurate realization of the seal, from which was created an engraved metal stamp (die) for endorsing official documents.

Members of the first Congress committee appointed to work on the Great Seal included Benjamin Franklin, Thomas Jefferson, and John Adams. They produced a complicated design that was immediately rejected. However, one of its features was included in the final seal: the Latin motto *E Pluribus Unum*, meaning "Out of Many, One."

The second committee's design, produced in 1780, was also rejected, although once again some of its features were retained—an olive branch with 13 olives and 13 leaves, 13 arrows, a constellation of stars, and a shield of red and white stripes on a blue field.

In 1782 a third committee introduced the eagle into the design. Finally, the first three designs were passed to Charles Thomson, secretary of the Congress, who created a fourth design, subsequently amended by William Barton, a Philadelphian who had studied heraldry. This design was finally officially accepted on June 20, 1782.

In its final form, the seal included ten symbols and three mottoes, specifically selected to express America's ideals. A written description of these symbols and mottoes produced by Charles Thomson constitutes the only official explanation ever offered of the individual elements that make up the seal. He said that the unsupported bald eagle showed that the United States of America ought to rely on their own virtue. On its breast, the eagle bears a shield, made up of 13 stripes representing the 13 states that had joined together. The motto that the eagle holds in its beak, *E Pluribus Unum*, also refers to the Union. In its right talon the eagle holds an olive branch with 13 olives and 13 leaves (symbolizing peace) and in its left, 13 arrows (signifying war), demonstrating that the power of peace and war is in the sole hands of Congress. Above the

THE BALD EAGLE

The bald eagle was regarded as a sacred bird by several Native American peoples, and had already been adopted as a symbol by some states before its image was incorporated in the Great Seal of the new United States of America. On the seal itself, it turns its head significantly towards the olive branch (signifying peace) held in its right talon. Benjamin Franklin famously denounced the use of the bald eagle in the seal, although not altogether seriously, stating that another native bird, the wild turkey, would be a more accurate signifier of American values.

Charles Thomson's sketch for the Great Seal, showing elements from all three previous attempts merged together.

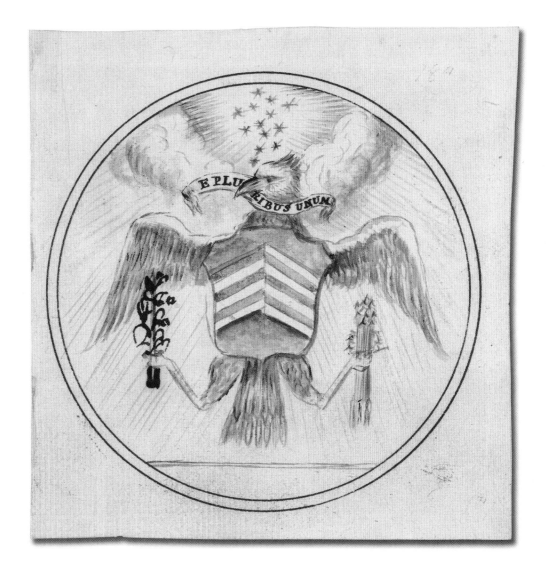

eagle's head is a constellation of 13 stars, indicating a new state taking its place among other sovereign powers.

On the seal's reverse is a pyramid, representing strength and duration. The eye above it and the motto *Annuit Coeptis* ("Providence has favored our undertakings") indicate the Founding Fathers' belief that God had intervened on many occasions in favor of the American cause. Below this, in roman numerals, is 1776, the date of the Declaration of Independence, and under it the words *Novus Ordo Seclorum* ("A new order of the ages"), meaning the starting point of a new American era.

The seal is still used today, some 3,000 times a year, when the Department of State receives official documents. Americans are familiar with the obverse from its appearance on coins, stamps, passports, monuments, and flags. Although it was never used as a seal, the reverse is also well known because in 1935 President Franklin D. Roosevelt asked for both sides of the seal to be reproduced on the dollar bill.

The Peace of Paris, by Benjamin West (1738–1820),
showing, from left to right, John Jay, John Adams,
Benjamin Franklin, Henry Laurens, and
William Temple Franklin

THE TREATY
OF PARIS

Between the Kingdom of Great Britain
and the United States of America

September 3, 1783

FOLLOWING THE SURRENDER of the British commander, Lord Cornwallis, after the decisive siege of Yorktown in 1781, the British were forced to accept that they could not win the Revolutionary War—a war for which they had largely lacked a coherent strategy. Conversely, America's state militias had performed well alongside the Continental Army under General George Washington, and the country had benefited from military and naval support from France—all of which enabled America to take advantage of British disorganization. Peace negotiations were complex because other countries had also been at war with Britain. Treaties needed to be drawn up between Britain and America, France, Spain, and Holland.

■ *Benjamin West's* The Peace of Paris, *a depiction of the negotiators and signatories of the Treaty, was left unfinished after the British delegation refused to sit for the painter. The half-completed painting shows only the five American representatives. The British refusal to participate indicates that divisions between America and Britain were still strongly felt.*

Thanks to the skill and tactics of the three American negotiators—Benjamin Franklin, John Adams, and John Jay—the United States was to achieve very favorable terms in its treaty with Britain, including British recognition of their independence and the establishment of new boundaries that would allow the young nation to expand westwards. The treaty would go down in history as a triumph of diplomatic skill, critical to the subsequent growth of the American nation.

By 1781, after six years of fighting, there was serious opposition in Britain to the war in America. Shortly after the defeat at Yorktown, the British Parliament voted to cease further prosecution of the war, and the Prime Minister, Lord North, under whose administration the war had been conducted, resigned. Although King George III wanted the war to continue, the new British government, led by Lord Shelburne, wanted peace with the United States.

The following year, Benjamin Franklin refused informal British proposals for a settlement that would give the 13 states some autonomy within the British empire. The Americans wanted complete independence, access to fishing grounds in Newfoundland, the evacuation of British forces from all areas of occupation, and a western boundary on the Mississippi, far beyond the existing boundary along the Appalachians. Franklin negotiated secretly with representatives from London, and his suggested articles for a workable treaty were close to those finally agreed. Their effectiveness was conditional on peace agreements being reached between Britain and France, still a strong American ally.

In November 1782 an Anglo-American agreement, the Preliminary Treaty of Paris, was signed, ending the fighting in America. In September 1783 three other treaties were signed—the Treaty of Paris between Britain and the United States, and the two Treaties of Versailles, in which Britain made peace with both France and Spain. The Netherlands and Britain signed a separate peace treaty in May

MORE IS LESS
An earlier treaty agreed between Britain, France, and Spain in 1763 had transferred French Canada to Britain and French Louisiana to Spain, which lost Florida to the British. But these major acquisitions for the British empire were more than countered by the loss of the 13 former British colonies in 1783.

1784. The Revolutionary War had shaken the most powerful countries in Europe. The new United States of America had dented the supremacy of the nations of the Old World, and established itself as a major player on the international stage.

The American Continental Congress ratified the Treaty of Paris in January 1784, and British ratification followed in April. As well as formally recognizing the United States, the Treaty of Paris set the geographical parameters of the new nation: America would extend from the Atlantic Ocean in the east to the Mississippi River in the west, and from the northern boundary of Florida in the south to approximately the same northern boundaries it has today. The Mississippi River was made freely accessible to both nations. Britain agreed to remove its troops from America, while the United States agreed to treat fairly those American colonials who had remained loyal to Britain. Under the terms of the Treaty, Britain retained Canada.

Some clauses, including those that restored the rights and property of loyalists and agreed the payment of pre-war debts to British merchants, caused trouble later. After the war, up to 80,000 loyalists migrated to Canada, England, and the British West Indies, although some eventually returned. Those who stayed in the United States became citizens of the new nation.

The Treaty of Paris marked the recognition of a new nation, the United States of America, by Britain, the former colonial power, and the rest of the world. It was signed by John Adams, Benjamin Franklin, and John Jay for the U.S., and by David Hartley, a member of Parliament, on behalf of Britain.

Transcript of THE TREATY OF PARIS

'In the name of the most holy and undivided Trinity.

It having pleased the Divine Providence to dispose the hearts of the most serene and most potent Prince George the Third, by the grace of God, king of Great Britain, France, and Ireland, defender of the faith, duke of Brunswick and Lunebourg, arch-treasurer and prince elector of the Holy Roman Empire etc., and of the United States of America, to forget all past misunderstandings and differences that have unhappily interrupted the good correspondence and friendship which they mutually wish to restore, and to establish such a beneficial and satisfactory intercourse, between the two countries upon the ground of reciprocal advantages and mutual convenience as may promote and secure to both perpetual peace and harmony; and having for this desirable end already laid the foundation of peace and reconciliation by the Provisional Articles signed at Paris on the 30th of November 1782, by the commissioners empowered on each part, which articles were agreed to be inserted in and constitute the Treaty of Peace proposed to be concluded between the Crown of Great Britain and the said United States, but which treaty was not to be concluded until terms of peace should be agreed upon between Great Britain and France and his Britannic Majesty should be ready to conclude such treaty accordingly; and the treaty between Great Britain and France having since been concluded, his Britannic Majesty and the United States of America, in order to carry into full effect the Provisional Articles above mentioned, according to the tenor thereof, have constituted and appointed, that is to say his Britannic Majesty on his part, David Hartley, Esqr., member of the Parliament of Great Britain, and the said United States on their part, John Adams, Esqr., late a commissioner of the United States of America at the court of Versailles, late delegate in Congress from the state of Massachusetts, and chief justice of the said state, and minister plenipotentiary of the said United States to their high mightinesses the States General of the United Netherlands; Benjamin Franklin, Esqr., late delegate in Congress from the state of Pennsylvania, president of the convention of the said state, and minister plenipotentiary from the United States of America at the court of Versailles; John Jay, Esqr., late president of Congress and chief justice of the state of New York, and minister plenipotentiary from the said United States at the court of Madrid; to be plenipotentiaries for the concluding and signing the present definitive treaty; who after having reciprocally communicated their respective full powers have agreed upon and confirmed the following articles.

> "His Britannic Majesty acknowledges the said United States . . . to be free sovereign and independent states, that he treats with them as such, and for himself, his heirs, and successors, relinquishes all claims to the government, propriety, and territorial rights of the same and every part thereof."

Article 1:
His Britannic Majesty acknowledges the said United States, viz., New Hampshire, Massachusetts Bay, Rhode Island and Providence Plantations,

Connecticut, New York, New Jersey, Pennsylvania, Maryland, Virginia, North Carolina, South Carolina and Georgia, to be free sovereign and independent states, that he treats with them as such, and for himself, his heirs, and successors, relinquishes all claims to the government, propriety, and territorial rights of the same and every part thereof.

Article 2:

And that all disputes which might arise in future on the subject of the boundaries of the said United States may be prevented, it is hereby agreed and declared, that the following are and shall be their boundaries, viz.; from the northwest angle of Nova Scotia, viz., that angle which is formed by a line drawn due north from the source of St. Croix River to the highlands; along the said highlands which divide those rivers that empty themselves into the river St. Lawrence, from those which fall into the Atlantic Ocean, to the northwesternmost head of Connecticut River; thence down along the middle of that river to the forty-fifth degree of north latitude; from thence by a line due west on said latitude until it strikes the river Iroquois or Cataraquy; thence along the middle of said river into Lake Ontario; through the middle of said lake until it strikes the communication by water between that lake and Lake Erie; thence along the middle of said communication into Lake Erie, through the middle of said lake until it arrives at the water communication between that lake and Lake Huron; thence along the middle of said water communication into Lake Huron, thence through the middle of said lake to the water communication between that lake and Lake Superior; thence through Lake Superior northward of the Isles Royal and Phelipeaux to the Long Lake; thence through the middle of said Long Lake and the water communication between it and the Lake of the Woods, to the said Lake of the Woods; thence through the said lake to the most northwesternmost point thereof, and from thence on a due west course to the river Mississippi; thence by a line to be drawn along the middle of the said river Mississippi until it shall intersect the northernmost part of the thirty-first degree of north latitude, South, by a line to be drawn due east from the determination of the line last mentioned in the latitude of thirty-one degrees of the equator, to the middle of the river Apalachicola or Catahouche; thence along the middle thereof to its junction with the Flint River, thence straight to the head of Saint Mary's River; and thence down along the middle of Saint Mary's River to the Atlantic Ocean; east, by a line to be drawn along the middle of the river Saint Croix, from its mouth in the Bay of Fundy to its source, and from its source directly north to the aforesaid highlands which divide the rivers that fall into the Atlantic Ocean from those which fall into the river Saint Lawrence; comprehending all islands within twenty leagues of any part of the shores of the United States, and lying between lines to be drawn due east from the points where the aforesaid boundaries between Nova Scotia on

> "And that all disputes which might arise in future on the subject of the boundaries of the said United States may be prevented, it is hereby agreed ... that the following ... shall be their boundaries ..."

the one part and East Florida on the other shall, respectively, touch the Bay of Fundy and the Atlantic Ocean, excepting such islands as now are or heretofore have been within the limits of the said province of Nova Scotia.

Article 3:

It is agreed that the people of the United States shall continue to enjoy unmolested the right to take fish of every kind on the Grand Bank and on all the other banks of Newfoundland, also in the Gulf of Saint Lawrence and at all other places in the sea, where the inhabitants of both countries used at any time heretofore to fish . . .

> "There shall be a firm and perpetual peace between his Britannic Majesty and the said states, and between the subjects of the one and the citizens of the other, wherefore all hostilities both by sea and land shall from henceforth cease."

Article 4:

It is agreed that creditors on either side shall meet with no lawful impediment to the recovery of the full value in sterling money of all bona fide debts heretofore contracted.

. . .

Article 7:

There shall be a firm and perpetual peace between his Britannic Majesty and the said states, and between the subjects of the one and the citizens of the other, wherefore all hostilities both by sea and land shall from henceforth cease. All prisoners on both sides shall be set at liberty, and his Brittanic Majesty shall with all convenient speed, and without causing any destruction, or carrying away any Negroes or other property of the American inhabitants, withdraw all his armies, garrisons, and fleets from the said United States, and from every post, place, and harbor within the same; leaving in all fortifications, the American artillery that may be therein; and shall also order and cause all archives, records, deeds, and papers belonging to any of the said states, or their citizens, which in the course of the war may have fallen into the hands of his officers, to be forthwith restored and delivered to the proper states and persons to whom they belong.

Article 8:

The navigation of the river Mississippi, from its source to the ocean, shall forever remain free and open to the subjects of Great Britain and the citizens of the United States . . .

Done at Paris, this third day of September in the year of our Lord, one thousand seven hundred and eighty-three.

D. HARTLEY (SEAL)
JOHN ADAMS (SEAL)
B. FRANKLIN (SEAL)
JOHN JAY (SEAL)

*Scene at the signing of the Constitution of the United States,
1787, by Howard Chandler Christy (1873–1952)*

The

CONSTITUTION

OF THE

UNITED STATES

ACCEPTED BY THE PHILADELPHIA CONVENTION

SEPTEMBER 17, 1787

THE FIRST GOVERNING document of the newly united former colonies was a Congressional agreement, the Articles of Confederation of 1781. However, it rapidly became clear that the Articles did not provide a strong enough legal basis for national government. In May 1787, 55 state delegates gathered in Independence Hall in Philadelphia to discuss how they could be amended. The delegates concluded that the Articles needed to be replaced by a completely new document, one that enshrined the principle of a strong federal government, an idea that had been previously outlined in James Madison's Virginia Plan. The new Constitution was a compromise between various regional interests in the Convention. It was finally ratified by all 13 states when ten amendments, known collectively as the Bill of Rights, were passed in 1791.

■ *Notable radicals were absent from the Philadelphia Convention. In 1788, the anti-Federalist Patrick Henry asked of the delegates, "Who authorized them to speak the language of 'We, the People,' instead of 'We, the States'?" Henry was instrumental in the drafting of the Bill of Rights (1791).*

The weaknesses of the Articles of Confederation provided a valuable learning experience for the new nation. Four main problems made it impossible for Congress to carry out its duties under these Articles, and these problems were cogently summarized in *The Federalist*—a set of political essays written by lobbyists for a completely new U.S. Constitution in 1787.

Under the Articles, Congress could only legislate for states, not individuals, and so could not enforce legislation. It had no power to tax the population, and could only apportion its expenses among states and request they be paid—a requirement that was not often complied with. Congress had no power to regulate commerce and so could not establish successful foreign relations, which were usually based on trade. Finally, any amendments necessary to correct the first three problems required the agreement of all 13 state legislatures, and this degree of mutuality had never occurred.

The lack of power in central government caused increased problems, as demonstrated by Shay's Rebellion in Massachusetts in 1786–7, and the ability of one state to block legislation desired by the other 12 inevitably weakened the whole. In 1786 the Annapolis Convention addressed the increasing problem of interstate commerce, and proposed the summoning of a constitutional convention. Twelve states, excepting Rhode Island, sent delegates to attend the Constitutional Convention in Philadelphia. The Convention leaders included political moderates like George Washington, James Madison, and Benjamin Franklin; more radical statesmen, such as Patrick Henry and Thomas Jefferson, were markedly absent.

In *The Federalist*, James Madison summarized the problem that the Constitution had to resolve: "In framing a government which is to be administered by men over men, the great difficulty lies in this: you must first enable the government to control the governed; and in the next place oblige it to control itself." The chief issues were the degree of power to be allocated to central government; the number of representatives each state should have in Congress; and how they should be elected—by the people or by state legislators.

A landmark document in the history of democracy, the United States Constitution sets out the legal basis for federal government. It is the oldest written national constitution still in operation, outlining the structure of government and, through its first ten amendments, the fundamental rights of American citizens.

Congress may by general Laws prescribe the Manner in which such Acts, Records and Proceedings shall be proved, and the Effect thereof.

Section. 2. The Citizens of each State shall be entitled to all Privileges and Immunities of Citizens in the several States.

A Person charged in any State with Treason, Felony, or other Crime, who shall flee from Justice, and be found in another State, shall on Demand of the executive Authority of the State from which he fled, be delivered up, to be removed to the State having Jurisdiction of the Crime.

No Person held to Service or Labour in one State, under the Laws thereof, escaping into another, shall, in Consequence of any Law or Regulation therein, be discharged from such Service or Labour, but shall be delivered up on Claim of the Party to whom such Service or Labour may be due.

Section. 3. New States may be admitted by the Congress into this Union; but no new State shall be formed or erected within the Jurisdiction of any other State; nor any State be formed by the Junction of two or more States, or Parts of States, without the Consent of the Legislatures of the States concerned as well as of the Congress.

The Congress shall have Power to dispose of and make all needful Rules and Regulations respecting the Territory or other Property belonging to the United States; and nothing in this Constitution shall be so construed as to Prejudice any Claims of the United States, or of any particular State.

Section. 4. The United States shall guarantee to every State in this Union a Republican Form of Government, and shall protect each of them against Invasion; and on Application of the Legislature, or of the Executive (when the Legislature cannot be convened) against domestic Violence.

Article. V.

The Congress, whenever two thirds of both Houses shall deem it necessary, shall propose Amendments to this Constitution, or, on the Application of the Legislatures of two thirds of the several States, shall call a Convention for proposing Amendments, which, in either Case, shall be valid to all Intents and Purposes, as Part of this Constitution, when ratified by the Legislatures of three fourths of the several States, or by Conventions in three fourths thereof, as the one or the other Mode of Ratification may be proposed by the Congress; Provided that no Amendment which may be made, prior to the Year One thousand eight hundred and eight shall in any Manner affect the first and fourth Clauses in the Ninth Section of the first Article; and that no State, without its Consent, shall be deprived of its equal Suffrage in the Senate.

Article. VI.

All Debts contracted and Engagements entered into, before the Adoption of this Constitution, shall be as valid against the United States under this Constitution, as under the Confederation.

This Constitution, and the Laws of the United States which shall be made in Pursuance thereof; and all Treaties made, or which shall be made, under the Authority of the United States, shall be the supreme Law of the Land; and the Judges in every State shall be bound thereby, any Thing in the Constitution or Laws of any State to the Contrary notwithstanding.

The Senators and Representatives before mentioned, and the Members of the several State Legislatures, and all executive and judicial Officers, both of the United States and of the several States, shall be bound by Oath or Affirmation, to support this Constitution; but no religious Test shall ever be required as a Qualification to any Office or public Trust under the United States.

Article. VII.

The Ratification of the Conventions of nine States, shall be sufficient for the Establishment of this Constitution between the States so ratifying the Same.

The Word "the" being interlined between the seventh and eighth Lines of the first Page, The Word "Thirty" being partly written on an Erazure in the fifteenth Line of the first Page. The Words "is tried" being interlined between the thirty second and thirty third Lines of the first Page and the Word "the" being interlined between the forty third and forty fourth Lines of the second Page.

done in Convention by the Unanimous Consent of the States present the Seventeenth Day of September in the Year of our Lord one thousand seven hundred and Eighty seven and of the Independance of the United States of America the Twelfth In witness whereof We have hereunto subscribed our Names,

Attest William Jackson Secretary

G⁰. Washington—Presidt. and deputy from Virginia

Delaware
Geo: Read
Gunning Bedford jun
John Dickinson
Richard Bassett
Jaco: Broom

Maryland
James McHenry
Dan of St Thos. Jenifer
Danl Carroll

Virginia
John Blair—
James Madison Jr.

North Carolina
Wm. Blount
Richd. Dobbs Spaight.
Hu Williamson

South Carolina
J. Rutledge
Charles Cotesworth Pinckney
Charles Pinckney
Pierce Butler.

Georgia
William Few
Abr Baldwin

New Hampshire
John Langdon
Nicholas Gilman

Massachusetts
Nathaniel Gorham
Rufus King

Connecticut
Wm. Saml. Johnson
Roger Sherman

New York
Alexander Hamilton

New Jersey
Wil: Livingston
David Brearley
Wm. Paterson
Jona: Dayton

Pennsylvania
B Franklin
Thomas Mifflin
Robt Morris
Geo. Clymer
Thos. FitzSimons
Jared Ingersoll
James Wilson
Gouv Morris

By September 1787 the drafting of the Constitution was complete. Benjamin Franklin, who favored leadership by executive committee rather than by a President, declared that he was not completely happy with the Constitution. However, he accepted that perfection could never be achieved, supported the draft, and urged others to accept it too. The new government outlined in the Constitution came into existence when, in keeping with its own Article 7, the Constitution had been ratified by nine states. Although unusually democratic for the times, the Constitution was badly received in some states, where it was felt that national government had been strengthened at the cost of individual citizens' rights. In June 1788, New Hampshire became the ninth state to ratify the Constitution. However, many other states only ratified it after James Madison ensured that the Bill of Rights, championed by Thomas Jefferson and many others, was passed four years later.

In its final form, the Constitution was composed of a preamble, seven Articles, and ten Amendments. Its resounding opening words, "We the People," established the citizens of the United States at the center of their new system of democratic government.

Article I decrees that the American people will control government through the electoral process, and be represented in a Congress made up of a Senate and House of Representatives. Article II describes procedures for selecting the President, defines the role of Vice-President, and determines the processes required for their impeachment and removal from office. The court system, the judicial branch of government, is described in Article III. Article IV covers the relationships between the states and the Federal government, and between the states themselves, including freedom of movement. Article V outlines the process necessary for proposing amendments to the Constitution, and Article VI forbids any form of religious test being required as qualification for those seeking office. Article VII simply states that the Constitution requires the ratification of nine states to come into force.

Because the Constitution was more a statement of national principles than a detailed plan of how government would operate, it had an inbuilt flexibility that has ensured its continued use and relevance. The British Prime Minister, William Gladstone (1809–98), later described it as "the most wonderful work ever struck off at a given time by the brain and purpose of man."

Transcript of THE CONSTITUTION OF THE UNITED STATES

'We the People of the United States, in Order to form a more perfect Union, establish Justice, insure domestic Tranquility, provide for the common defense, promote the general Welfare, and secure the Blessings of Liberty to ourselves and our Posterity, do ordain and establish this Constitution for the United States of America.

Article. I.

Section. 1.

All legislative Powers herein granted shall be vested in a Congress of the United States, which shall consist of a Senate and House of Representatives.

Section. 2.

The House of Representatives shall be composed of Members chosen every second Year by the People of the several States, and the Electors in each State shall have the Qualifications requisite for Electors of the most numerous Branch of the State Legislature.

> "We the people of the United States, in Order to form a more perfect Union, establish Justice, . . . and secure the Blessings of Liberty to ourselves and our Posterity, do ordain and establish this Constitution for the United States of America."

No Person shall be a Representative who shall not have attained to the Age of twenty five Years, and been seven Years a Citizen of the United States, and who shall not, when elected, be an Inhabitant of that State in which he shall be chosen.

Representatives and direct Taxes shall be apportioned among the several States which may be included within this Union, according to their respective Numbers, which shall be determined by adding to the whole Number of free Persons, including those bound to Service for a Term of Years, and excluding Indians not taxed, three fifths of all other Persons. The actual Enumeration shall be made within three Years after the first Meeting of the Congress of the United States, and within every subsequent Term of ten Years, in such Manner as they shall by Law direct. The Number of Representatives shall not exceed one for every thirty Thousand, but each State shall have at Least one Representative; and until such enumeration shall be made, the State of New Hampshire shall be entitled to chuse three, Massachusetts eight, Rhode-Island and Providence Plantations one, Connecticut five, New-York six, New Jersey four, Pennsylvania eight, Delaware one, Maryland six, Virginia ten, North Carolina five, South Carolina five, and Georgia three.

. . .

Section. 3.

The Senate of the United States shall be composed of two Senators from each State, chosen by the Legislature thereof for six Years; and each Senator shall have one Vote.

Immediately after they shall be assembled in Consequence of the first Election, they shall be divided as equally as may be into three Classes. The Seats of the Senators of the first Class shall be vacated at the Expiration of the second Year, of the second Class at the Expiration of the fourth Year, and of the third Class at the Expiration of the sixth Year, so that one third may be chosen every second Year; and if Vacancies happen by Resignation, or otherwise, during the Recess of the Legislature of any State, the Executive thereof may make temporary Appointments until the next Meeting of the Legislature, which shall then fill such Vacancies.

No Person shall be a Senator who shall not have attained to the Age of thirty Years, and been nine Years a Citizen of the United States, and who shall not, when elected, be an Inhabitant of that State for which he shall be chosen.

The Vice President of the United States shall be President of the Senate, but shall have no Vote, unless they be equally divided.

The Senate shall chuse their other Officers, and also a President pro tempore, in the Absence of the Vice President, or when he shall exercise the Office of President of the United States.

The Senate shall have the sole Power to try all Impeachments. When sitting for that Purpose, they shall be on Oath or Affirmation. When the President of the United States is tried, the Chief Justice shall preside: And no Person shall be convicted without the Concurrence of two thirds of the Members present.

Judgment in Cases of Impeachment shall not extend further than to removal from Office, and disqualification to hold and enjoy any Office of honor, Trust or Profit under the United States: but the Party convicted shall nevertheless be liable and subject to Indictment, Trial, Judgment and Punishment, according to Law.

. . .

> "The Senate shall have the sole Power to try all Impeachments. When sitting for that Purpose, they shall be on Oath or Affirmation. When the President of the United States is tried, the Chief Justice shall preside: And no Person shall be convicted without the Concurrence of two thirds of the Members present."

Section. 5.

Each House shall be the Judge of the Elections, Returns and Qualifications of its own Members, and a Majority of each shall constitute a Quorum to do Business; but a smaller Number may adjourn from day to day, and may be authorized to compel the Attendance of absent Members, in such Manner, and under such Penalties as each House may provide.

Each House may determine the Rules of its Proceedings, punish its Members for disorderly Behaviour, and, with the Concurrence of two thirds, expel a Member.

Each House shall keep a Journal of its Proceedings, and from time to time publish the same, excepting such Parts as may in their Judgment require Secrecy; and the Yeas and Nays of the Members of either House on any question shall, at the Desire of one fifth of those Present, be entered on the Journal.

. . .

> "Each House may determine the Rules of its Proceedings, punish its Members for disorderly Behaviour, and, with the Concurrence of two thirds, expel a Member."

Section. 6.

The Senators and Representatives shall receive a Compensation for their Services, to be ascertained by Law, and paid out of the Treasury of the United States. They shall in all Cases, except Treason, Felony and Breach of the Peace, be privileged from Arrest during their Attendance at the Session of their respective Houses, and in going to and returning from the same; and for any Speech or Debate in either House, they shall not be questioned in any other Place.

No Senator or Representative shall, during the Time for which he was elected, be appointed to any civil Office under the Authority of the United States, which shall have been created, or the Emoluments whereof shall have been increased during such time; and no Person holding any Office under the United States, shall be a Member of either House during his Continuance in Office . . .

. . .

Section. 8.

The Congress shall have Power To lay and collect Taxes, Duties, Imposts and Excises, to pay the Debts and provide for the common Defence and general Welfare of the United States; but all Duties, Imposts and Excises shall be uniform throughout the United States;

To borrow Money on the credit of the United States;

To regulate Commerce with foreign Nations, and among the several States, and with the Indian Tribes;

To establish an uniform Rule of Naturalization, and uniform Laws on the subject of Bankruptcies throughout the United States;

To coin Money, regulate the Value thereof, and of foreign Coin, and fix the Standard of Weights and Measures;

To provide for the Punishment of counterfeiting the Securities and current Coin of the United States;

To establish Post Offices and post Roads;

To promote the Progress of Science and useful Arts, by securing for limited Times to Authors and Inventors the exclusive Right to their respective Writings and Discoveries;

To constitute Tribunals inferior to the supreme Court;

To define and punish Piracies and Felonies committed on the high Seas, and Offences against the Law of Nations;

To declare War, grant Letters of Marque and Reprisal, and make Rules concerning Captures on Land and Water;

To raise and support Armies, but no Appropriation of Money to that Use shall be for a longer Term than two Years;

To provide and maintain a Navy;

To make Rules for the Government and Regulation of the land and naval Forces;

To provide for calling forth the Militia to execute the Laws of the Union, suppress Insurrections and repel Invasions;

To provide for organizing, arming, and disciplining, the Militia, and for governing such Part of them as may be employed in the Service of the United States, reserving to the States respectively, the Appointment of the Officers, and the Authority of training the Militia according to the discipline prescribed by Congress;

> "The Congress shall have Power ... to define and punish Piracies and Felonies committed on the high Seas, and Offences against the Law of Nations."

To exercise exclusive Legislation in all Cases whatsoever, over such District (not exceeding ten Miles square) as may, by Cession of particular States, and the Acceptance of Congress, become the Seat of the Government of the United States, and to exercise like Authority over all Places purchased by the Consent of the Legislature of the State in which the Same shall be, for the Erection of Forts, Magazines, Arsenals, dock-Yards, and other needful Buildings ...

...

Section. 10.

No State shall enter into any Treaty, Alliance, or Confederation; grant Letters of Marque and Reprisal; coin Money; emit Bills of Credit; make any Thing but gold and silver Coin a Tender in Payment of Debts; pass any Bill of Attainder, ex post facto Law, or Law impairing the Obligation of Contracts, or grant any Title of Nobility.

No State shall, without the Consent of the Congress, lay any Imposts or Duties on Imports or Exports, except what may be absolutely necessary for executing its inspection Laws: and the net Produce of all Duties and Imposts, laid by any State on Imports or Exports, shall be for the Use of the Treasury of the United States; and all such Laws shall be subject to the Revision and Controul of the Congress.

No State shall, without the Consent of Congress, lay any Duty of Tonnage, keep Troops, or Ships of War in time of Peace, enter into any Agreement or Compact with another State, or with a foreign Power, or engage in War, unless actually invaded, or in such imminent Danger as will not admit of delay.

Article. II.

Section. 1.

The executive Power shall be vested in a President of the United States of America. He shall hold his Office during the Term of four Years, and, together with the Vice President, chosen for the same Term, be elected, as follows:

Each State shall appoint, in such Manner as the Legislature thereof may direct, a Number of Electors, equal to the whole Number of Senators and Representatives to which the State may be entitled in the Congress: but no Senator or Representative, or Person holding an Office of Trust or Profit under the United States, shall be appointed an Elector.

The Electors shall meet in their respective States, and vote by Ballot for two Persons, of whom one at least shall not be an Inhabitant of the same State with themselves. And they shall make a List of all the Persons voted for, and of the Number of Votes for each; which List they shall sign and certify, and transmit sealed to the Seat of the Government of the United States, directed to the President of the Senate. The President of the Senate shall, in the Presence of the Senate and House of Representatives, open all the Certificates, and the Votes shall then be counted. The Person having the greatest Number of Votes shall be the President, if such Number be a Majority of the whole Number of Electors appointed; and if there be more than one who have such Majority, and have an equal Number of Votes, then the House of Representatives shall immediately chuse by Ballot one of them for President; and if no Person have a Majority, then from the five highest on the List the said House shall in like Manner chuse the President. But in chusing the President, the Votes shall be taken by States, the Representation from each State having one Vote; A quorum for this purpose shall consist of a Member or Members from two thirds of the States, and a Majority of all the States shall be necessary to a Choice. In every Case, after the Choice of the President, the Person having the greatest Number of Votes of the Electors shall be the Vice President. But if there should remain two or more who have equal Votes, the Senate shall chuse from them by Ballot the Vice President.

The Congress may determine the Time of chusing the Electors, and the Day on which they shall give their Votes; which Day shall be the same throughout the United States.

No Person except a natural born Citizen, or a Citizen of the United States, at the time of the Adoption of this Constitution, shall be eligible to the Office of President; neither shall any Person be eligible to that Office who shall not have attained to the Age of thirty-five Years, and been fourteen Years a Resident within the United States.

In Case of the Removal of the President from Office, or of his Death, Resignation, or Inability to discharge the Powers and Duties of the said Office,

> "The executive Power shall be vested in a President of the United States of America."

the Same shall devolve on the Vice President, and the Congress may by Law provide for the Case of Removal, Death, Resignation or Inability, both of the President and Vice President, declaring what Officer shall then act as President, and such Officer shall act accordingly, until the Disability be removed, or a President shall be elected.

> "The President shall be Commander in Chief of the Army and Navy of the United States, and of the Militia of the several States."

Section. 2.

The President shall be Commander in Chief of the Army and Navy of the United States, and of the Militia of the several States, when called into the actual Service of the United States; he may require the Opinion, in writing, of the principal Officer in each of the executive Departments, upon any Subject relating to the Duties of their respective Offices, and he shall have Power to grant Reprieves and Pardons for Offences against the United States, except in Cases of Impeachment.

He shall have Power, by and with the Advice and Consent of the Senate, to make Treaties, provided two thirds of the Senators present concur; and he shall nominate, and by and with the Advice and Consent of the Senate, shall appoint Ambassadors, other public Ministers and Consuls, Judges of the supreme Court, and all other Officers of the United States, whose Appointments are not herein otherwise provided for, and which shall be established by Law: but the Congress may by Law vest the Appointment of such inferior Officers, as they think proper, in the President alone, in the Courts of Law, or in the Heads of Departments . . .

The President shall have Power to fill up all Vacancies that may happen during the Recess of the Senate, by granting Commissions which shall expire at the End of their next Session.

. . .

Section. 4.

The President, Vice President and all civil Officers of the United States, shall be removed from Office on Impeachment for, and Conviction of, Treason, Bribery, or other high Crimes and Misdemeanors.

Article. III.

Section. 1.

The judicial Power of the United States shall be vested in one supreme Court, and in such inferior Courts as the Congress may from time to time ordain and establish. The Judges, both of the supreme and inferior Courts, shall hold their Offices during good Behaviour, and shall, at stated Times, receive for their Services a Compensation, which shall not be diminished during their Continuance in Office . . .

. . .

Section. 3.

Treason against the United States, shall consist only in levying War against them, or in adhering to their Enemies, giving them Aid and Comfort. No Person shall be convicted of Treason unless on the Testimony of two Witnesses to the same overt Act, or on Confession in open Court.

The Congress shall have Power to declare the Punishment of Treason, but no Attainder of Treason shall work Corruption of Blood, or Forfeiture except during the Life of the Person attainted.

Article. IV.

Section. 1.

Full Faith and Credit shall be given in each State to the public Acts, Records, and judicial Proceedings of every other State. And the Congress may by general Laws prescribe the Manner in which such Acts, Records and Proceedings shall be proved, and the Effect thereof.

> "The Citizens of each State shall be entitled to all Privileges and Immunities of Citizens in the several States."

Section. 2.

The Citizens of each State shall be entitled to all Privileges and Immunities of Citizens in the several States.

A Person charged in any State with Treason, Felony, or other Crime, who shall flee from Justice, and be found in another State, shall on Demand of the executive Authority of the State from which he fled, be delivered up, to be removed to the State having Jurisdiction of the Crime.

No Person held to Service or Labour in one State, under the Laws thereof, escaping into another, shall, in Consequence of any Law or Regulation therein, be discharged from such Service or Labour, but shall be delivered up on Claim of the Party to whom such Service or Labour may be due . . .

Article. V.

The Congress, whenever two thirds of both Houses shall deem it necessary, shall propose Amendments to this Constitution, or, on the Application of the Legislatures of two thirds of the several States, shall call a Convention for proposing Amendments, which, in either Case, shall be valid to all Intents and Purposes, as Part of this Constitution, when ratified by the Legislatures of three fourths of the several States, or by Conventions in three fourths thereof, as the one or the other Mode of Ratification may be proposed by the Congress; Provided that no Amendment which may be made prior to the Year One thousand eight hundred and eight shall in any Manner affect the first and fourth Clauses in the Ninth Section of the first Article; and that no State, without its Consent, shall be deprived of its equal Suffrage in the Senate . . .

Article. VI.

The Senators and Representatives before mentioned, and the Members of the several State Legislatures, and all executive and judicial Officers, both of the United States and of the several States, shall be bound by Oath or Affirmation, to support this Constitution; but no religious Test shall ever be required as a Qualification to any Office or public Trust under the United States.

Article. VII.

The Ratification of the Conventions of nine States, shall be sufficient for the Establishment of this Constitution between the States so ratifying the Same.
. . .

Attest William Jackson Secretary

Done in Convention by the Unanimous Consent of the States present the Seventeenth Day of September in the Year of our Lord one thousand seven hundred and Eighty seven and of the Independence of the United States of America the Twelfth. In witness whereof We have hereunto subscribed our Names,

George Washington
President and Deputy from Virginia

DELAWARE
George Read
Gunning Bedford, Jr.
John Dickinson
Richard Bassett
Jacob Broom

NORTH CAROLINA
William Blount
Richard Dobbs Spaight
Hugh Williamson

NEW HAMPSHIRE
John Langdon
Nicholas Gilman

NEW YORK
Alexander Hamilton

MARYLAND
James McHenry
Daniel of St Thos. Jenifer
Daniel Carroll

SOUTH CAROLINA
John Rutledge
Charles Cotesworth Pinckney
Charles Pinckney
Pierce Butler

MASSACHUSETTS
Nathaniel Gorham
Rufus King

NEW JERSEY
William Livingston
David Brearley
William Paterson
Jonathan Dayton

VIRGINIA
John Blair
James Madison, Jr.

GEORGIA
William Few
Abraham Baldwin

CONNECTICUT
William Samuel Johnson
Roger Sherman

PENNSYLVANIA
Benjamin Franklin
Thomas Mifflin
Robert Morris
George Clymer
Thomas FitzSimons
Jared Ingersoll
James Wilson
Gouverneur Morris

George Washington
(1732–99), first President of the
United States of America, painted in
1796 by Gilbert Stuart (1755–1828)

The first inaugural address of

PRESIDENT GEORGE WASHINGTON

New York

April 30, 1789

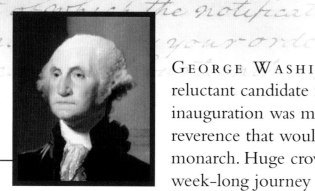

GEORGE WASHINGTON was a war hero and initially a reluctant candidate for the Presidency. Nevertheless, his inauguration was marked with the sort of ceremony and reverence that would not have disgraced the coronation of a monarch. Huge crowds and lavish celebrations punctuated his week-long journey from his home in Virginia to New York, where the inauguration took place. Outside Philadelphia he mounted a white horse so that 20,000 observers could watch his progress. Later, his path was strewn with flowers by a choir of white-robed girls, while on his head, like a victorious Roman general, he wore a crown of laurels. As his barge approached New York harbor, it was accompanied by a fleet of decorated ships.

■ *George Washington is the only President in U.S. history to be elected unanimously by members of the Electoral College. And it happened twice, as he also won his second term with a unanimous vote in 1792.*

Having led the Americans to victory in the Revolutionary War, Washington would now lead them in peace. As the first chief executive of the United States, he took his oath of office on the balcony of the Senate Chamber at Federal Hall on Wall Street, and delivered his inaugural address at a joint session of the two Houses of Congress gathered inside the Senate Chamber.

Born in February 1732, the son of a Virginia planter, George Washington inherited property and social position from his family. He was appointed county surveyor in 1749, and the experience he gained on the frontier led to his appointment as a major in the Virginia militia in 1752 and early military experience in the French and Indian War (1754–63). In 1758 he resigned his commission to work on his estate at Mount Vernon in Virginia, where he established his future political base. Washington was one of many landowners who objected vociferously to what they regarded as the injustices and oppressions of British rule. Through his marriage to Martha Custis, a rich young widow, Washington became extremely wealthy, and established himself as a respected and powerful public figure.

Tall, handsome, dignified, and energetic, Washington exuded competence, despite being a poor orator. His strengths lay in his powers of organization, his personal bravery, and his wisdom. At times his reticence and formality made him seem a rather distant personality. Chosen to represent Virginia at the first and second Continental Congresses in 1774 and 1775, he went on to become commander-in-chief of the American forces during the Revolutionary War.

After the war Washington retired from public life, intending to work as a gentleman farmer. He wrote to a friend, "I have not only retired from all public employments but I am retiring within myself." He wanted to sit "under the shadow of my own view and my own fig tree."

However, his quiet life was disrupted by his concerns about the weakness of the Articles of Confederation then governing the new United States. In 1786 he attended

WASHINGTON D.C.

George Washington chose the location on the Potomac River for the national capital, a new settlement whose design, site, and name would be highly significant for the new country. The city was officially named Washington in September 1791, although Washington himself always referred to it as "the Federal city." The District of Columbia was a 100-square mile area designated for the seat of government. It included the new city of Washington, and the existing towns of Georgetown and Alexandria.

the Annapolis Convention, held ostensibly to discuss interstate trade relations but aimed at strengthening national unity. He then presided over the subsequent Constitutional Convention in Philadelphia in 1787, where his support of the proposed Constitution secured its ratification.

When the Convention delegates created the new role of President, they had Washington very much in mind. One of the Founding Fathers stated the Convention would not have made the executive powers of the President so great "had not many of the members cast their eyes towards General Washington as President and shaped their ideas of the powers to be given a president by their opinions of his virtue." He was unanimously elected to office in 1789, at the age of 57.

Washington established the ceremonial nature of the presidential role, but ensured that the trappings associated with it never resembled European royal courts. His preferred form of address was "Mr. President." He declined to accept the large salary the first U.S. Congress proposed for the President, not only because he was already very rich, but also because he had a keen appreciation of the symbolic value of his gesture of refusal.

As President, Washington created an enduring system of cabinet government and worked hard to establish the United States as a nation in a world still dominated by the warring European powers of Britain and France. He quelled a rebellion in Pennsylvania when federal authority was threatened, becoming a Federalist hero in the process.

Determined not to stand for office a third time in 1796, in his farewell address Washington urged his fellow Americans to work for unity and to avoid all alliances with foreign powers. He spent his remaining years on his estate at Mount Vernon.

George Washington delivered his inaugural address in New York, at the time the capital of the United States and the seat of Congress. Washington took the opportunity to reassure his listeners about the constitutional responsibilities of the President, aware that many citizens feared the position might become monarchical.

Transcript of GEORGE WASHINGTON'S INAUGURAL ADDRESS

 Fellow-Citizens of the Senate and of the House of Representatives:

Among the vicissitudes incident to life no event could have filled me with greater anxieties than that of which the notification was transmitted by your order, and received on the 14th day of the present month. On the one hand, I was summoned by my Country, whose voice I can never hear but with veneration and love, from a retreat which I had chosen with the fondest predilection, and, in my flattering hopes, with an immutable decision, as the asylum of my declining years—a retreat which was rendered every day more necessary as well as more dear to me by the addition of habit to inclination, and of frequent interruptions in my health to the gradual waste committed on it by time. On the other hand, the magnitude and difficulty of the trust to which the voice of my country called me, being sufficient to awaken in the wisest and most experienced of her citizens a distrustful scrutiny into his qualifications, could not but overwhelm with despondence one who (inheriting inferior endowments from nature and unpracticed in the duties of civil administration) ought to be peculiarly conscious of his own deficiencies. In this conflict of emotions all I dare aver is that it has been my faithful study to collect my duty from a just appreciation of every circumstance by which it might be affected. All I dare hope is that if, in executing this task, I have been too much swayed by a grateful remembrance of former instances, or by an affectionate sensibility to this transcendent proof of the confidence of my fellow-citizens, and have thence too little consulted my incapacity as well as disinclination for the weighty and untried cares before me, my error will be palliated by the motives which mislead me, and its consequences be judged by my country with some share of the partiality in which they originated.

> "I was summoned by my Country, whose voice I can never hear but with veneration and love, from a retreat which I had chosen with the fondest predilection, and, in my flattering hopes, with an immutable decision, as the asylum of my declining years."

. . . By the article establishing the executive department it is made the duty of the President "to recommend to your consideration such measures as he shall judge necessary and expedient." The circumstances under which I now meet you will acquit me from entering into that subject further than to refer to the great constitutional charter under which you are assembled, and which, in defining your powers, designates the objects to which your attention is to be given. It will be more consistent with those circumstances, and far more congenial with the feelings which actuate me, to substitute, in place of a recommendation of particular measures, the tribute that is due to the talents, the rectitude, and the patriotism which adorn the characters selected to devise and adopt them. In these honorable qualifications I behold the surest pledges that as on one side no local prejudices or attachments, no separate views nor party animosities, will misdirect the comprehensive and equal eye which ought to watch over this great assemblage of communities and interests, so, on another, that the foundation of our national policy will be laid in the pure and immutable principles of private morality, and the preeminence of free government be exemplified by all the attributes which can win the affections of its citizens and command the respect of the world. I dwell on this prospect with every satisfaction which an ardent love for my country can inspire, since there is no truth more thoroughly established than that there exists in the economy and course of nature an indissoluble union between virtue and happiness; between duty and advantage; between the genuine maxims of an honest and magnanimous policy and the solid rewards of public prosperity and felicity; since we ought to be no less persuaded that the propitious smiles of Heaven can never be expected on a nation that disregards the eternal rules of order and right which Heaven itself has ordained; and since the preservation of the sacred fire of liberty and the destiny of the republican model of government are justly considered, perhaps, as deeply, as finally, staked on the experiment entrusted to the hands of the American people.

"I must decline as inapplicable to myself any share in the personal emoluments which may be indispensably included in a permanent provision for the executive department."

. . . To the foregoing observations I have one to add, which will be most properly addressed to the House of Representatives. It concerns myself, and will therefore be as brief as possible. When I was first honored with a call into the service of my country, then on the eve of an arduous struggle for its liberties, the light in which I contemplated my duty required that I should renounce every pecuniary compensation. From this resolution I have in no instance departed; and being still under the impressions which produced it, I must decline as inapplicable to myself any share in the personal emoluments which may be indispensably included in a permanent provision for the executive department, and must accordingly pray that the pecuniary estimates for the station in which I am placed may during my continuance in it be limited to such actual expenditures as the public good may be thought to require.

Having thus imparted to you my sentiments as they have been awakened by the occasion which brings us together, I shall take my present leave; but not without resorting once more to the benign Parent of the Human Race in humble supplication that, since He has been pleased to favor the American people with opportunities for deliberating in perfect tranquillity, and dispositions for deciding with unparalleled unanimity on a form of government for the security of their union and the advancement of their happiness, so His divine blessing may be equally conspicuous in the enlarged views, the temperate consultations, and the wise measures on which the success of this Government must depend.

PRESIDENTIAL PORTRAIT OF
JAMES MADISON BY GILBERT STUART
(1755–1828)

The

BILL OF
RIGHTS

DECEMBER 15, 1791

ALTHOUGH THEY HAD fought hard for independence from Britain, the Americans had expectations of government that were strongly influenced by the British heritage of their forebears. In Britain, individual rights had been protected since Magna Carta (1215) and the Bill of Rights (1689). The latter was based on philosopher John Locke's views of man's natural rights and government's task to protect them. Locke's ideas had also influenced the 1776 Virginia Declaration of Rights, and subsequently the Declaration of Independence. At stake in the debate over the U.S. Constitution was the issue of a balance of power between national government and the rights of individuals only recently freed from British tyranny.

James Madison (1751–1836), nicknamed the "Father of the Constitution", was the leading theorist of republican government and the fourth President of the United States.

During the process of ratifying the U.S. Constitution, opinion was strongly divided between the Federalists, who wanted a strong government and no Bill of Rights, and the anti-Federalists, who wanted more power for the states and a Bill of Rights specifying the rights of individual citizens. Paradoxically, it was the memory of British violation of their civil rights before, and during, the Revolutionary War that made opponents of the U.S. Constitution so concerned about the absence of any discussion in it of individual rights. Virginia delegate George Mason, author of the Virginia Declaration of Rights, refused to vote for the Constitution at the Constitutional Convention in Philadelphia in 1787 when his last-minute attempt to include a bill of rights in the Constitution failed.

Those drafting the Constitution saw no need for guaranteed civil rights to be specifically spelled out as they did not think the new federal government would have the power to restrict them. They also argued that any list of rights would always be incomplete. However, it was clear that many delegates at the Constitutional Convention disagreed. Like Mason, they felt that central government would not protect personal rights unless these were actually stated in a bill. Some states only ratified the Constitution on the understanding that such a bill would be passed.

James Madison, a Federalist Virginian Congressman who had contributed to the Virginia Declaration, and who later became fourth President of the United States, was one of those who saw that compromise was necessary. He therefore prepared a series of 17 amendments incorporating British precedents concerning personal liberty in an American context. Of these, ten were eventually ratified.

Many Americans were religious dissenters who had left their homeland in search of liberty of worship, and this freedom is protected by the First Amendment to the

DEDICATED TO DEMOCRACY
In 1991, the original document of the Bill of Rights toured the country in honor of its bicentennial, visiting the capitals of 50 states. It is now on permanent display in the Rotunda at the National Archives and Records Administration Center in Washington D.C. When the National Archives were rededicated in 2003, President George W. Bush stated that the American Revolution declared the principles of "the quality of each person before God, and the responsibility of government to secure the rights of all."

Essential to acceptance of the U.S. Constitution (1789) was a series of amendments required by its opponents, who feared an over-powerful central government. Although they were proposed when the Constitution was debated, these amendments protecting civil rights were only adopted in 1791, when they were passed collectively as the Bill of Rights.

Constitution. The Revolutionary War had also placed the right of representation and self-determination firmly in American minds. Other amendments reflected controversial issues before and during the war: there was a ruling guaranteeing people's right to bear arms, another against standing armies, and another placing limits on soldiers being quartered in private homes. The Fourth Amendment protected people against general warrants and unreasonable searches and seizures, requiring warrants to be specific and only issued on "probable cause."

Some amendments based on British principles are now fundamental to the U.S. legal system. These are trial by jury, and protection from cruel and unusual punishment and self-incrimination. Grand-jury indictments are required in major criminal prosecutions, and there is a ban on trying a person twice on the same charge (double jeopardy). The Sixth Amendment protects criminal defendants, guaranteeing the accused a speedy trial by jury, the right to be informed of the accusation, and the right to be assisted by counsel. The Bill of Rights also bans the taking of private property for public use without just compensation, and forbids the deprivation of life, liberty, and property without due process of law. The concept of "due process" became the main constitutional tool for protecting any rights not specifically defined in the Bill of Rights.

The First and Second Amendments became obsolete shortly after adoption. However, the Fourth, Fifth, and Sixth Amendments have been described as the "workhorses" of the Bill of Rights, which was later extended to 24 amendments. The U.S. Supreme Court today is often called upon to hear cases relating to people's rights as laid down in the Bill of Rights, which is legally binding. Acts of Congress in conflict with the Bill of Rights can be rendered void if challenged on constitutional grounds.

Transcript of THE BILL OF RIGHTS

PREAMBLE
Congress of the United States begun and held at the City of New-York, on Wednesday the fourth of March, one thousand seven hundred and eighty nine.

THE Conventions of a number of the States, having at the time of their adopting the Constitution, expressed a desire, in order to prevent misconstruction or abuse of its powers, that further declaratory and restrictive clauses should be added: And as extending the ground of public confidence in the Government, will best ensure the beneficent ends of its institution.

RESOLVED by the Senate and House of Representatives of the United States of America, in Congress assembled, two thirds of both Houses concurring, that the following Articles be proposed to the Legislatures of the several States, as amendments to the Constitution of the United States, all, or any of which Articles, when ratified by three fourths of the said Legislatures, to be valid to all intents and purposes, as part of the said Constitution; viz.

ARTICLES in addition to, and Amendment of the Constitution of the United States of America, proposed by Congress, and ratified by the Legislatures of the several States, pursuant to the fifth Article of the original Constitution.

First amendment
Congress shall make no law respecting an establishment of religion, or prohibiting the free exercise thereof; or abridging the freedom of speech, or of the press; or the right of the people peaceably to assemble, and to petition the Government for a redress of grievances.

> "Congress shall make no law respecting an establishment of religion, or prohibiting the free exercise thereof."

Second amendment
A well regulated militia being necessary to the security of a free State, the right of the People to keep and bear arms shall not be infringed.

Third amendment
No Soldier shall, in time of peace be quartered in any house, without the consent of the Owner, nor in time of war, but in a manner to be prescribed by law.

Fourth amendment
The right of the people to be secure in their persons, houses, papers, and effects, against unreasonable searches and seizures, shall not be violated, and no Warrants shall issue, but upon probable cause, supported by oath or affirmation, and particularly describing the place to be searched, and the persons or things to be seized.

Fifth amendment
No person shall be held to answer for a capital, or otherwise infamous crime, unless on a presentment or indictment of a Grand Jury, except in cases arising in the land or naval forces, or in the Militia, when in actual service in time of War or public danger; nor shall any person be subject for the same offense to be twice put in jeopardy of life or limb; nor shall be compelled in any criminal case to be a witness against himself, nor be deprived of life, liberty, or property, without due process of law; nor shall private property be taken for public use, without just compensation.

> "In all criminal prosecutions, the accused shall enjoy the right to a speedy and public trial, by an impartial jury."

Sixth amendment
In all criminal prosecutions, the accused shall enjoy the right to a speedy and public trial, by an impartial jury of the State and district wherein the crime shall have been committed, which district shall have been previously ascertained by law, and to be informed of the nature and cause of the accusation; to be confronted with the witnesses against him; to have compulsory process for obtaining witnesses in his favor, and to have the Assistance of Counsel for his defense.

Seventh amendment
In suits at common law, where the value in controversy shall exceed twenty dollars, the right of trial by jury shall be preserved, and no fact tried by a jury, shall be otherwise reexamined in any court of the United States, than according to the rules of the common law.

Eighth amendment
Excessive bail shall not be required, nor excessive fines imposed, nor cruel and unusual punishments inflicted.

Ninth amendment
The enumeration in the Constitution, of certain rights, shall not be construed to deny or disparage others retained by the people.

Tenth amendment
The powers not delegated to the United States by the Constitution, nor prohibited by it to the States, are reserved for the States respectively, or to the people.

William Henry Harrison (1773–1841),
ninth President of the United States,
19th-century portrait from the
American school

The

HARRISON LAND ACT

An act providing for the sale of the lands
of the United States, in the territory
northwest of the Ohio, and above
the mouth of Kentucky river

May 10, 1800

THE HARRISON LAND ACT, 1800, was one of the most significant pieces of U.S. legislation in the nineteenth century. It set out the full details for the division, sale, and purchase of land in the Northwest Territory, reducing the minimum amount of land that could be purchased from the Federal Government from 640 acres to 320 acres, at a price of two dollars an acre, and introducing a credit feature. However, the act now has to be assessed in the wider context of land taken from the Native American peoples, either by purchase or force. William Henry Harrison, as a soldier and politician, participated in both these methods of replacing Native Americans with white settlers, making him a hero in the eyes of many at the time and helping to win him the Presidency in 1841. His actions are now viewed very differently.

■ *William Henry Harrison took office as ninth U.S. President in 1841 at the age of 68. He held the record as the oldest elected President until Ronald Reagan, the fortieth President, took office at the age of 69 nearly a century and a half later. His grandson, Benjamin Harrison, became the twenty-third President in 1889.*

William Henry Harrison, as his Presidential campaign loudly proclaimed, was the kind of man magazine illustrators and popular historians loved to portray: a buckskin pioneer; a frontiersman who drank cider in log cabins, but who made it to the Presidency; a war hero with a string of exotically named victories; a man who made treaties with Native Americans; and above all a champion of the settler—the little man standing up to the big, corrupt land speculators. Unhappily, the facts tell a very different story.

Harrison actually came from a patrician political family from Virginia. His father, Benjamin Harrison V, was one of the Founding Fathers, and had signed the Declaration of Independence and been governor of Virginia. On his father's death, William Henry Harrison gave up training as a doctor to enter the army, and as an ensign raised a troop to fight the Native Americans in the Northwest Territory, serving under General "Mad" Anthony Wayne. He fought in the Battle of Fallen Timbers in 1794, the final decisive battle in the Northwest Indian War, and was a signatory to the Treaty of Greenville. In this treaty, which white settlers later broke, the indigenous peoples, including the Wyandot, Delaware, Ottawa, and Miami, were paid to give up their claims to a large area of Ohio.

It was as delegate for the Northwest Territory to the U.S. Congress that Harrison helped pass the Land Act, enabling more settlers than ever before to buy land from the federal government. Thousands of people were encouraged to buy land on credit, in installments, and in smaller plots than had previously been possible, thus greatly increasing the settlement of the Northwest Territory. However, there were downsides to this apparently generous act. Firstly, squatters already occupying the land prior to the Act had no entitlement to ownership unless they had built a mill on the land they farmed. Secondly, settlers who could not keep up their credit payments lost everything they owned when the government foreclosed on the loans after four years. The credit provision was repealed in 1820.

Soon after the passing of the Land Act, Harrison became governor of the Indiana Territory and built a mansion, Grouseland, in the territorial capital, Vincennes. He is said to have favored the reintroduction of slavery and a plantation

society—something his friends did their best to conceal during his Presidential campaign. As Governor, he oversaw many treaties with the Native Americans, which extended white settlement into their lands. However, this continual encroachment—in particular the Treaty of Fort Wayne, by which the U.S. purchased approximately three million acres of Native American land in return for annuities ranging from $220 to $500 for each tribe—provoked a Native American resistance movement. It was led by two brothers from the Shawnee tribe, Tecumseh and Tenskwatawa, whom Harrison defeated at the Battle of Tippecanoe, outside Prophetstown, earning himself the nicknames "Old Tip" or "the Hero of Tippecanoe." Harrison went on to defeat a combined Native American and British force at the Battle of the Thames on October 5, 1813.

His distinguished war career led Harrison naturally into politics. He served in the U.S. House of Representatives (1816–19), the Ohio Senate (1819–21), and was a U.S. senator from 1825 until 1828, after which he made two bids for the Presidency. The first, in 1836, was unsuccessful, but he won at the second attempt, at the age of 68, after mounting the first modern-style Presidential campaign, with huge election rallies, catchy slogans, and a focus on personality, playing up his concocted image as a pioneering frontiersman. Harrison's inaugural speech was the longest in U.S. history, lasting over two hours. He delivered it on a bitterly cold day, and as a result fell ill with pneumonia. He died after only 30 days in office.

The Harrison Land Act, 1800, brought more land under white settlement in the Northwest Territory—a vast area taking in the present-day states of Ohio, Indiana, Michigan, Illinois, and Wisconsin.

Transcript of THE HARRISON LAND ACT

'*An ACT to amend the act, intituled, "An act providing for the sale of the lands of the United States, in the territory north-west of the Ohio, and above the mouth of Kentucky river."*

Sec. 1. *Be it enacted by the Senate and House of Representatives of the United States of America, in Congress assembled,* That for the disposal of the lands of the United States, directed to be sold by the act, intituled, "An act providing for the sale of the lands of the United States, in the territory north-west of the Ohio, and above the mouth of Kentucky river," there shall be four land-offices established in the said territory: One at Cincinnati, for lands below the Little Miami which have not heretofore been granted; one at Chilicothe, for lands east of the Sciota, south of the lands appropriated for satisfying military bounties to the late army of the United States, and west of the fifteenth range of townships; one at Marietta, for the lands east of the sixteenth range of townships, south of the before-mentioned military lands, and south of a line drawn due west from the north-west corner of the first township of the second range, to the said military lands; and one at Steubenville, for the lands north of the last mentioned line, and east or north of the said military lands: Each of the said offices shall be under the direction of an officer, to be called "The Register of the Land-Office," who shall be appointed by the President of the United States, by and with the advice and consent of the Senate, and shall give bond to the United States, with approved security, in the sum of ten thousand dollars, for the faithful discharge of the duties of his office; and shall reside at the place where the land-office is directed to be kept. . . .

Sec. 3. *And be it further enacted,* That the Surveyor-General shall cause the townships west of the Muskingum, which by the above-mentioned act are directed to be sold in quarter townships, to be subdivided into half sections of three hundred and twenty acres each, as nearly as may be, by running parallel lines through the same from east to west, and from south to north, at the distance of one mile from each other, and marking corners, at the distance of each half mile on the lines running from east to west . . .

"... no lands shall be sold by virtue of this act ... for less than two dollars per acre ..."

Sec. 5. *And be it further enacted,* That no lands shall be sold by virtue of this act, at either public or private sale, for less than two dollars per acre, and payment may be made for the same by all purchasers, either in specie, or in evidences of the public debt of the United States, at the rates prescribed by the act, intituled, "An act to authorize the receipt of evidences of the public debt in payment for the lands of the United States;" and shall be made in the following manner, and under the following conditions, to wit:

1. At the time of purchase, every purchaser shall, exclusively of the fees hereinafter-mentioned, pay six dollars for every section, and three dollars

for every half section, he may have purchased, for surveying expenses, and deposit one-twentieth part of the amount of the purchase money, to be forfeited, if within forty days one fourth part of the purchase money, including the said twentieth part, is not paid.

2. One-fourth part of the purchase money shall be paid within forty days after the day of sale as aforesaid and other fourth part shall be paid within two years; another fourth part within three years; and another fourth part within four years after the day of sale.

3. Interest, at the rate of six per cent. a year, from the day of sale, shall be charged upon each of the three last payments, payable as they respectively become due . . .

6. If any tract shall not be completely paid for within one year after the date of the last payment, the tract shall be advertised for sale by the Register of the land-office within whose district it may lie . . . ; but if the sum due, with interest, be not bidden and paid, then the land shall revert to the United States. All monies paid therefore shall be forfeited, and the Register of the land-office may proceed to dispose of the same to any purchaser, as in case of other lands at private sale . . .

> "If any tract shall not be completely paid for within one year after the date of the last payment, the tract shall be advertised for sale . . . ; but if the sum due, with interest, be not bidden and paid, then the land shall revert to the United States."

Sec. 16. *And be it further enacted,* That each person who before the passing of this act shall have erected, or begun to erect, a grist-mill or saw-mill upon any of the lands herein directed to be sold, shall be entitled to the pre-emption of the section including such mill, at the rate of two dollars per acre: Provided, The person or his heirs, claiming such right of pre-emption, shall produce to the Register of the land-office satisfactory evidence that he or they are entitled thereto, and shall be subject to and comply with the regulations and provisions by this act prescribed for other purchasers.

Sec. 17. *And be it further enacted,* That so much of the "act providing for the sale of the lands of the United States in the territory north-west of the river Ohio, and above the mouth of Kentucky river," as comes within the purview of this act, be and the same is hereby repealed.

THEODORE SEDGWICK,
Speaker of the House of Representatives.

TH: JEFFERSON,
*Vice-President of the United States, and
President of the Senate
Approved-May 10th, A.D. 1800.*

JOHN ADAMS,
President of the United States.

Bonaparte discussing the Louisiana Purchase Treaty with Talleyrand and Barbé-Marbois, print by André Castaigne (1861–1929)

The
LOUISIANA PURCHASE

Treaty between the United States of America and the French Republic

May 2, 1803

THE LOUISIANA PURCHASE was the largest land deal in the history of the United States, and is largely responsible for creating the shape of the U.S.A. we know today. It came about through events more connected with the Old World than the New, as France, Britain, and Spain contended for power and global domination. Under the terms of the treaty, signed in 1803, the United States bought the port of New Orleans and the vast French territory to the west of the Mississippi. The gains doubled the size of the U.S., encouraged expansion to the west, secured valuable trading routes, and tested the scope of the federal Constitution.

■ *Opportunism, and the confidence to act independently, marked the skills of the negotiators on both sides of the Louisiana Purchase deal. The Americans gained valuable territory and much-needed security, while the French rid themselves more or less honorably of an expensive obligation, raising essential funds in the process.*

The deal came about almost by accident. The American representatives, Robert Livingston and James Monroe, had only been authorized to negotiate the purchase of the port of New Orleans. Under Spanish rule, American merchants had the right to free use of the Mississippi River and could deposit their goods for export in the port of New Orleans. These rights, highly important to the American economy, were briefly revoked between 1798 and 1801, and the United States became worried that they would be lost once more when they heard that the Spanish king, Charles IV, had ceded the Louisiana territory (including New Orleans) to the French, under Napoleon Bonaparte, in a secret treaty signed at San Ildefonso in Spain in 1800. Napoleon had hoped to create a French empire in the New World, centered on Hispaniola (Haiti), using New Orleans and the Mississippi valley as its food and trade center. However, a slave rebellion and an outbreak of yellow fever that decimated the French army forced Napoleon to abandon Haiti to concentrate on the impending war with Britain in Europe. He no longer needed Louisiana, which he would not be able to defend from the British, but he did need money. The American negotiators, who were prepared to pay $10 million for New Orleans, were suddenly offered the whole of the Louisiana lands for $15 million, and immediately negotiated the treaty.

Under the terms of the treaty, signed on May 2 and antedated to April 30, the United States purchased more than 800,000 square miles of land extending from the Mississippi River in the east to the Rocky Mountains in the west, and from the Gulf of Mexico in the south to headwaters of the Missouri River in the north. The price, in the currency of the day, was less than three cents an acre. The new territory covered what is now New Orleans, Louisiana, Missouri, Arkansas, Iowa, North and South Dakota, Nebraska, Oklahoma, most of Kansas, most of Colorado, Wyoming, Montana, and Minnesota, and parts of New Mexico and north Texas: 22.3 percent of the land area of the modern United States. It also included small areas of territory that would eventually become part of the Canadian provinces of Manitoba, Saskatchewan, and Alberta.

However, the treaty did not specify the boundaries in detail, partly because France did not wish to anger Spain, and partly because at the time much of the land still remained unknown. Spain contested the loss of Texas and half of New Mexico and the ownership of West Florida. It was not until the 1819 Adams-Onis

Treaty that the dispute was settled, by which Spain ceded all of Florida, and the boundary between the Louisiana territory and the Spanish colonies was set along the Sabine, Red, and Arkansas rivers and the 42nd parallel.

The Louisiana Purchase treaty, 1803. Under the terms of the Franco-American treaty, the United States acquired—for just under three cents an acre—territory that makes up one-fifth of the total area of the present-day U.S.A.

Transcript of THE LOUISIANA PURCHASE

'The President of the United States of America and the First Consul of the French Republic in the name of the French People desiring to remove all Source of misunderstanding relative to objects of discussion mentioned in the Second and fifth articles of the Convention of the 8th Vendémiaire[1] an 9/30 September 1800 relative to the rights claimed by the United States in virtue of the Treaty concluded at Madrid the 27 of October 1795, between His Catholic Majesty & the Said United States, & willing to Strengthen the union and friendship which at the time of the Said Convention was happily reestablished between the two nations have respectively named their Plenipotentiaries to wit The President of the United States, by and with the advice and consent of the Senate of the Said States; Robert R. Livingston Minister Plenipotentiary of the United States and James Monroe Minister Plenipotentiary and Envoy extraordinary of the Said States near the Government of the French Republic; And the First Consul in the name of the French people, Citizen Francis Barbé Marbois Minister of the public treasury who after having respectively exchanged their full powers have agreed to the following Articles.

Article I

Whereas by the Article the third of the Treaty concluded at St Ildefonso the 9th Vendémiaire an 9/1st October 1800 between the First Consul of the French Republic and his Catholic Majesty it was agreed as follows.

The First Consul of the French Republic desiring to give to the United States a strong proof of his friendship doth hereby cede to the United States in the name of the French Republic for ever and in full Sovereignty the said territory with all its rights and appurtenances as fully and in the Same manner as they have been acquired by the French Republic in virtue of the above mentioned Treaty concluded with his Catholic Majesty.

> "The First Consul of the French Republic desiring to give to the United States a strong proof of his friendship doth hereby cede to the United States in the name of the French Republic for ever and in full Sovereignty the said territory with all its rights and appurtenances ..."

Art: II

In the cession made by the preceeding article are included the adjacent Islands belonging to Louisiana all public lots and Squares, vacant lands and all public buildings, fortifications, barracks and other edifices which are not private property.—The Archives, papers & documents relative to the domain and Sovereignty of Louisiana and its dependances will be left in the possession of the Commissaries of the United States, and copies will be afterwards given in due form to the Magistrates and Municipal officers of such of the said papers and documents as may be necessary to them.

Art: III

The inhabitants of the ceded territory shall be incorporated in the Union of the United States and admitted as soon as possible according to the principles of the federal Constitution to the enjoyment of all these rights, advantages and immunities of citizens of the United States, and in the mean time they shall be maintained

"The inhabitants of the ceded territory shall be incorporated in the Union of the United States and admitted as soon as possible . . . to the enjoyment of all these rights, advantages and immunities of citizens of the United States."

and protected in the free enjoyment of their liberty, property and the Religion which they profess.

Art: IV

There Shall be Sent by the Government of France a Commissary to Louisiana to the end that he do every act necessary as well to receive from the Officers of his Catholic Majesty the Said country and its dependances in the name of the French Republic . . .

Art: V

Immediately after the ratification of the present Treaty by the President of the United States and in case that of the first Consul's shall have been previously obtained, the commissary of the French Republic shall remit all military posts of New Orleans and other parts of the ceded territory to the Commissary or Commissaries named by the President to take possession—the troops whether of France or Spain who may be there shall cease to occupy any military post from the time of taking possession and shall be embarked as soon as possible in the course of three months after the ratification of this treaty.

Art: VI

The United States promise to execute Such treaties and articles as may have been agreed between Spain and the tribes and nations of Indians until by mutual consent of the United States and the said tribes or nations other Suitable articles Shall have been agreed upon.

Art: VII

As it is reciprocally advantageous to the commerce of France and the United States to encourage the communication of both nations for a limited time in the country ceded by the present treaty until general arrangements relative to commerce of both nations may be agreed on; it has been agreed between the contracting parties that the French Ships coming directly from France or any of her colonies loaded only with the produce and manufactures of France or her Said Colonies; and the Ships of Spain coming directly from Spain or any of her colonies loaded only with the produce or manufactures of Spain or her Colonies shall be admitted during the Space of twelve years in the Port of New-Orleans and in all other legal ports-of-entry within the ceded territory in the Same manner as the Ships of the United States coming directly from France or Spain or any of their Colonies without being Subject to any other or greater duty on merchandize or other or greater tonnage than that paid by the citizens of the United States.

During that Space of time above mentioned no other nation Shall have a right to the Same privileges in the Ports of the ceded territory—the twelve years Shall commence three months after the exchange of ratifications if it Shall take place in France or three months after it Shall have been notified at Paris to the French Government if it Shall take place in the United States; It is however well understood that the object of the above article is to favor the manufactures, Commerce, freight and navigation of France and of Spain So far as relates to the importations that the French and Spanish Shall make into the Said Ports of the United States without in any Sort affecting the regulations that the United States may make concerning the exportation of the produce and merchandize of the United States, or any right they may have to make Such regulations.

Art: VIII

In future and for ever after the expiration of the twelve years, the Ships of France shall be treated upon the footing of the most favored nations in the ports above mentioned.

Art: IX

The particular Convention Signed this day by the respective Ministers, having for its object to provide for the payment of debts due to the Citizens of the United States by the French Republic prior to the 30th Sept. 1800 (8th Vendémiaire an 9) is approved and to have its execution in the Same manner as if it had been inserted in this present treaty, and it Shall be ratified in the same form and in the Same time So that the one Shall not be ratified distinct from the other.

Art: X

The present treaty Shall be ratified in good and due form and the ratifications Shall be exchanged in the Space of Six months after the date of the Signature by the Ministers Plenipotentiary or Sooner if possible.

In faith whereof the respective Plenipotentiaries have Signed these articles in the French and English languages; declaring nevertheless that the present Treaty was originally agreed to in the French language; and have thereunto affixed their Seals.

Done at Paris the tenth day of Floréal[2] in the eleventh year of the French Republic; and the 30th of April 1803.

Robt R Livingston [seal]
Jas. Monroe [seal]
Barbé-Marbois [seal]

The French Revolutionary calendar comprised 12 months of 30 days each, which were given new names derived from nature:

1 Vendémiaire ("vintage month") was the first month of the French Revolutionary year, from September 22 to October 21.

2 Floréal ("blossom month") was the second month of the spring quarter. It started on April 20 or 21 and ended on May 19 or 20.

Henry Clay (1777–1852),
proposer of the Missouri
Compromise, painted in 1843 by
John Neagle (1796–1865)

The

MISSOURI COMPROMISE

March 5–6, 1820

IN 1820 THE American Senate was finely balanced, with an equal number of Senators from slave states (those in which slavery was legal) and Senators from free states. The issue of slavery smoldered in Congressional debates, and had to be confronted when Missouri, one of the new Louisiana Purchase lands where slavery was practiced, asked to be admitted to the Union. When a Northern representative tried to add an antislavery amendment to the act of admission, the federal government's right to impose conditions on new admissions to the Union was angrily contested. This led to the formulation of the Missouri Compromise, allowing slavery in Missouri but prohibiting it in other states to the north of the 36° 30′ line of latitude. A second Compromise in 1821 disastrously affected the status of black people as U.S. citizens.

Henry Clay is known as the "Great Compromiser" for his promotion of compromise between North and South prior to the Civil War. Almost universally popular, Clay was the first person to lie in state in the Capitol after his death in 1852. Clay's biographer, the German-born Carl Schurz, said that the key to Clay's success lay in "his persuasiveness as an orator and his charming personality."

On the face of it, the act of admission for Missouri was a perfectly ordinary act, full of legal jargon, laying down the conditions to admit a new state to the Union, dealing with boundaries, numbers of representatives, taxes, salt springs, schools, roads, and canals. The final section stated that slavery was to be prohibited in all the Louisiana Purchase lands above the 36° 30′ latitude—but Missouri, whose southern border lay along this line, was excepted. This compromise was designed to maintain the balance of free and slave states in the Union, and to appease both the proslavery and antislavery factions. It allowed Missouri to enter the Union as a slave state, while simultaneously admitting Maine as a free state. However, its effect was to establish a fault line between the Northern and Southern states, one that would later open up and eventually lead to the Civil War.

Many of the settlers in Missouri came from the slave-owning South and so expected Missouri to remain a slave territory. However, when Missouri applied for statehood in 1817, the New York representative, James Tallmadge, tried to add an antislavery amendment. This provoked an angry dispute over the federal government's right to restrict slavery and to impose conditions on new states that did not apply to states already in the Union. Although Tallmadge's amendment was passed in the Northern-dominated House of Representatives in February 1819, it failed in the Senate.

Senator Jesse B. Thomas of Illinois then came up with the compromise amendment, allowing Missouri to be a slave state. This was strongly backed by the influential speaker of the House, Henry Clay, and accepted in 1820. Missouri's borders often ran down the middle of rivers, most significantly the Mississippi. This meant that a river would be bordered on one side by a slave state and on the other bank by a free state. Slaves who managed to escape across the river to the free state could still be "lawfully reclaimed."

The controversial compromise was not enough for Missouri, however. Its new constitutional convention excluded "free negroes and mulattoes" from the state, provoking a new storm in Congress as many Northern states objected to this racial provision. Henry

THOMAS JEFFERSON'S WARNING

"This momentous question, like a fire bell in the night, awakened and filled me with terror. I considered it at once as the knell of the Union. It is hushed, indeed, for the moment. But this is a reprieve only, not a final sentence. A geographical line, coinciding with a marked principle, moral and political, once conceived and held up to the angry passions of men, will never be obliterated; and every new irritation will mark it deeper and deeper." Letter to John Holmes, April 22, 1820

The committee of conference of the Senate and of the House of Representatives, on the subject of the disagreeing votes of the Two Houses, upon the Bill entitled an "Act for the admission of the State of Maine into the Union";

Report the following Resolution.

Resolved.

1st. That they recommend to the Senate to recede from their amendments to the said Bill

2d. That they recommend to the two Houses to agree to strike out of the fourth section of the Bill from the House of Representatives, now pending in the Senate, entitled an "Act to authorize the people of the Missouri Territory to form a Constitution and State Government, and for the admission of such State into the Union upon an equal footing with the original States" the following proviso in the following words — and shall ordain and establish, that there shall be neither Slavery nor involuntary servitude otherwise than in the

The Missouri Compromise was actually two amendments to the act allowing Missouri statehood and admission to the Union. These Compromises of 1820 and 1821 concerned slavery and the status of black people—the powder that later ignited the American Civil War.

Clay then formulated the second Missouri Compromise, which stated that Missouri would not be admitted to the Union unless it agreed that the exclusionary clause in its constitution should "never be constructed to authorize the passage of any law" affecting the privileges and immunities of any U.S. citizen. This apparently undermined the racial exclusion, and when Missouri accepted it, the state was in turn admitted into the Union in August 1821. In fact, the wording was deliberately ambiguous and was interpreted to mean that blacks of African origin did not qualify as U.S. citizens.

In 1857 the Supreme Court ruled the first Compromise unconstitutional, and ratified the second Compromise. This inflamed antislavery feeling in the North and contributed directly to the outbreak of the Civil War in 1861.

Transcript of THE MISSOURI COMPROMISE

Be it enacted by the Senate and House of Representatives of the United States of America, in Congress assembled, That the inhabitants of that portion of the Missouri territory included within the boundaries herein after designated, be, and they are hereby, authorized to form for themselves a constitution and state government, and to assume such name as they shall deem proper; and the said state, when formed, shall be admitted into the Union, upon an equal footing with the original states, in all respects whatsoever.

SEC. 2. And be it further enacted, That the said state shall consist of all the territory included within the following boundaries, to wit: Beginning in the middle of the Mississippi river, on the parallel of thirty-six degrees of north latitude; thence west, along that parallel of latitude, to the St. Francois river; thence up, and following the course of that river, in the middle of the main channel thereof, to the parallel of latitude of thirty-six degrees and thirty minutes; thence west, along the same, to a point where the said parallel is intersected by a meridian line passing through the middle of the mouth of the Kansas river, where the same empties into the Missouri river, thence, from the point aforesaid north, along the said meridian line, to the intersection of the parallel of latitude which passes through the rapids of the river Des Moines, making the said line to correspond with the Indian boundary line; thence east, from the point of intersection last aforesaid, along the said parallel of latitude, to the middle of the channel of the main fork of the said river Des Moines; thence down and along the middle of the main channel of the said river Des Moines, to the mouth of the same, where it

> "... the inhabitants of that portion of the Missouri territory included within the boundaries herein after designated ... are hereby authorized to form for themselves a constitution and state government."

empties into the Mississippi river; thence, due east, to the middle of the main channel of the Mississippi river; thence down, and following the course of the Mississippi river, in the middle of the main channel thereof, to the place of beginning: Provided, The said state shall ratify the boundaries aforesaid. And provided also, That the said state shall have concurrent jurisdiction on the river Mississippi, and every other river bordering on the said state so far as the said rivers shall form a common boundary to the said state; and any other state or states, now or hereafter to be formed and bounded by the same, such rivers to be common to both; and that the river Mississippi, and the navigable rivers and waters leading into the same, shall be common highways, and for ever free, as well to the inhabitants of the said state as to other citizens of the United States, without any tax, duty impost, or toll, therefor, imposed by the said state.

SEC. 3. And be it further enacted, That all free white male citizens of the United States, who shall have arrived at the age of twenty-one years, and have resided in said territory: three months previous to the day of election, and all other persons qualified to vote for representatives to the general assembly of the said territory, shall be qualified to be elected and they are hereby qualified and authorized to vote, and choose representatives to form a convention, who shall be apportioned amongst the several counties as follows:

> "And be it further enacted, That the members of the convention thus duly elected, shall be, and they are hereby authorized to meet at the seat of government of said territory on the second Monday of the month of June next."

From the county of Howard, five representatives. From the county of Cooper, three representatives. From the county of Montgomery, two representatives. From the county of Pike, one representative. From the county of Lincoln, one representative. From the county of St. Charles, three representatives. From the county of Franklin, one representative. From the county of St. Louis, eight representatives. From the county of Jefferson, one representative. From the county of Washington, three representatives. From the county of St. Genevieve, four representatives. From the county of Madison, one representative. From the county of Cape Girardeau, five representatives. From the county of New Madrid, two representatives. From the county of Wayne, and that portion of the county of Lawrence which falls within the boundaries herein designated, one representative.

And the election for the representatives aforesaid shall be holden on the first Monday, and two succeeding days of May next, throughout the several counties aforesaid in the said territory, and shall be, in every respect, held and conducted in the same manner, and under the same regulations as is prescribed by the laws of the said territory regulating elections therein for members of the general assembly, except that the returns of the election in that portion of Lawrence county included in the boundaries aforesaid, shall be made to the county of Wayne, as is provided in other cases under the laws of said territory.

SEC. 4. And be it further enacted, That the members of the convention thus duly elected, shall be, and they are hereby authorized to meet at the seat of government of said territory on the second Monday of the month of June next; and the said convention, when so assembled, shall have power and authority to adjourn to any other place in the said territory, which to them shall seem best for the convenient transaction of their business; and which convention, when so met, shall first determine by a majority of the whole number elected, whether it be, or be not, expedient at that time to form a constitution and state government for the people within the said territory, as included within the boundaries above designated; and if it be deemed expedient, the convention shall be, and hereby is, authorized to form a constitution and state government; or, if it be deemed more expedient, the said convention shall provide by ordinance for electing representatives to form a constitution or frame of government; which said representatives shall be chosen in such manner, and in such proportion as they shall designate; and shall meet at such time and place as shall be prescribed by the said ordinance; and shall then form for the people of said territory, within the boundaries aforesaid, a constitution and state government: Provided, That the same, whenever formed, shall be republican, and not repugnant to the constitution of the United States; and that the legislature of said state shall never interfere with the primary disposal of the soil by the United States, nor with any regulations Congress may find necessary for securing the title in such soil to the bona fide purchasers . . .

SEC. 7. And be it further enacted, That in case a constitution and state government shall be formed for the people of the said territory of Missouri, the said convention or representatives, as soon thereafter as may be, shall cause a true and attested copy of such constitution or frame of state government, as shall be formed or provided, to be transmitted to Congress.

SEC. 8. And be it further enacted, That in all that territory ceded by France to the United States, under the name of Louisiana, which lies north of thirty-six degrees and thirty minutes north latitude, not included within the limits of the state, contemplated by this act, slavery and involuntary servitude, otherwise than in the punishment of crimes, whereof the parties shall have been duly convicted, shall be, and is hereby, forever prohibited: Provided always, That any person escaping into the same, from whom labour or service is lawfully claimed, in any state or territory of the United States, such fugitive may be lawfully reclaimed and conveyed to the person claiming his or her labour or service as aforesaid.

APPROVED, March 6, 1820

James Monroe (1758–1831),
fifth President of the United States,
painted by Asher Brown Durand
(1796–1886)

The

MONROE
DOCTRINE

President James Monroe's State of the
Union address to Congress

December 2, 1823

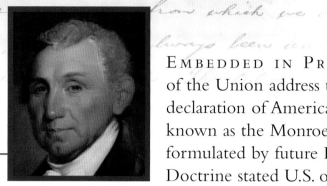

EMBEDDED IN PRESIDENT James Monroe's seventh State of the Union address to Congress in 1823 was the first major declaration of American foreign policy. This has always been known as the Monroe Doctrine, although it was originally formulated by future President John Quincy Adams. The Doctrine stated U.S. opposition to European intervention in the Western hemisphere, opposing any further colonization while respecting existing European colonies. It also stated U.S. neutrality in European quarrels. Implicitly, the Doctrine was a declaration of U.S. hegemony throughout the Americas.

■ *James Monroe (1758–1831) protégé and friend of Thomas Jefferson and fifth U.S. President. His two administrations (1817–25) were marked by his skill in foreign policy and benefited from a period of relative calm in U.S. politics, known as "the Era of Good Feelings."*

By 1823, many Latin American nations, including Argentina, Chile, and Venezuela, had asserted their independence from Spain, and were anxious that the United States recognize them as republics. Although sympathetic to their cause, the United States had refrained from intervening in the wars between the former Spanish colonies and Spain. However, Russia and France were now threatening to help Spain recover her colonies, hoping to establish or increase their own power in North and South America. Britain, on the other hand, wanted to prevent her old European rivals from regaining power in the New World, and regarded the potential for trade with the Latin American nations as more important than making a stand for imperialism. When Britain approached the United States with a proposal to form an alliance against the other European powers, many politicians, including Thomas Jefferson and James Madison, were in favor of the idea. However, President James Monroe and Secretary of State John Quincy Adams did not want to risk war with the European nations.

President Monroe's State of the Union address stated that European powers could no longer colonize or interfere in the affairs of the Americas, and that if they did, the United States would see their actions "as the manifestation of an unfriendly disposition toward the United States . . . endangering our peace and happiness." At the same time, the U.S. would remain neutral in the present dispute between Spain and the new Latin American governments (although the U.S. did not consider continued sales of naval vessels to the rebel armies as compromising that neutrality). The U.S. also affirmed its policy of non interference in purely European matters.

The Doctrine is significant for the stance the United States took against the European powers, and for the explicit identification it made with the rest of the American continent. Its powerful warning was heeded from the start, although the success of U.S. foreign policy for the next half-century owed a great deal to support from the British, whose own interests were served by it. However, it is the ways in which the Monroe Doctrine has been interpreted since 1823 that have made it so famous. It has been used to justify the United States' long period of isolationism, as well as its decisions to intervene in other countries in more

JOHN QUINCY ADAMS *saw President Monroe's State of the Union address as an opportunity for the United States to state its diplomatic position and assert its determination to preserve its independent sovereignty. At a Cabinet meeting on November 7, 1823, he argued, "It would be more candid, as well as more dignified, to avow our principles explicitly to Russia and France, than to come in as a cockboat in the wake of the British man-of-war."*

recent times. Many Latin American states have long been rightly suspicious of their increasingly powerful neighbor taking such a close interest in their affairs. President Theodore Roosevelt's famous 1904 Corollary to the Doctrine explicitly stated the right of the U.S. to exercise "international police power" in Latin America. Since 1846, the Doctrine and its corollary have been used to back numerous interventions there, such as the military occupation of the Dominican Republic from 1916 to 1922. In 1962 President Kennedy used the Monroe Doctrine to justify his trade embargo on Cuba, which he regarded as a Soviet puppet, and in the 1980s the Director of the CIA cited the Doctrine to justify the training of "Contra" rebels to fight against the left-wing Sandinista government in Nicaragua.

The Monroe Doctrine has been the backbone of U.S. foreign policy for nearly 200 years. A warning to the European powers not to embark on further colonial ventures in the Western Hemisphere, it can be seen as the first statement of America's great-power ambitions.

Transcript of THE MONROE DOCTRINE

' At the proposal of the Russian Imperial Government, made through the minister of the Emperor residing here, a full power and instructions have been transmitted to the minister of the United States at St. Petersburg to arrange by amicable negotiation the respective rights and interests of the two nations on the northwest coast of this continent. A similar proposal has been made by His Imperial Majesty to the Government of Great Britain, which has likewise been acceded to. The Government of the United States has been desirous by this friendly proceeding of manifesting the great value which they have invariably attached to the friendship of the Emperor and their solicitude to cultivate the best understanding with his Government. In the discussions to which this interest has given rise and in the arrangements by which they may terminate the occasion has been judged proper for asserting, as a principle in which the rights and interests of the United States are involved, that the American continents, by the free and independent condition which they have assumed and maintain, are henceforth not to be considered as subjects for future colonization by any European powers . . .

"The American continents, by the free and independent condition which they have assumed and maintain, are henceforth not to be considered as subjects for future colonization by any European powers."

It was stated at the commencement of the last session that a great effort was then making in Spain and Portugal to improve the condition of the people of those countries, and that it appeared to be conducted with extraordinary moderation. It need scarcely be remarked that the results have been so far very different from what was then anticipated. Of events in that quarter of the globe, with which we have so much intercourse and from which we derive our origin, we have always been anxious and interested spectators. The citizens of the United States cherish sentiments the most friendly in favor of the liberty and happiness of their fellow-men on that side of the Atlantic. In the wars of the European powers in matters relating to themselves we have never taken any part, nor does it comport with our policy to do so. It is only when our rights are invaded or seriously menaced that we resent injuries or make preparation for our defense. With the movements in this hemisphere we are of necessity more immediately connected, and by causes which must be obvious to all enlightened and impartial observers. The political system of the allied powers is essentially different in this respect from that of America. This difference proceeds from that which exists in their respective Governments; and to the defense of our own, which has been achieved by the loss of so much blood and treasure, and matured by the wisdom of their most enlightened citizens, and under which we have enjoyed unexampled felicity, this whole nation is devoted. We owe it, therefore, to candor and to the amicable relations existing between the United States and those powers to declare that we should consider any attempt on their part to extend their system to any portion of this hemisphere as dangerous to our peace and safety. With the existing colonies or dependencies of any European power we have not interfered and shall not interfere. But with the Governments who have declared their independence and maintain it, and whose independence we have, on great consideration and on just principles, acknowledged, we could not view any interposition for the purpose of oppressing them, or controlling in any other manner their destiny, by any European power in any other light than as the manifestation of an unfriendly disposition toward the United States. In the war between those new Governments and Spain we declared our neutrality at the time of their recognition, and to this we have adhered, and shall continue to adhere, provided no change shall occur which, in the judgement of the competent authorities of this Government, shall make a corresponding change on the part of the United States indispensable to their security.

The late events in Spain and Portugal shew that Europe is still unsettled. Of this important fact no stronger proof can be adduced than that the allied powers should have thought it proper, on any principle satisfactory to themselves, to have interposed by force in the internal concerns of Spain.

> "It is impossible that the allied powers should extend their political system to any portion of either continent without endangering our peace and happiness . . . It is equally impossible, therefore, that we should behold such interposition in any form with indifference."

To what extent such interposition may be carried, on the same principle, is a question in which all independent powers whose governments differ from theirs are interested, even those most remote, and surely none of them more so than the United States. Our policy in regard to Europe, which was adopted at an early stage of the wars which have so long agitated that quarter of the globe, nevertheless remains the same, which is, not to interfere in the internal concerns of any of its powers; to consider the government de facto as the legitimate government for us; to cultivate friendly relations with it, and to preserve those relations by a frank, firm, and manly policy, meeting in all instances the just claims of every power, submitting to injuries from none. But in regard to those continents circumstances are eminently and conspicuously different.

It is impossible that the allied powers should extend their political system to any portion of either continent without endangering our peace and happiness; nor can anyone believe that our southern brethren, if left to themselves, would adopt it of their own accord. It is equally impossible, therefore, that we should behold such interposition in any form with indifference. If we look to the comparative strength and resources of Spain and those new Governments, and their distance from each other, it must be obvious that she can never subdue them. It is still the true policy of the United States to leave the parties to themselves, in hope that other powers will pursue the same course . . .

ANDREW JACKSON (1767–1845),
SEVENTH PRESIDENT OF THE
UNITED STATES, PAINTED BY
THOMAS SULLY (1783–1872)

President Andrew Jackson's address to Congress on

INDIAN REMOVAL

DECEMBER 6, 1830

IT IS DIFFICULT now to read the self-congratulatory opening sentences of President Andrew Jackson's Congressional address on Indian removal, knowing what we do of the treachery, abuse, and sufferings inflicted on the Native peoples at the time. Jackson's policy was designed to appease white settlers by granting them valuable land, through the forcible removal of the indigenous tribes. Jackson portrayed it as a generous move, one in the best interests of the resettled peoples, designed to protect and "civilize savages," for which they should be grateful.

■ *Andrew Jackson, self-made man, military hero, and founder of the Democratic Party, served two terms as President. Confrontational, egalitarian, and controversial, he strengthened the executive role of the Presidency.*

Given that Jackson had spent much of his military career waging war on Native American peoples, he was never, as President, likely to be a respecter of their rights. He had made his name when he inflicted a crushing defeat on the Creek people in 1814, and sparked an international incident when he pursued the Seminole into Spanish Florida in 1818. The Creek lost 22 million acres in southern Georgia and central Alabama during the War of 1812. Jackson had also been instrumental in negotiating a number of treaties to persuade the southern tribes to move west, outside the existing borders of the United States, so vacating their land for white settlers to grow cotton and prospect for gold. Very few actually moved.

The Indian Removal Act of 1830 was the first major piece of legislation to override the legal and political rights of the Native Americans. It provided a framework for the removal of the tribes of the southeast; the dispossessed tribes were to be offered payment, and resettlement in unsettled prairies in the west, in present-day Oklahoma. Ostensibly, there was to be negotiation, but in fact, if they refused, they were sometimes forcibly removed or so mistreated that they were eventually left no choice but to leave. Andrew Jackson's presentation of this as a "benevolent policy" was an effective whitewash of the act's implications. The purchase of tribal homelands and the evacuation of their peoples beyond the national frontier assured domestic security (Native Americans in the past allied themselves with Britain and Spain in wars with the United States). It also freed fertile territory for the expanding population of white settlers. Jackson did not advocate forcible evacuation: the removal was to be effected through legal treaties, more of which were signed during Jackson's Presidency than under any other administration.

Jackson characterized the Native Americans as "a few thousand savages" ranging through forest, contrasting them with "12,000,000 happy people" in cities, towns, and farms, "filled with all the blessings of liberty, civilization, and religion." This was disingenuous: many of the so-called "five civilized tribes"—Chickasaw, Choctaw, Seminole, Cherokee, and Creek—were engaged in large-scale

AN OFFICIAL APOLOGY *to the Native Peoples was introduced in Congress by Representatives from Ohio and Kansas in 2004. The document proposes that the government "apologizes on behalf of the people of the United States to all Native Peoples for the many instances of violence, maltreatment, and neglect inflicted on Native Peoples by citizens of the United States."*

farming. They also had Western education, trades, and representative government, and even kept slaves—although some, such as the Seminole, further enraged white farmers by taking in runaway slaves. The Cherokee in Georgia had tried to coexist with white settlers; in 1827 they had adopted a written constitution, and considered themselves a sovereign nation. Far from being "unwilling to submit to the laws of the States and mingle with their population," they tried to use the courts to combat the settlers who stole their livestock and burned their towns. Although the Cherokee eventually won a Supreme Court appeal in 1831, prohibiting whites from settling on their land without license from the state, Georgia refused to enforce the law.

Most Native resistance to removal was non-violent, but over the next 28 years forced removal provoked two more Seminole wars and countless deaths. In the 1830s, about 100,000 people were forced by the U.S. military to march westward, some in manacles, with up to 25 percent dying on the way. The most infamous incident was the 1838–9 trek of 16,000 Cherokee, who had been tricked into a fraudulent treaty and then forcibly removed. In what has become known as the Trail of Tears, approximately 4,000 died from sickness and starvation.

In the end, even the promised "title in perpetuity" to their new lands—some of them too poor to sustain more than subsistence farming—was taken away as more white settlers moved west. Today, the removal of Native Americans from their homelands is viewed as one of the most shameful episodes in U.S. history.

The Indian Removal Act, 1830, advocated the removal of Native Americans from their southeastern homelands to unsettled territory in the west. Andrew Jackson considered the act a humane and civilizing policy necessary for security and prosperity.

Transcript of PRESIDENT JACKSON'S ADDRESS ON INDIAN REMOVAL

'It gives me pleasure to announce to Congress that the benevolent policy of the Government, steadily pursued for nearly thirty years, in relation to the removal of the Indians beyond the white settlements is approaching to a happy consummation. Two important tribes have accepted the provision made for their removal at the last session of Congress, and it is believed that their example will induce the remaining tribes also to seek the same obvious advantages.

The consequences of a speedy removal will be important to the United States, to individual States, and to the Indians themselves. The pecuniary advantages which it promises to the Government are the least of its recommendations. It puts an end to all possible danger of collision between the authorities of the General and State Governments on account of the Indians. It will place a dense and civilized population in large tracts of country now occupied by a few savage hunters. By opening the whole territory between Tennessee on the north and Louisiana on the south to the settlement of the whites it will incalculably strengthen the southwestern frontier and render the adjacent States strong enough to repel future invasions without remote aid. It will relieve the whole State of Mississippi and the western part of Alabama of Indian occupancy, and enable those States to advance rapidly in population, wealth, and power. It will separate the Indians from immediate contact with settlements of whites; free them from the power of the States; enable them to pursue happiness in their own way and under their own rude institutions; will retard the progress of decay, which is lessening their numbers, and perhaps cause them gradually, under the protection of the Government and through the influence of good counsels, to cast off their savage habits and become an interesting, civilized, and Christian community.

"What good man would prefer a country covered with forests and ranged by a few thousand savages to our extensive Republic, studded with cities, towns, and prosperous farms?"

What good man would prefer a country covered with forests and ranged by a few thousand savages to our extensive Republic, studded with cities, towns, and prosperous farms embellished with all the improvements which art can devise or industry execute, occupied by more than 12,000,000 happy people, and filled with all the blessings of liberty, civilization and religion?

The present policy of the Government is but a continuation of the same progressive change by a milder process. The tribes which occupied the countries now constituting the Eastern States were annihilated or have melted away to make room for the whites. The waves of population and civilization are rolling to the westward, and we now propose to acquire the countries occupied by the red men of the South and West by a fair exchange, and, at the expense of the United States, to send them to land where their existence may be prolonged and perhaps made perpetual. Doubtless it will be painful to leave the graves of their fathers; but what do they more than our ancestors did or than our children are now doing? To better their condition in an unknown land our forefathers left all that was dear in earthly objects. Our children by thousands yearly leave the land of their birth to seek new homes in distant regions. Does Humanity weep at these painful separations from everything, animate and inanimate, with which the young heart has become entwined? Far from it. It is rather a source of joy that our country affords scope where our young population may range unconstrained in body or in mind, developing the power and facilities of man in their highest perfection. These remove hundreds and almost thousands of miles at their own expense, purchase the lands they occupy, and support themselves at their new homes from the moment of their arrival. Can it be cruel in this Government when, by events which it can not control, the Indian is made discontented in his ancient home to purchase his lands, to give him a new and extensive territory, to pay the expense of his removal, and support him a year in his new abode? How many thousands of our own people would gladly embrace the opportunity of removing to the West on such conditions! If the offers made to the Indians were extended to them, they would be hailed with gratitude and joy.

> "The policy of the General Government toward the red man is not only liberal, but generous . . . The General Government kindly offers him a new home, and proposes to pay the whole expense of his removal and settlement."

And is it supposed that the wandering savage has a stronger attachment to his home than the settled, civilized Christian? Is it more afflicting to him to leave the graves of his fathers than it is to our brothers and children? Rightly considered, the policy of the General Government toward the red man is not only liberal, but generous. He is unwilling to submit to the laws of the States and mingle with their population. To save him from this alternative, or perhaps utter annihilation, the General Government kindly offers him a new home, and proposes to pay the whole expense of his removal and settlement.

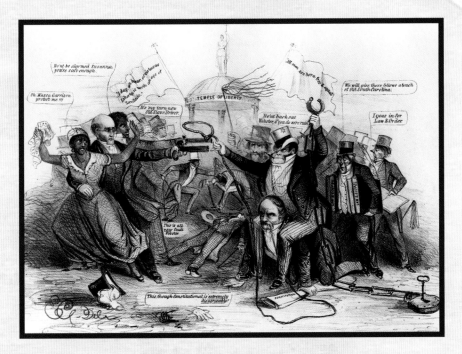

Practical illustration of the fugitive slave law,
1851 drawing by Edward Williams (1799–1857)

The

COMPROMISE

of

1850

September 9–20, 1850

THE COMPROMISE OF 1850 was the second attempt to paper over the differences between the proslavery and antislavery factions in the Union. Did the Compromise of 1850 postpone the Civil War by a decade, or did it further expose the deep divisions in the Union? Either way, it touched on the foundation stone of American democracy, enshrined in the Declaration of Independence: "We hold these truths to be self-evident . . . that all men are created equal." Should all people have human rights, or could some be treated as the property of others?

■ *The Compromise of 1850, like the Missouri Compromise a generation earlier, aggravated tensions over the nationally divisive practice of slavery in the United States. It merely put a brake on civil war, which looked increasingly inevitable.*

The Missouri Compromise of 1820 appeared to maintain the status quo by balancing the numbers of free and slave states in Congress and drawing a geographical line between them. However, as the United States acquired more land after the Mexican-American war of 1846–8, and new territories continued to apply to join the Union, the issue was constantly being raised.

The Wilmot Proviso in 1846 proposed outlawing slavery in any new territory acquired from Mexico as a result of the war. Northerners saw the rights of free soil and free labor as fundamental aspects of political freedom. However, Senator John C. Calhoun of South Carolina defended the right of slave states such as Texas to expand, and the right of slave owners to move into the new territories and take their "property" with them. The Proviso was never passed, but its supporters, the Free Soil Party, formed the basis of the new Republican Party, founded in 1854.

When California applied to join the Union as a free state in 1849, matters came to a head once more. Senator Henry Clay, the "Great Compromiser," tried to pacify both factions. He drafted resolutions that moved away from creating free or slave states toward the doctrine of popular sovereignty, in which each new state could decide its own position on slavery.

After seven months of occasionally violent debate, five statutes were adopted to determine several important issues. California was admitted to the Union as a free state; the inhabitants of the territory of New Mexico were allowed to decide for themselves on slavery; and New Mexico received disputed land from Texas. The U.S. government assumed Texas' pre-annexation debts, and ended the slave trade, although not slavery itself, in Washington D.C. Enough moderates agreed on these compromises to pass them, but the adjunct to the Compromise—the Amendment to the Fugitive Slave Act—angered abolitionists.

FREDERICK DOUGLASS, *the black abolitionist campaigner, spoke passionately against the Compromise: "This reproach, the Fugitive Slave Act, must be wiped out, and nothing short of resistance on the part of the colored man can wipe it out. Every slavehunter who meets a bloody death in his infernal business is an argument in favor of the manhood of our race."*

The Amendment implicated even the free states in slavery by requiring all U.S. citizens to co-operate in the return of fugitive slaves to their "owners." This made even free blacks in the North fearful. About 300 alleged fugitives were returned to slavery in the South under the terms of this act.

The next ten years could not even be described as a truce. Harriet Beecher Stowe's novel *Uncle Tom's Cabin* (1852) powerfully awoke the conscience of many Americans to the moral degradation of all involved

The five statutes of the Compromise of 1850 were based on a bill entered by Senator Stephen A. Douglas of Illinois. The final version contained the inflammatory Amendment to the Fugitive Slave Act.

in slavery. The 1854 Kansas-Nebraska Act reversed the provisions of the Missouri Compromise by allowing the territories of Kansas and Nebraska to decide for themselves on slavery. The 1857 decision in the Dred Scott case ruled that people of African descent, whether slaves or not, could never be U.S. citizens. In 1859 John Brown and his followers tried but failed to start a slave uprising. By the time Abraham Lincoln became President in 1860, South Carolina had already withdrawn from the Union, and civil war was inevitable. If the Compromise had delayed the war by ten years, it was to the advantage of the North, which had industrialized and strengthened in that time, giving it a technological advantage over the South.

Transcript of THE COMPROMISE OF 1850

'It being desirable, for the peace, concord, and harmony of the Union of these States, to settle and adjust amicably all existing questions of controversy between them arising out of the institution of slavery upon a fair, equitable and just basis: therefore,

1. Resolved, That California, with suitable boundaries, ought, upon her application to be admitted as one of the States of this Union, without the imposition by Congress of any restriction in respect to the exclusion or introduction of slavery within those boundaries.

2. Resolved, That as slavery does not exist by law, and is not likely to be introduced into any of the territory acquired by the United States from the republic of Mexico, it is inexpedient for Congress to provide by law either for its introduction into, or exclusion from, any part of the said territory; and that appropriate territorial governments ought to be established by Congress in all of the said territory, not assigned as the boundaries of the proposed State of California, without the adoption of any restriction or condition on the subject of slavery.

> "Resolved, That Congress has no power to promote or obstruct the trade in slaves between the slaveholding States; but that the admission or exclusion of slaves ... depends exclusively upon their own particular laws ..."

3. Resolved, That the western boundary of the State of Texas ought to be fixed on the Rio del Norte, commencing one marine league from its mouth, and running up that river to the southern line of New Mexico; thence with that line eastwardly, and so continuing in the same direction to the line as established between the United States and Spain, excluding any portion of New Mexico, whether lying on the east or west of that river.

5. Resolved, That it is inexpedient to abolish slavery in the District of Columbia whilst that institution continues to exist in the State of Maryland, without the consent of that State, without the consent of the people of the District, and without just compensation to the owners of slaves within the District.

6. But, resolved, That it is expedient to prohibit, within the District, the slave trade in slaves brought into it from States or places beyond the limits of the District, either to be sold therein as merchandise, or to be transported to other markets without the District of Columbia.

8. Resolved, That Congress has no power to promote or obstruct the trade in slaves between the slaveholding States; but that the admission or exclusion of slaves brought from one into another of them, depends exclusively upon their own particular laws ...

An Act to amend, and supplementary to, the Act entitled "An Act respecting Fugitives from Justice, and Persons escaping from the Service of their Masters," approved February twelfth, one thousand seven hundred and ninety-three.

Be it enacted by the Senate and House of Representatives of the United States of America in congress assembled, That the persons who have been, or may hereafter be, appointed commissioners, in virtue of any act of Congress, by the Circuit Courts of the United States and who, in consequence of such appointment, are authorized to exercise the powers that any justice of the peace, or other magistrate of any of the United States, may exercise in respect to offenders for any crime or offence against the United States, by arresting, imprisoning, or bailing the same under and by virtue of the thirty-third section of the act of the twenty-fourth of September seventeen hundred and eighty-nine, entitled "An Act to establish the Judicial courts of the United States," shall be, and are hereby, authorized and required to exercise and discharge all the powers and duties conferred by this act.

"... it shall be the duty of all marshals and deputy marshals to obey and execute all warrants and precepts issued under the provisions of this act ..."

SEC. 2. And be it further enacted, That the Superior Court of each organized Territory of the United States shall have the same power to appoint commissioners to take acknowledgements of bail and affidavits and to take depositions of witnesses in civil causes, which is now possessed by the Circuit Court of the United States; and all commissioners who shall hereafter be appointed for such purposes by the Superior Court of any organized Territory of the United States, shall possess all the powers, and exercise all the duties, conferred by law upon the commissioners appointed by the Circuit Courts of the United States for similar purposes, and shall moreover exercise and discharge all the powers and duties conferred by this act.

SEC. 3. And be it further enacted, That the Circuit Courts of the United States, and the Superior Courts of each organized Territory of the United States, shall from time to time enlarge the number of commissioners, with a view to afford reasonable facilities to reclaim fugitives from labor, and to the prompt discharge of the duties imposed by this act.

SEC. 5. And be it further enacted, That it shall be the duty of all marshals and deputy marshals to obey and execute all warrants and precepts issued under the provisions of this act, when to them directed; and should any marshal or deputy marshal refuse to receive such warrant, or other process, when tendered, or to use all proper means diligently to execute the same, he shall, on conviction thereof, be fined in the sum of one thousand dollars, to the use of such claimant, on the motion of such claimant, by the Circuit or District Court for the district of such marshal; and after arrest of such fugitive, by such marshal or his deputy, or whilst at any time in his custody under the provisions of this act, should such fugitive escape, whether with or without the assent of such marshal or his deputy, such marshal shall be liable, on his official bond, to be prosecuted for the benefit of such claimant, for the full value of the service or labor of said fugitive in the State, Territory, or District whence he escaped: and the better to enable the said commissioners, when thus appointed, to execute their duties faithfully and efficiently, in conformity with the requirements of the Constitution of the United States and of this act, they are hereby authorized and empowered, within their counties respectively, to appoint, in writing under their hands, anyone or more suitable persons, from time to time, to execute all such warrants and other process as may be issued by them in the lawful performance of their respective duties; with authority to such commissioners, or the persons to be appointed by them, to execute process as aforesaid, to summon and call to their aid the bystanders, or posse comitatus of the proper county, when necessary to ensure a faithful observance of the clause of the Constitution referred to, in conformity with the provisions of this act; and all good citizens are hereby commanded to aid and assist in the prompt and efficient execution of this law, whenever their services may he required, as aforesaid, for that purpose; and said warrants shall run, and be executed by said officers, any where in the State within which they are issued.

SEC. 7. And be it further enacted, That any person who shall knowingly and willingly obstruct, hinder, or prevent such claimant, his agent or attorney, or any person or persons lawfully assisting him, her, or them, from arresting such a fugitive from service or labor, either with or without process as aforesaid, or shall rescue, or attempt to rescue such fugitive from service or labor, from the custody of such claimant, his or her agent or attorney, or other person or persons lawfully assisting as aforesaid, when so arrested, pursuant to the authority herein given and declared; or shall aid, abet, or assist such person so owing service or labor as aforesaid, directly or indirectly, to escape from such claimant, his agent or attorney, or other person or persons legally authorized as aforesaid; or shall harbor or conceal such fugitive, so as to prevent the discovery and arrest of such person, after notice or knowledge of the fact that such person was a fugitive from service or labor as aforesaid, shall, for either of said offences, be subject to a fine not exceeding one thousand dollars, and imprisonment not exceeding six months, by indictment and conviction before the District Court of the United States for the district in which such offence may have been committed, or before the proper court of criminal jurisdiction, if committed within anyone of the organized Territories of the United States; and shall moreover forfeit and pay, by way of civil damages to the party injured by such illegal conduct, the sum of one thousand dollars, for each fugitive so lost as aforesaid, to be recovered by action of debt, in any of the District or Territorial Courts aforesaid, within whose jurisdiction the said offence may have been committed.

HAMMERING IN THE GOLDEN SPIKE AT PROMONTORY, UTAH—
THE CEREMONY TO MARK THE COMPLETION OF THE FIRST
TRANSCONTINENTAL RAILROAD, MAY 10, 1869

The
PACIFIC
RAILWAY ACT

JULY 1, 1862

ALTHOUGH THE COUNTRY was in the midst of civil war, in 1862 the federal government launched a major project to improve communications across the country—reflecting the strong commitment of President Lincoln and the Republican Party to further open up America. The Pacific Railway Acts made federal subsidies and loans available to help railroad companies with construction costs. Under the first act, the Union Pacific Railroad was authorized to build westwards from Nebraska and the Central Pacific Railroad to build eastwards from California, both to meet at Utah. This was achieved in 1869. The second act (1864) provided more land and money to complete the project.

■ *On May 10, 1869 the Golden Spike—the final spike that joined the two halves of the new railroad—was hammered in by Leland Stanford, President of the Central Pacific Railroad and later founder of Stanford University in California.*

Throughout the nineteenth century, millions of people were to settle in the western United States. This process was vastly accelerated by the coming of the railroads, which gave would-be migrants easier means of reaching the American interior. This migration ultimately led to the transformation of the United States from an undeveloped rural nation into an industrial giant, with a communications infrastructure that stretched from the Atlantic Ocean to the Pacific coast.

Railroads had been established in the United States since 1830, and their popularity meant that, by 1850, railroad investment had exceeded $300 million. The years after 1850 were of vital importance in the growth of the railroad system: a few short tracks grew rapidly into a network serving all the states east of the Mississippi. Railroads were now accepted as superior to earlier forms of transport—cheaper than wagon, faster than canal packet and more direct than river steamboats. When the Civil War broke out in 1861, railroads were quickly commissioned to play a major role in moving and supplying troops.

It was clear that building a railroad to cross the whole country would bring huge benefits, but also that the cost would be enormous. Congress commissioned surveys of the West to establish the best route for a railroad, but private companies were unwilling to undertake the work without some federal aid. The passing of the 1862 Pacific Railway Act changed the situation, providing a means by which the railroad could be funded, and specifying that the first transcontinental railroad should broadly follow the 32nd parallel. In passing the act, Congress aimed to create both a rail route and a telegraph line running from the Missouri river to the Pacific, both of which could then be put to government use.

THE GOLDEN SPIKE
The final spike that completed the transcontinental railroad was not made from pure gold, which would have flattened under a hammer blow, but a copper alloy. It is engraved with the dates that work began and ended on the railroad and the names of the directors of the railroad companies. It still shows the marks of the blows from the silver hammer that was used to drive it in.

To give the railroad companies an incentive for undertaking such a financially risky and physically dangerous project, they were allocated grants of land on either side of the track, which they could later sell to would-be settlers at a sizeable profit. Land closest to the tracks made the

OPPOSITE: *The first Pacific Railway Act provided for the building of a massive railroad across America connecting the east and west coasts—the first transcontinental route. Together with a second act in 1864, this legislation enabled railroads to fund the huge cost by selling portions of land to the many settlers migrating westwards.*

Thirty Seventh

Congress of the United States,

At the Second Session

BEGUN AND HELD AT THE CITY OF WASHINGTON

in the District of Columbia

on Monday the second day of December one thousand eight hundred and sixty one

---

AN ACT To aid in the construction of a railroad and telegraph line from the Missouri river to the Pacific ocean; and to secure to the government the use of the same for postal, military, and other purposes.

Be it Enacted by the Senate and House of Representatives of the United States of America in Congress assembled,

That Walter S. Burges, William P. Blodget, Benjamin W. Cheever, Charles Fosdick Fletcher, of Rhode Island; Augustus Brewster, Henry P. Haven, Cornelius S. Bushnell, Henry Hammond, of Connecticut; Isaac Sherman, Dean Richmond, Royal Phelps, William H. Ferry, Henry L. Paddock, Lewis L. Stancliff, Charles A. Secor, Samuel R. Campbell, Alfred E. Tilton, John Anderson, Azariah Boody, John S. Kennedy, H. Carver, Joseph Field, Benjamin F. Camp, Orville W. Childs, Alexander J. Bergen, Ben. Holliday, D. N. Barney, S. De Witt Bloodgood, William H. Grant, Thomas W. Olcott, Samuel B. Ruggles, James B. Wilson, of New York; Ephraim Marsh, Charles M. Harker, of New Jersey; John Edgar Thompson, Benjamin Haywood, Joseph H. Scranton, Joseph Harrison, George W. Cass, John H. Bryant, Daniel J. Morrell, Thomas W. Howe, William F. Johnson, Robert Finney, John A. Green, E. R. Myer, Charles F. Wells, junior, of Pennsylvania; Noah L. Wilson, Amasa Stone, William H. Clement, S. S. L'Hommedieu, John Brough, William Dennison, Jacob Blickensderfer, of Ohio; William M. McPherson, R. W. Wells, Willard P. Hall, Armstrong Beatty, John Corby, of Missouri; S. J. Hensley, Peter Donahue, C. P. Huntington, T. D. Judah, James Bailey, James T. Ryan, Charles Hosmer, Charles Marsh, D. O. Mills, Samuel Bell, Louis McLane, George W. Mowe, Charles McLaughlin, Timothy Dame, John R. Robinson, of California; John Atchison, and John D. Winters, of the Territory of Nevada; John D. Campbell, R. N. Rice, Charles A. Trowbridge, and Ransom Gardner, Charles W. Penny, Charles T. Gorham, William McConnell, of Michigan; William F. Coolbaugh, Lucius H. Langworthy, Hugh T. Reid, Hoyt Sherman, Lyman Cook, Samuel R. Curtis, Lewis A. Thomas, Platt Smith, of Iowa; William B. Ogden, Charles G. Hammond, Henry Farnum, Amos C. Babcock, W. Seldon Gale, Nehemiah Bushnell and Lorenzo Bull, of Illinois; William H. Swift, Samuel T. Dana, John Bertram, Franklin L. Stevens,

railroads the most money because farmers and ranchers wanted to be near railway stations. Under the first acts, the companies were granted ten square miles of land for every mile constructed, plus loan bonds. The loans were repayable in 30 years and the dollars per mile increased in proportion to the difficulty of the terrain being worked.

However, two years into the project, the railroads were still struggling to raise enough capital. Congress, therefore, doubled the size of the land grants and allowed the railroads to sell their own bonds. After the completion of the railroad in 1869, a Congressional investigation found that some railroad entrepreneurs had made illegal profits from the favorable terms of the acts.

The construction of the transcontinental railroad was a huge engineering achievement involving backbreaking work. Thousands of laborers worked in gangs using picks, shovels, and explosives. The Union Pacific employed mostly Irish workers, many of them recent immigrants who had fled the Irish Potato Famine, some of them veterans of the Civil War. Laying track across flat plains was fairly straightforward, but workers were often attacked by Native American peoples angry at the "iron horse" invading the land.

The Central Pacific railroad had to negotiate different territory: the wild Sierra Nevada mountains. This company used more than 12,000 Chinese laborers, brought to California to work on the railroad because they were rightly reputed to be hard and fearless workers. They used hand tools, wheelbarrows and horse-drawn wagons to build tunnels and bridges through cliffs and across valleys—slow and dangerous work. Many hundreds of workers died in accidents, such as rock falls set off as the engineers blasted their way through the sides of mountains. Both companies also faced problems from severe weather.

Finally, on May 10, 1869, the two railroad tracks met at Promontory in Utah. Nationwide celebrations marked the historic occasion. However, although many white settlers were able to build their lives and fortunes through the advent of the 1,776 mile railroad tracks, for the Native Americans the transatlantic rail route spelled disaster. They were finally overwhelmed as the trickle of white settlers onto their ancient homelands turned into a flood.

Transcript of THE
PACIFIC RAILWAY ACT

CHAP. CXX. — An Act to aid in the Construction of a Railroad and Telegraph Line from the Missouri River to the Pacific Ocean, and to secure to the Government the Use of the same for Postal, Military, and Other Purposes.

Be it enacted by the Senate and House of Representatives of the United States of America in Congress assembled, That Walter S. Burgess [and others] ... together with commissioners to be appointed by the Secretary of the

Interior, and all persons who shall or may be associated with them, and their successors, are hereby created and erected into a body corporate and politic in deed and in law, by the name, style, and title of "The Union Pacific Railroad Company;" and by that name shall have perpetual succession, and shall be able to sue and to be sued, plead and be impleaded, defend and be defended, in all courts of law and equity within the United States, and may make and have a common seal; and the said corporation is hereby authorized and empowered to layout, locate, construct, furnish, maintain, and enjoy a continuous railroad and telegraph, with the appurtenances, from a point on the one hundredth meridian of longitude west from Greenwich, between the south margin of the valley of the Republican River and the north margin of the valley of the Platte River, in the Territory of Nebraska, to the western boundary of Nevada Territory, upon the route and terms hereinafter provided, and is hereby vested with all the powers, privileges, and immunities necessary to carry into effect the purposes of this act as herein set forth. The capital stock of said company shall consist of one hundred thousand shares of one thousand dollars each, which shall be subscribed for and held in not more than two hundred shares by anyone person, and shall be transferable in such manner as the by-laws of said corporation shall provide. The persons hereinbefore named, together with those to be appointed by the Secretary of the Interior, are hereby constituted and appointed commissioners, and such body shall be called the Board of Commissioners of the Union Pacific Railroad and Telegraph Company, and twenty-five shall constitute a quorum for the transaction of business. The first meeting of said board shall be held at Chicago at such time as the commissioners from Illinois herein named shall appoint, not more than three nor less than one month after the passage of this act, notice of which shall be given by them to the other commissioners by depositing a call thereof in the post office at Chicago, post paid, to their address at least forty days before said meeting, and also by publishing said notice in one daily newspaper in each of the cities of Chicago and Saint Louis . . .

> "... the said corporation is hereby authorized and empowered to layout, locate, construct, furnish, maintain, and enjoy a continuous railroad and telegraph ..."

SEC. 2. And be it further enacted, That the right of way through the public lands be, and the same is hereby, granted to said company for the construction of said railroad and telegraph line; and the right, power, and authority is hereby given to said company to take from the public lands adjacent to the line of said road, earth, stone, timber, and other materials for the construction thereof; said right of way is granted to said railroad to the extent of two hundred feet in width on each side of said railroad where it may pass over the public lands, including all necessary grounds for stations, buildings, workshops, and depots, machine shops, switches, side tracks, turntables, and, water stations. The United States shall extinguish as rapidly as may be the Indian titles to all lands falling under the operation of this act and required for the said right of way and grants hereinafter made . . .

SEC. 7. And be it further enacted, That said company shall file their assent to this act, under the seal of said company, in the Department of the Interior, within one year after the passage of this act, and shall complete said railroad and telegraph from the point of beginning, as herein provided, to the western boundary of Nevada Territory before the first day of July, one thousand eight hundred and seventy-four: Provided, That within two years after the passage of this act said company shall designate the general route of said road, as near as may be, and shall file a map of the same in the Department of the Interior, whereupon the Secretary of the Interior shall cause the lands within fifteen miles of said designated route or routes to be withdrawn from preemption, private entry, and sale; and when any portion of said route shall be finally located, the Secretary of the Interior shall cause the said lands herein-before granted to be surveyed and set off as fast as may be necessary for the purposes herein named: Provided, That in fixing the point of connection of the main trunk with the eastern connections, it shall be fixed at the most practicable point for the construction of the Iowa and Missouri branches, as hereinafter provided.

> "The United States shall extinguish as rapidly as may be the Indian titles to all lands falling under the operation of this act and required for the said right of way and grants hereinafter made."

SEC. 20. And be it further enacted, That the corporation hereby created and the roads connected therewith, under the provisions of this act, shall make to the Secretary of the Treasury an annual report wherein shall be set forth-

First. The names of the stockholders and their places of residence, so far as the same can be ascertained;

Second. The names and residences of the directors, and all other officers of the company;

Third. The amount of stock subscribed, and the amount thereof actually paid in;

Fourth. A description of the lines of road surveyed, of the lines thereof fixed upon for the construction of the road, and the cost of such surveys;

Fifth. The amount received from passengers on the road;

Sixth. The amount received for freight thereon;

Seventh. A statement of the expense of said road and its fixtures;

Eighth. A statement of the indebtedness of said company, setting forth the various kinds thereof. Which report shall be sworn to by the president of the said company, and shall be presented to the Secretary of the Treasury on or before the first day of July in each year.

APPROVED, July 1, 1862.

ABRAHAM LINCOLN (1809–65),
16TH PRESIDENT OF THE
UNITED STATES, GIVES HIS
GETTYSBURG ADDRESS, 1863

The

GETTYSBURG ADDRESS

DELIVERED AT THE DEDICATION OF THE SOLDIERS'
NATIONAL CEMETERY AT GETTYSBURG, PENNSYLVANIA

NOVEMBER 19, 1863

THE BATTLE OF GETTYSBURG, the decisive battle of the Civil War, took place on July 1–3, 1863. The Confederate commander, General Robert E. Lee, had invaded Pennsylvania with his army of 75,000, and then came up against a 90,000-strong Union Army led by General George G. Meade. The battle ended in defeat for the southern forces, and left more than 51,000 Confederate and Union soldiers wounded, missing, or dead. For months afterwards Gettysburg was overwhelmed by the stench of 7,500 human corpses and several thousand dead horses. However, when Lincoln visited the site in November he focused not on the battle but on the greater importance of the war as a "new birth of freedom" for the nation.

■ *During the Civil War, many threats were made to President Abraham Lincoln's life. In the euphoria following the official ending of the war in April 1865, the high level of protection the President had been given lapsed. John Wilkes Booth, an actor and Confederate sympathizer who had previously plotted to kidnap Lincoln, shot the President in the head as he watched a play at Ford's Theater in Washington, D.C.*

Burial of the dead with dignity was a critical priority for Gettysburg residents. Soon after the battle, the state of Pennsylvania bought 17 acres of land on which to build a cemetery to honor those who had died during those awful July days. David Wills, the wealthy attorney who organized the purchase, also planned a dedication ceremony to take place in September. He invited Edward Everett, ex-Governor of Massachusetts and previous Secretary of State, who was president of Harvard University, to be the main speaker on the occasion. As Everett was unable to prepare what he considered a suitable speech in time he asked for the event to be postponed until November.

The organizing committee then decided that a public figure should also be asked to attend, so they invited President Abraham Lincoln to make a few suitable remarks after the main speech. Lincoln agreed, and traveled to Gettysburg by train from Washington. On the morning of the event he joined a procession marching to the grounds of the cemetery. The ceremony was attended by about 15,000 people, including governors of six of the 24 Union states. Reinterment in the cemetery of the bodies taken from temporary graves on the battlefield was only half complete by the day of the dedication.

The ceremony began with music and prayers, after which Everett gave a two-hour oration. His 13,607-word speech is now virtually forgotten—in stark contrast to the brief speech of approximately 300 words then delivered by the President. Lincoln took a copy of his carefully considered words from his coat pocket and read from it in his distinctive high-pitched Kentucky accent. His speech lasted for less than three minutes. Newspapers reported that the President was interrupted five times by clapping and that the speech was followed by long, continued applause. Other eyewitness accounts record that the speech was received in silence, the crowd hushed by its simple profundity. Everett lost no time in writing to Lincoln, praising him generously: "I should be glad if I could flatter myself that I came as near to the central idea of the occasion, in two hours, as you did in two minutes."

Lincoln's prediction in the speech that "the world will little note nor long remember what we say here . . ." could not have

DE MORTUIS NIL NISI BONUM
The first bodies to be reinterred in Gettysburg National Cemetery were those of Union soldiers. The remains of Confederate soldiers were reburied seven years later. The dead were originally to be interred randomly, to symbolize their equality as citizens and in death, but this was resisted, and the graves are grouped by state.

been more wrong. His Gettysburg Address has come to be regarded not only as a literary masterpiece, but also as a defining statement of democracy. The speech put a different interpretation on the aims of the Civil War, redefining it as a battle for the survival of liberty. Lincoln used the word "nation" five times but avoided the word "union," as this might have been misinterpreted as referring only to the North. He also referred to the year 1776, to the Revolutionary War, and cited the famous words of the Declaration of Independence, that "all men are created equal."

Elected twice as President, Lincoln's tenure in office was dominated by the Civil War. He believed the country could not survive "half slave and half free" and was convinced of the political dangers of allowing the practice to continue—if initially equivocal about the moral iniquity

Following the carnage of the Battle of Gettysburg, a cemetery was built to provide a proper final resting place for thousands of dead who lay in makeshift graves on the battlefield. On November 19, 1863, President Abraham Lincoln delivered this brief and now world-famous speech dedicating the national burial site.

of slavery. He was later to alter his stance and issue the famous Emancipation Proclamation (1863), bringing freedom to millions of slaves.

Although mild-mannered, Lincoln had an iron will, and proved a strong leader of the Northern states during the war. However, he was also notably charitable after the Southern states' bid to cede from the Union was defeated, making a plea for "malice towards none" in his second inaugural address, and concerning himself with restructuring the governments of the vanquished states. Lincoln's life and second term, however, were cut tragically short when he was shot by Confederate sympathizer John Wilkes Booth on Good Friday 1865 in Washington, D.C.

Transcript of THE GETTYSBURG ADDRESS

Four score and seven years ago our fathers brought forth, upon this continent, a new nation, conceived in liberty, and dedicated to the proposition that "all men are created equal."

Now we are engaged in a great civil war, testing whether that nation, or any nation so conceived, and so dedicated, can long endure. We are met on a great battle field of that war. We have come to dedicate a portion of it, as a final resting place for those who died here, that the nation might live. This we may, in all propriety do. But, in a larger sense, we cannot dedicate, we cannot consecrate—we cannot hallow—this ground. The brave men, living and dead, who struggled here, have hallowed it far above our poor power to add or detract. The world will little note, nor long remember what we say here; while it can never forget what they did here.

AN ORIGINAL VERSION?

There are five extant manuscript versions of Abraham Lincoln's Gettysburg Address, written by the President himself and named for the people to whom Lincoln gave them. They all vary in small details, indicating that Lincoln continued to refine his words whenever he revisited them. The imagery, language, and style of this short speech continue to be analyzed at great length by scholars.

It is rather for us, the living, we here be dedicated to the great task remaining before us—that, from these honored dead we take increased devotion to that cause for which they here, gave the last full measure of devotion—that we here highly resolve these dead shall not have died in vain; that the nation, shall have a new birth of freedom, and that government of the people by the people for the people, shall not perish from the earth.

PRESIDENT LINCOLN RIDES THROUGH RICHMOND,
VIRGINIA, IN 1865

The

13th
AMENDMENT

to the U.S. Constitution:
the abolition of slavery

JANUARY 31, 1865

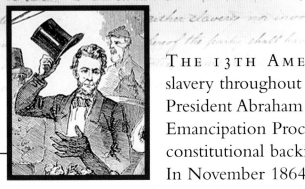

THE 13TH AMENDMENT to the Constitution abolished slavery throughout the United States. It was promoted by President Abraham Lincoln, who recognized that the Emancipation Proclamation he had issued in 1863 had to have constitutional backing if slaves were to become "forever free." In November 1864 Lincoln was re-elected as President on this pledge. Three months later, the formal abolition of slavery was accomplished with the words: "Neither slavery nor involuntary servitude . . . shall exist within the United States, or any place subject to their jurisdiction." However, even before the Amendment's ratification by Congress, Abraham Lincoln—its chief instigator— had been assassinated by Confederate sympathizer John Wilkes Booth.

■ *On April 11, 1865, two days after the South surrendered in the Civil War, John Wilkes Booth was outside the White House when Abraham Lincoln gave an impromptu address to the crowd. When Lincoln spoke about his support for the ending of slavery in the U.S., Wilkes attempted to persuade a fellow sympathizer, whom he knew to be armed, to shoot the President. His friend refused, and three days later Booth, acting alone, killed Lincoln himself.*

Slave traders began carrying their human cargo in tightly packed ships to America in the seventeenth century. As early as 1724 the Quakers had protested against slavery, and although there were slave markets in both the North and South, colonists in the North increasingly viewed slavery as undesirable and immoral. Some states, such as Rhode Island in 1774, had unilaterally abolished it. However, the demand for slaves was boosted in 1793 when New Englander Eli Whitney invented his improved cotton-harvesting machine, which created a huge demand for field laborers.

In 1833 the Abolitionist movement was formally established with the founding of the American Anti-Slavery Society in Philadelphia. By 1840 a huge network of people known as the "Underground Railroad" was helping fugitive slaves escape to freedom in the North or Canada. Despite the growing strength of the Abolitionist cause, the annexation of Texas in 1845 created a huge new slave state, and in 1854 Congress passed the Kansas-Nebraska Act, which repealed a ban on slavery in the northwest. All new territories seemed likely to be opened up for slave labor. There was guerrilla warfare in Kansas as Northern and Southern partisans struggled to impose their differing views on slavery in the territory.

Previously unwilling to endanger the Union by disputing the slave question, in 1854 many Northerners joined the new Republican Party, which demanded a federal ban on the spread of slavery. The issue split the Democratic Party into Northern and Southern factions—then in 1860, a Republican, Abraham Lincoln, won the Presidential election. As early as 1854, Lincoln had said, "The monstrous injustice of slavery . . . deprives our republican example of its just influence in the world—enables the enemies of free institutions, with plausibility, to taunt us as hypocrites." Fearing Lincoln would outlaw slavery, seven Deep South states led by Jefferson Davis seceded from the Union and became an independent Confederacy.

In 1861, civil war broke out. At stake was the issue of the individual rights of the states—in particular, the right of each state to make its own decision about slavery. When the Union army opened its ranks to black soldiers, many fugitive slaves joined up. Lincoln identified the slavery issue as the "heart of the rebellion." In peacetime, the President had no constitutional power to

THE RATIFICATION PROCESS
The 13th Amendment was ratified by three-quarters of the states, as required for it to become part of the Constitution, within a year of being proposed. However, it was not until 1995 that Mississippi ratified it—the last of the 36 states in existence in 1865 to do so.

The 13th Amendment was the first unconditional constitutional action to end slavery right across the United States. It was to be followed by three further amendments—the 14th, 15th, and 24th—all aimed at establishing equality for black people in the U.S.

Rec.d 2 Feb

Thirty-Eighth **Congress of the United States of America;**

At the _Second_ Session,

an and held at the City of Washington, on Monday, the _fifth_ day of December, one thousand eight hundred and sixty-_four_

A RESOLUTION

Submitting to the legislatures of the several States a proposition to amend the Constitution of the United States.

Resolved by the Senate and House of Representatives of the United States of America in Congress assembled, (two-thirds of both houses concurring), that the following article be proposed to the legislatures of the several States as an amendment to the constitution of the United States, which, when ratified by three-fourths of said legislatures shall be valid, to all intents and purposes, as a part of the said Constitution, namely: Article XIII. Section 1. Neither slavery nor involuntary servitude, except as a punishment for crime whereof the party shall have been duly convicted, shall exist within the United States, or any place subject to their jurisdiction. Section 2. Congress shall have power to enforce this article by appropriate legislation.

Schuyler Colfax
Speaker of the House of Representatives.

H. Hamlin
Vice President of the United States,
and President of the Senate

Abraham Lincoln

Approved February 1. 1865.

emancipate slaves in every state. However, as wartime commander, Lincoln had the constitutional right to seize any enemy property that was used to wage war—and slaves, integral to the Southern states' campaign, qualified as such property.

In September 1862, Lincoln issued a warning that he would apply his war powers in all states still in rebellion against the federal government on January 1, 1863, proclaiming their slaves "then, thenceforward and forever free." In January he issued the Emancipation Proclamation, stating, "I never, in my life, felt more certain that I was doing right than I do in signing this paper." The Emancipation Proclamation was a Presidential executive order, rather than a law passed by Congress, issued under the wartime powers that the Constitution accorded the President.

In terms of slave liberation, the Proclamation was initially limited. It did not apply to slave states in the Union, or slaves in Southern areas already under Union control—although by the summer of 1865, nearly four million had been freed. Its immediate significance lay elsewhere, in realigning the war aims of the North: the Civil War was now being fought to end slavery. The ratification of the 13th Amendment in December 1865 completed the process of abolition that Lincoln's Proclamation had begun, extending emancipation to those slave states (Missouri, Kentucky, Maryland and Delaware) that had not seceded.

The 13th Amendment went to Congress at the end of the Civil War, before the Southern states had been restored to the Union. Although passed by the Senate in April 1864, it failed to get through the House of Representatives. Lincoln made the passing of the Amendment an election issue during his second Presidential campaign. His determination meant that it was voted through the House of Representatives in January 1866, by a vote of 119 to 56.

Transcript of THE 13TH AMENDMENT TO THE U.S. CONSTITUTION

❛ AMENDMENT XIII

Section 1.
Neither slavery nor involuntary servitude, except as a punishment for crime whereof the party shall have been duly convicted, shall exist within the United States, or any place subject to their jurisdiction.

Section 2.
Congress shall have power to enforce this article by appropriate legislation.

Passed by Congress January 31, 1865. Ratified December 6, 1865. ❜

THE FIRST VOTE, 1867 DRAWING BY
ALFRED R. WAUD (1828–91), DEPICTING
BLACK VOTERS GOING TO THE POLLS FOR
THE FIRST STATE ELECTION

The
15th
AMENDMENT

to the U.S. Constitution:
voting rights

FEBRUARY 3, 1870

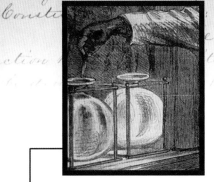

XV.

AFTER THE ASSASSINATION of Abraham Lincoln in April 1865, Andrew Johnson became President. A pro-Union Southerner from Tennessee, Johnson believed white people to be superior to blacks "in point of intellect" and thought only white men should govern. However, in the 1866 elections Radical Republicans won enough seats in Congress to thwart Johnson's approach to the Reconstruction of the South (begun by Lincoln and lasting until 1877). Radical Republicans wanted Southern society reorganized before Southern delegates were readmitted to Congress. Together with moderate Republicans, the Radicals forced the federal government to grant full citizenship to black Americans through the 14th Amendment, and to grant the right to vote through the 15th.

■ *Alfred R. Waud, an English-born illustrator who covered the Civil War and its aftermath for* Harper's Weekly, *drew this idealistic picture of black voters in 1867, three years before ratification of the 15th Amendment. On March 31, 1870, Thomas Mundy Peterson of New Jersey became the first African American to vote in an election. However, the swift introduction of "Jim Crow" laws curtailed black people's rights, and the scene Waud depicted would remain imaginary for nearly a century.*

One of the driving forces behind the introduction of the 15th Amendment was the Republicans' determination to establish their power in both the North and the South of the United States. Black votes would help achieve that goal. Passed in 1869, the 15th Amendment was ratified by the required number of states in 1870. Opposition from Southern states could not be mobilized because Republicans controlled the state governments in the South. Furthermore, ratification of the 15th Amendment was made a condition for readmission for those Southern states still excluded from the Union.

Although the 15th Amendment gave the vote to blacks in the Northern states and to Southern blacks for a period, it was ultimately ineffective. The former Confederate states undermined it by introducing into their state constitutions voting qualifications that effectively disenfranchised black voters. Through voter intimidation, Southern states ensured that it would be nearly a century before blacks in the South benefited from the Amendment through the Civil Rights legislation of the 1960s. Despite the legislation implied in the 13th, 14th, and 15th Amendments, Southern states passed laws in the 1890s that led to the firm establishment of racial segregation and confirmed the second-class status of black Americans.

At the end of the Civil War, black Americans were finally free from slavery, but their struggle for equal citizenship was far from over. Nine out of ten black people in the U.S. lived in the rural South, and they hoped to receive land along with their freedom. They rarely did so. Many simply swapped slavery for sharecropping—working for white plantation owners for a share of the crop rather than for wages.

During the 11 years of Reconstruction, the federal government attempted to rebuild the South and guarantee black civil rights. By 1867 the South had 735,000 black voters. Congress established the Freedman's Bureau in 1865, a federal agency set up to help ex-slaves find work and to provide them with education, training, and hospitals. Some state lands in the South were also opened to black settlers.

RESPECTING THE AMENDMENT
In 1965, President Lyndon B. Johnson, a Southerner, urged Congress to pass legislation "which will make it impossible to thwart the 15th Amendment," stating, "We cannot have government for all the people until we first make certain it is government of and by all the people." The Voting Rights Act of 1965 abolished all outstanding impediments to general suffrage, and authorized federal supervision of voter registration where needed.

Northern educators and black clergy established schools throughout the South, initially with white teachers, although by 1870 over a third of the teaching staff was black. This led to the founding of the first black colleges, and nearly 50 were established between 1865 and 1877. Black candidates were elected to Congress, state governments, and city councils, and blacks set up farms and businesses, and attended schools and universities.

Reaction from Southern whites was extreme. In 1865, they formed the terror organization known as the Ku Klux Klan (KKK). The KKK set out to oppose Reconstruction by intimidating Northern abolitionists and reformers who had moved south (derisively labeled "Carpetbaggers"), as well as Southern Republicans ("Scalawags"). There was a wave of murder, lynching, rape, and arson. Blacks were often prevented from exercising their right to vote by gangs of white thugs.

Recognizing the financial opportunities in the South, the federal government gradually sought "reconciliation" with the Southern states. Congress closed the Freedman's Bureau, and in 1875 rejected a Bill protecting black voting rights. When the Northern officials who had controlled the Southern states during Reconstruction finally left in 1877, the Southern states introduced the "Jim Crow" laws, banning black people from white schools, restaurants, public transport, and housing.

The 15th Amendment aimed to prevent federal or state governments from infringing the right of citizens to vote "on account of race, color, or previous condition of servitude." One of three civil rights amendments proposed after the Civil War, it allowed federal government to determine voting qualifications, previously a matter for state governments.

In the 1890s, various means were used by the Southern states to establish white supremacy. They introduced literacy tests for voters and "grandfather clauses," excluding from voting all those whose ancestors had not voted in the 1860s. In 1896, the famous court case *Plessy v. Ferguson* declared the Jim Crow laws to be constitutional, a decision upheld by the Supreme Court. Between 1901 and 1929 no blacks were elected to Congress, and by 1910 it was impossible for most blacks to vote. Many lost their property and returned to poverty. Within 30 years of the end of the Civil War and the abolition of slavery, black civil rights had been seriously undermined.

Transcript of THE 15TH AMENDMENT

Fortieth Congress of the United States of America;

At the third Session, Begun and held at the city of Washington, on Monday, the seventh day of December, one thousand eight hundred and sixty-eight.

A Resolution Proposing an amendment to the Constitution of the United States.

Resolved by the Senate and House of Representatives of the United States of America in Congress assembled, (two-thirds of both Houses concurring) that the following article be proposed to the legislature of the several States as an amendment to the Constitution of the United States which, when ratified by three-fourths of said legislatures shall be valid as part of the Constitution, namely:

Article XV.

Section 1. The right of citizens of the United States to vote shall not be denied or abridged by the United States or by any State on account of race, color, or previous condition of servitude.

Section 2. The Congress shall have the power to enforce this article by appropriate legislation.

The Grand Canyon of the Yellowstone,
painted in 1872 by Thomas Moran (1837–1926)

Act establishing

YELLOWSTONE NATIONAL PARK

March 1, 1872

EXPLORERS OF THE WEST in the early 1800s returned with stories of an extraordinary region of huge geysers, hot springs, mud volcanoes, spectacular waterfalls, vast lakes and rivers, rich and varied wildlife, and immense areas of wilderness. These tales were largely dismissed as fantastic inventions. However, after the Civil War the government sponsored fact-finding expeditions to journey westward and survey the area's potential for development and wealth generation. As more was discovered about the Yellowstone region, people realized that the land's unique geological features were too important to exploit for private gain and should be preserved for public use. The idea grew in popularity and was eventually adopted by Congress.

■ *Congress bought Thomas Moran's painting of the Grand Canyon of the Yellowstone for $10,000 in 1872. Born in England in 1837, Moran came to the United States as a child, and became a member of the Hudson River School of painters. His sketches of Yellowstone were the first color images of the region to be shown in the East.*

One of the first non-Native American adventurers to bring back tales of the amazing sights of the Yellowstone region was the trapper-explorer John Colter, who went into the area alone in 1806–7. By the 1820s trappers ocasionally found their way to the Yellowstone, but it was usually bypassed by migrants making their way westward. One of four great government surveys, the Folsom-Cook Expedition, explored the area extensively in 1869. The following year the Washburn-Langford-Doane Expedition confirmed the extraordinary natural features of the Yellowstone region. One member of the expedition, Cornelius Hedges, suggested that the area should be established as a national park rather than developed for settlers.

Hedges was not the first to want to conserve land in the West in its natural state. In 1833 George Catlin, famous for his paintings of Native Americans and scenes of the West, expressed his hope that the western regions could be protected in their natural beauty. Others, including the writer and philosopher Ralph Waldo Emerson, campaigned for the preservation of the disappearing wilderness. The eventual wording of Section 2 of the 1872 Act protecting Yellowstone reflected their fears for environmental survival: "If this bill fails to become a law this session, the vandals who are now waiting to enter into this wonderland will, in a single season despoil, beyond recovery, these remarkable curiosities which have required all the cunning skill of nature thousands of years to prepare."

JOHN COLTER

Colter was a breakaway member of one of the earliest expeditions into Yellowstone, which had gone there to hunt and trap. Colter's accounts of the astonishing geothermal activity in the area were dismissed by many as hallucinations brought on by his extended periods of isolation. For many years, Yellowstone was considered a mythical region, and was nicknamed Colter's Hell.

In 1871 another surveyor of Yellowstone, Ferdinand Hayden, started a campaign to publicize and protect the area. His work, together with the paintings of Thomas Moran, a member of Hayden's expedition, did much to persuade Congress and the nation of the area's wonders. On March 1, 1872, Congress passed into law an act that made Yellowstone "a public park or pleasuring-ground for the benefit and enjoyment of the people."

The Yellowstone Act provided for the "preservation, from injury or spoliation, of all timber, mineral deposits, natural curiosities or wonders within said park and their retention in their natural condition." In so doing, it laid down a pattern adopted across the world for the preservation of wild areas of great natural beauty.

Forty-second Congress of the United States of America;

At the Second Session,

Begun and held at the City of Washington, on Monday, the Fourth day of December, one thousand eight hundred and seventy-one.

AN ACT

To set apart a certain tract of land lying near the head-waters of the Yellowstone River as a public park.

Be it enacted by the Senate and House of Representatives of the United States of America in Congress assembled,

That the tract of land in the Territories of Montana and Wyoming lying near the head-waters of the Yellowstone River, and described as follows, to wit, commencing at the junction of Gardiner's River with the Yellowstone River, and running east to the meridian passing ten miles to the eastward of the most eastern point of Yellowstone Lake; thence south along said meridian to the parallel of latitude passing ten miles south of the most southern point of Yellowstone Lake; thence west along said parallel to the meridian passing fifteen miles west of the most western point of Madison Lake; thence north along said meridian to the latitude of the junction of the Yellowstone and Gardiner's Rivers; thence east to the place of beginning is hereby reserved and withdrawn from settlement, occupancy, or sale under the laws of the United States, and dedicated and set apart as a public park or pleasuring-ground for the benefit and enjoyment of the people; and all persons who shall locate or settle upon or occupy the same, or any part thereof, except as hereinafter provided, shall be considered trespassers, and removed therefrom. Sec. 2. That said public park shall be under the exclusive control of the Secretary of the Interior, whose duty it shall be as soon as practicable, to make and publish such rules and regulations as he may deem necessary or proper for the care and management of the same. Such regulations shall provide for the preservation, from injury or spoliation, of all timber, mineral deposits, natural curiosities, or wonders within said park and their retention in their natural condition. The Secretary may, in his discretion, grant leases or building purposes for terms not exceeding ten years, of small parcels of ground, at such places in said park as shall require the erection of buildings for the accommodation of visitors; all of the proceeds of said leases, and all other revenues that may be derived from any source connected with said park, to be expended under his direction in the management of the same, and the construction of roads and bridle-paths therein. He shall provide against the wanton destruction of the fish and game found within said park, and against their capture or destruction for the purposes of merchandise or profit. He shall also cause all persons trespassing upon the same

---

Yellowstone National Park, occupying parts of the western states of Wyoming, Montana, and Idaho, was the first area of land in the world to be established as a national park. It gained this status through a Congressional Act in March 1872, under President Ulysses S. Grant. The park is a plateau, bordered by four mountain ranges, including the Rocky Mountains. Roughly square shaped, it is approximately 3,462 square miles in size.

Transcript of THE ACT ESTABLISHING YELLOWSTONE NATIONAL PARK

' Forty-Second Congress of the United States of America;

At the Second Session, Begun and held at the City of Washington, on Monday, the Fourth day of December, one thousand eight hundred and seventy-one.

AN ACT to set apart a certain tract of land lying near the headwaters of the Yellowstone River as a public park.

Be it enacted by the Senate and House of Representatives of the United States of America in Congress assembled, That the tract of land in the Territories of Montana and Wyoming, lying near the headwaters of the Yellowstone River, and described as follows, to wit, commencing at the junction of Gardiner's river with the Yellowstone river, and running east to the meridian passing ten miles to the eastward of the most eastern point of Yellowstone lake; thence south along said meridian to the parallel of latitude passing ten miles south of the most southern point of Yellowstone lake; thence west along said parallel to the meridian passing fifteen miles west of the most western point of Madison lake; thence north along said meridian to the latitude of the junction of Yellowstone and Gardiner's rivers; thence east to the place of beginning, is hereby reserved and withdrawn from settlement, occupancy, or sale under the laws of the United States, and dedicated and set apart as a public park or pleasuring-ground for the benefit and enjoyment of the people; and all persons who shall locate or settle upon or occupy the same, or any part thereof, except as hereinafter provided, shall be considered trespassers and removed therefrom.

> "... the tract of land in the Territories of Montana and Wyoming ... is hereby reserved ... for the benefit and enjoyment of the people."

SEC 2. That said public park shall be under the exclusive control of the Secretary of the Interior ... Such regulations shall provide for the preservation, from injury or spoliation, of all timber, mineral deposits, natural curiosities, or wonders within said park, and their retention in their natural condition. The Secretary may in his discretion, grant leases for building purposes for terms not exceeding ten years, of small parcels of ground, at such places in said park as shall require the erection of buildings for the accommodation of visitors ... He shall provide against the wanton destruction of the fish and game found within said park, and against their capture or destruction for the purposes of merchandise or profit. He shall also cause all persons trespassing upon the same after the passage of this act to be removed therefrom, and generally shall be authorized to take all such measures as shall be necessary or proper to fully carry out the objects and purposes of this act. '

A chromolithograph illustration of Thomas Alva Edison (1847–1931), American inventor, from *World's Inventors*, published in 1900 by Allen and Ginter

THOMAS ALVA EDISON'S

Patent drawing for the electric lamp

January 27, 1879

AFTER REVOLUTIONIZING THE world of sound with the invention of the phonograph (or gramophone) in 1877, Thomas Alva Edison applied his creative genius to producing cheap, safe, and reliable electric lighting. Other inventors, notably English scientist Joseph Swan, were also tackling the challenge of creating an electric light that would burn long enough to provide sustained illumination. Edison and his colleagues were to spend a year carrying out thousands of experiments before identifying the precise kind of carbon filament needed. After receiving its patent, Edison's light bulb went into production in 1880.

■ *In October 1879, American inventor Thomas Alva Edison, assisted by his research team, and with financial backing from J. P. Morgan, was the first to patent a commercially practical electric light bulb—thus becoming known forever as the man who brought the world out of the gaslight era into the age of electricity.*

ON DECEMBER 13, 2006, *a box containing 23 light bulbs used in Thomas Edison's court case when he defended his patent went on sale at London auction house Christie's. The light bulbs had disappeared after the clash over the U.S. patent, but were discovered by chance in an attic in 2002.*

Joseph Swan's later improvement on Edison's filament, which extended the potential life of a light bulb, was commercially produced from 1881. By then, however, Edison was tackling the problem of generating and distributing electricity for widespread use. He invented new dynamos and a wide range of apparatus to assist the generation of electricity. In 1882 he made another lasting contribution to the electrical age by establishing the world's first central generating plant for electric lighting.

Economic growth and rapid technological development characterized the years after the end of the Civil War in 1865. Inventions between 1867 and 1876 included barbed wire, air brakes for locomotives, reinforced concrete buildings, cable cars, illustrated daily newspapers, and electric dental drills. Edison was the most prolific contemporary inventor, producing innovations like the phonograph, the mimeograph (which made copies of documents), flexible celluloid film, the motion-picture projector, the alkaline storage battery, and the carbon microphone still used in telephones today. When he died in 1931, Edison had patented over 1,000 inventions.

Few could have predicted this of the child born in Ohio on February 11, 1847, the seventh son of a mill owner and a former schoolteacher. Edison was removed from school after only three months when a teacher described him as "addled." After that, he was taught by his mother, of whom he said: "My mother was the making of me. She was so true, so sure of me; and I felt I had something to live for, someone I must not disappoint." His mother had taught him all she could by the time Edison was nine, but he continued to educate himself through avid reading.

At 12, Edison was already a business entrepreneur, selling magazines and sweets on the Grand Trunk Railroad. He satisfied his endless curiosity by establishing his own laboratory and spending his earnings on books and apparatus. The railroad was to give him his initial professional training. One day he rescued the young son of a station agent from a runaway train, and out of gratitude the boy's father taught Edison telegraph code. By the age of 15 Edison was managing a telegraph office. Among his earliest inventions were a transmitter and receiver for the automatic telegraph.

At 21 Edison put a notice in the *Telegrapher* stating he was "giving up telegraphy to devote his time to bringing out inventions." He invented a

T. A. EDISON.
Electric-Lamp.

No. 223,898.   Patented Jan. 27, 1880.

"To all whom it may concern: Be it known that I, Thomas Alva Edison, of Menlo Park, in the State of New Jersey, United States of America, have invented an improvement on Electric Lamps, and in the method of manufacturing the same, (Case No. 186,) of which the following is a specification. The object of this invention is to produce electric lamps giving light by incandescence, which lamps shall have high resistance, so as to allow of the practical subdivision of the electric light."

stock ticker for printing stock-exchange quotations in brokers' offices and, with the $40,000 this brought him, established a small laboratory and manufacturing shop selling electrical goods in Newark, New Jersey.

In 1876 Edison established a team of talented associates at Menlo Park, near New York, in the first fully equipped industrial research laboratory, boasting he would produce inventions "to order." The steady stream of innovations—including an electron tube that led to the development of radio and television—that came from his laboratory led to him becoming known as "the Wizard of Menlo Park."

A prodigious worker himself, Edison made huge demands on his staff. He would often sleep in the workplace when caught up in an experiment, and his appetite for hard work is evident from his much-quoted remark: "Genius is one percent inspiration and ninety-nine percent perspiration."

In 1879, greatly disappointed by the fact that fellow inventor Alexander Graham Bell had beaten him in the race to patent the first authentic transmission of the human voice—the "articulating" telephone—Edison now trounced the competition by inventing the first incandescent electric light bulb suitable for commercial production. He went on to produce a ceaseless flow of inventions. In World War I, 45 further inventions helped the government's war effort, and he was rewarded with the Congressional Medal of Honor.

By the 1920s Edison was one of the most famous Americans in the world, and had received many foreign honors. He worked until his death, collapsing in his laboratory in 1931 while researching the production of synthetic rubber with the help of his great friend Henry Ford.

Soon after Edison's death, President Herbert Hoover asked Americans to turn out their lights and plunge themselves into darkness to commemorate the man who had brought electricity into their lives.

Edison became a folk hero in his own lifetime—the self-taught Yankee inventor who rose to riches as a gifted commercial developer. An eccentric and an egotist, he was regarded by some as anti-intellectual and reactionary, and his methods were criticized in certain quarters. However, many now regard his methodology as his greatest contribution to scientific development. Edison's establishment of the modern laboratory, using specialist teams to carry out systematic research, was a radical departure from the nineteenth-century model of the individual, maverick inventor working in isolation.

JOHN HOLLAND (1841–1914) STANDS IN
THE CONNING TOWER OF ONE OF HIS
"HOLLAND" DIVING TORPEDO BOATS

The prototype for the

FIRST
MILITARY
SUBMARINE

APRIL 11, 1900

EARLY SUBMARINES WERE used in both the Revolutionary War and the Civil War. By the 1890s the French and U.S. navies had demonstrated the potential of all-electric submarines. However, their effectiveness was severely hampered by the limited capacity of the batteries that powered the electric motors, which forced the submarines to return to port for the batteries to be recharged. After 25 years of experimentation, in 1900 Irish immigrant John Holland perfected a vessel that had an electric motor for underwater propulsion, and a gasoline engine for surface propulsion and battery recharging. The *Holland 6* was the first submarine that could travel underwater for long distances, which gave it real potential as a naval vessel. It had all the basic features of later submarines used in both World Wars.

■ *John Holland's idea for a submersible craft that could tackle modern warships grew out of his observations of the naval battles of the Civil War and his Irish-republican antipathy for the British: "It struck me very forcibly that . . . ironclad ships had come to stay forever. I reflected that with her tremendous facilities England would . . . become the chief naval power of the world; and I wondered how she could be retarded in her designs upon the other peoples of the world, and how they would protect themselves against those designs."*

In 1776 an American, David Bushnell, invented the first submarine to be used in war, the one-man USS *Turtle*. This had two features of modern submarines: a closed hull and screw propulsion (hand-worked in the case of the *Turtle*). However, in order to become an effective war machine submarines needed good undersea weaponry and a source of power.

In 1800 Robert Fulton built his *Nautilus,* the first all-metal submarine, and during the Civil War the Confederate navy used small submarines known as "Davids" (after the biblical David who killed the giant Goliath). These were armed with an explosive charge, and powered by hand or steam. The invention of the first self-propelled torpedo by Italian engineer Giovanni Luppis, a captain in the Austrian navy, in 1864 provided submarines with their first effective weapon. The viability of the submarine was then secured by the addition in the late nineteenth century of the internal-combustion engine, electric motors, and batteries.

Key to the story of submarine development was John Holland, an Irish schoolteacher committed to the Irish-republican cause, who had emigrated to New York in 1873. Holland submitted plans for a submarine to the U.S. navy in 1875, but they were rejected. Holland wanted to perfect his vessel but lacked sufficient funds.

However, the Fenian Brotherhood, an Irish republican organization, was keen to support Holland in developing a craft that could be sailed across the Atlantic and used against the British navy. With Fenian funding, he constructed his first successful full-sized submarine, a three-man craft nicknamed the *Fenian Ram*. This was tested successfully in New York Harbor between 1881 and 1883 and, after improvements, attracted technical, but not financial, interest from the U.S. navy.

By 1885 Holland had parted from the Fenians and, working alongside Edmund L. Zalinski (known for his part in the development of the pneumatic dynamite torpedo-gun), had built a fourth boat, with dynamite guns, and a primitive periscope. In 1888 this was selected by the U.S.

THE ECONOMICS OF DESTRUCTION
In 1914, less than three months after Holland's death, a German naval submarine torpedoed and sank three British cruisers in the North Sea. The vessel proved its formidable worth as a weapon: 26 men in a 450-ton vessel destroyed 36,000 tons of enemy shipping and cost the British navy the lives of 1,400 servicemen.

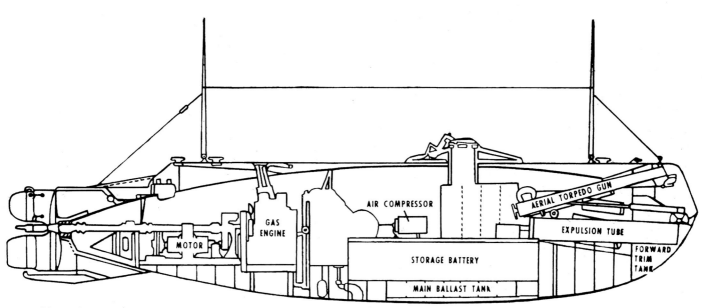

Plan of 53 foot HOLLAND

Labels on diagram: MOTOR · GAS ENGINE · AIR COMPRESSOR · AERIAL TORPEDO GUN · EXPULSION TUBE · STORAGE BATTERY · MAIN BALLAST TANK · FORWARD TRIM TANK

The Holland 6, the first modern submarine commissioned by the U.S. navy, was invented by Irish-American John Holland. Following the U.S. purchase of this new, fully practical underwater vessel, orders came from England, Japan, and Russia. From then on the submarine was a major element of many nations' navies.

navy over three other designs, but Holland was unable to fund its building until he was awarded a government contract following a second public competition. By 1895 Holland had designed a fifth boat, the *Plunger.* Against Holland's advice, the navy insisted that it should be driven by steam on the surface and electricity below, so he then withdrew to develop his own, privately financed *Holland 6,* completed by 1898. With its dual-propulsion system of a gasoline engine and battery-powered electric motors, the ship was able to travel at a speed of six knots when submerged.

After further design modifications, Holland sold his *Holland 6* to the U.S. government on April 11, 1900. It was the first U.S. naval submarine, and superior to any other current submarine in being able to dive rather than sink to a desired depth. This was the major contribution John Holland made to submarine technology—the use of "dynamic force" to maintain depth control. This force was produced by a combination of the craft's speed, angle of inclination, and diving planes. Its fat, cylindrical hull and minimal superstructure helped the submarine achieve maximum speed when submerged. The U.S. navy immediately ordered six more vessels, and Holland was soon asked to build similar ships by the navies of several other nations.

In his final years, like many other inventors who lacked private means for working capital, Holland encountered difficulties with the financiers who controlled his company. He abandoned submarines to experiment in aviation. After spending 57 of his 74 years working on submarines, Holland died in Newark, New Jersey in August 12, 1914, a few days after the outbreak of World War I—during which his weapon would prove its devastating effectiveness.

Henry Ford (center) with Thomas A. Edison (left)
and Harvey Firestone (right), c. 1930

Design of the

FORD
MODEL T

the "Farmer's Car"

October 1, 1908

ALTHOUGH THE GROWTH of the railroads had encouraged millions of Americans to migrate westwards, it was the creation of an affordable car that enabled many more to travel from the remote farms and small towns where many of the population lived. When Henry Ford was young, four Americans in every five lived on a farm: when he died in 1947, four in every five lived in cities, linked together by the best road system in the world. By then, too, automobile manufacturing was the chief industry in the U.S. Ford revolutionized manufacturing methods, increased production, maximized sales, and maintained profits—while the price of his famous Model T fell from $850 in 1908 to below $300 in 1925. It was the first car that ordinary Americans could afford.

■ *Ford recognized that the tedium of assembly-line work had to be tackled in order for employers and employees to benefit from its many advantages: specialized skills, improved safety, and increased production. Efficiency was rewarded with high wages, guaranteeing staff loyalty. Ford's system was copied in many different manufacturing industries.*

Although there were 30 U.S. automobile manufacturers by 1899, most Americans bought imported cars. In America generally the car was not the rich man's toy it was in Europe. Innovators like Henry Ford saw its potential for revolutionizing communications in a large country.

Born on July 30, 1864 on a farm in Michigan, the oldest of six children, Henry Ford was always more interested in machines than farming. At the age of 16 he walked to Detroit to become an apprentice in a machine shop. Unable to make his wages meet his living costs, Ford earned extra money by repairing clocks and watches at night. In Detroit he learned about European car production and began to dream of making his own "horseless carriage."

After his marriage in 1889, Ford returned to farming for two years, but in 1891 he joined the Edison Illuminating Company, and by 1893 was chief engineer. He spent his spare time building a car, finally producing his "quadricycle" in 1896. This pram-like "baby carriage," as Ford called it, was mounted on bicycle wheels, had a two-cylinder motor and no reverse gear, and was extremely light. From 1899 Ford started a number of unsuccessful car companies, but came to public awareness through the race cars he built, including the 999—which broke the U.S. speed record in 1901.

Success in racing won Ford a number of financial backers, including Edison, and in 1903 they formed the Ford Motor Company, which aimed to improve the lightweight car and reduce its price. After producing several prototypes, Ford and his team rolled out the first Model T on October 1, 1908. The Model T was light, relatively powerful, easy to drive, and could run on gasoline or ethanol. Because fuel relied on gravity to flow from the tank to the carburetor, the car could not climb steep hills when fuel was low. Instead, it had to drive up them in reverse—the source of many contemporary jokes. Although the Model T was originally available in several body styles and colors,

A UNIVERSAL ICON
Nearly 15,500,000 Model Ts were eventually sold in the U.S. alone, and at one stage in the 1920s nine out of ten cars in the world were Fords.

In his satirical novel Brave New World *(1932), the British novelist Aldous Huxley describes a mechanized totalitarian future society in which "Our Ford," rather than "Our Lord," is worshipped like a god.*

1909 drawing of the Ford Model T from the collection of the Benson Ford Research Center. Cheap, durable and easy to maintain, Henry Ford's Model T car—the "Tin Lizzie"—jump-started the automobile age in America. The manufacturing process Ford devised to mass-produce the car—the moving assembly line—changed the American lifestyle and economy as much as the car itself did.

from 1913 through 1925 Ford decided that people could "have the Model T in any color—so long as it's black," the reason being that black paint dried more quickly than any other color, which helped speed up assembly. The Model T's launch price of $850 hugely undercut the $2,000–3,000 cost of any competing car.

Over seven years Ford increased production phenomenally by perfecting a constantly moving assembly line at his manufacturing plant in Highland Park, Michigan. However, the new assembly process was tedious and led to high staff turnover. In an effort to retain skilled workers, in 1914 Ford began paying his employees five dollars a day, nearly twice the wages paid by other manufacturers. Not only did he keep his employees, but he also created a market for his cars among his own huge workforce.

At the end of World War I, Ford was a multi-millionaire, and in the period between the two World Wars the company expanded overseas, with manufacturing plants in India, Australia, and France, and dealerships around the globe. By the early 1930s, the Ford Motor Company was producing one-third of the world's automobiles and Ford himself had become an American hero: his hard work, self-reliance, and thrift recalled the Puritan values on which the still-young country had been founded. However, he tarnished his reputation by supporting for many years a newspaper that generated anti-Semitic propaganda. Energetic and extraordinarily fit, Ford continued to run his company autocratically until his death in 1947, at the age of 83. Although he was anti-intellectual and famously dismissive of history—once stating that "History is more or less bunk"—Ford changed the demographics of American society forever, and is frequently cited by historians as one of the key industrial and cultural figures of the Modern Era.

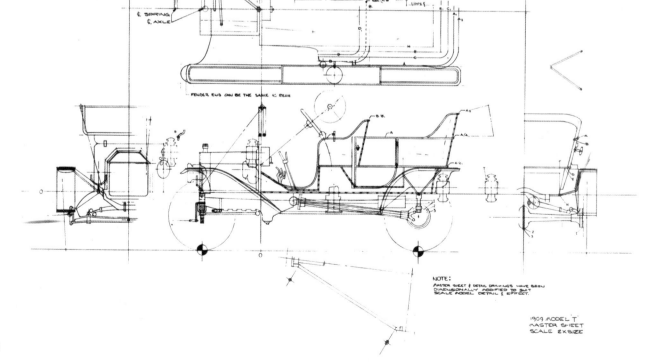

The *Titanic* goes down on April 15, 1912,
watched by survivors in lifeboats

Inquiry into the

SINKING

OF THE

RMS *TITANIC*

April 19–May 25, 1912

EVEN AS NEWS of the sinking of the *Titanic* was hitting American newspaper headlines, Senator William Alden Smith began preparations to investigate the causes of the disaster. Keen to gather eyewitness accounts while the events were still fresh in people's minds, Smith instigated an inquiry. It was held in the Waldorf-Astoria Hotel in New York, and began on April 19, just one day after the *Carpathia*, the ship carrying survivors of the *Titanic*, reached New York. The American inquiry, which lasted until May 25 and took 86 witness statements, was followed by a separate inquiry by the British Board of Trade. The U.S. inquiry placed responsibility for the disaster on the *Titanic*'s captain, and the captain of the SS *Californian*, a liner close by that failed to answer distress signals from the sinking ship.

■ *Although far worse maritime tragedies than that of the* Titanic *have happened during wartime, the loss of the "unsinkable" luxury liner has never loosened its grip on the public imagination. A film about the disaster made by the director James Cameron in 1997 became the highest-earning movie of all time, grossing $1.8 billion worldwide.*

In 1908, the White Star Company in Britain commissioned the *Titanic* and two sister ships, the *Olympic* and the *Britannic*, to compete in the profitable transatlantic passenger trade. The *Titanic* was the most lavishly appointed vessel ever built and, at 52,250 tons, the biggest ship in the world. It was a floating city, with First Class accommodation on the upper decks, Second Class in the middle, and Third Class at the bottom. It also had a swimming pool and gymnasium. Fittings in First Class were sumptuous, and even the Third Class facilities were the most luxurious ever installed on a ship. The *Titanic*'s maiden voyage attracted some of the most prominent people in the world as passengers—including industrialist Benjamin Guggenheim, Macy's department store owner Isador Strauss, U.S. Presidential aide Archibald Butt, multimillionaire John Jacob Astor IV, and streetcar magnate George Dunton Widener.

Despite its vast size, the *Titanic* was considered unsinkable because of the 16 watertight compartments and electronic watertight doors in its hull. If damage occurred to one part of the hull, flooding could be contained within the affected compartment. Up to four of these compartments could be flooded without compromising the ship's overall buoyancy.

There had been a record number of icebergs sighted in the North Atlantic in the winter of 1911–12, and the *Titanic*'s captain, Edward J. Smith, was well aware of the danger they represented. He was also keen to reach New York in record time, possibly urged on by the White Star Line managing director, J. Bruce Ismay, who was traveling First Class. On April 14, wireless operators on ship received several warnings of ice, but Captain Smith gave no order to reduce speed.

Just before midnight, about 400 miles south of Newfoundland, the *Titanic* hit an iceberg. Five of the ship's watertight compartments were ruptured—one more than the ship could safely sustain—and over the space of an hour and forty minutes the ship gradually sank, taking hundreds of passengers and crew to their death.

The deployment of lifeboats was chaotic, as the crew were unfamiliar with the equipment and lifeboat drill. Only 18

A TALE OF SURVIVAL

The last American survivor with first-hand memories of the sinking, Lillian Gertrud Asplund, died in Massachusetts in May 2006. Five at the time of the tragedy, she lost her twin brother, her father, and two other brothers. Her mother and another brother survived, but her mother died on the anniversary of the sinking in 1964.

lifeboats were launched, and most only partly filled—mainly with women and children among the First and Second Class passengers, as Third Class passengers had difficulty reaching the upper decks. Half the passengers were *de facto* doomed in the event of any disaster: the *Titanic's* lifeboats had places for only 1,178 people out of the 2,223 on board. Passengers without a place in the boats drowned or froze to death in the icy water.

At 4.10 a.m., two hours after the *Titanic* sank, the Cunard liner *Carpathia*, which had received a distress call, arrived at the scene to pick up survivors.

In the inquiry's final report, Senator Smith stated: "It is because Congress has jurisdiction to regulate commerce between the States and foreign countries that the committee has the right to undertake this investigation." In 1913 the first International Convention for Safety of Life at Sea led to the creation of the International Ice Patrol to warn ships of icebergs in the North Atlantic shipping lanes. It also ruled that all ships should carry lifeboat space for the full complement of persons on board, and that there should be constant radio watch at sea.

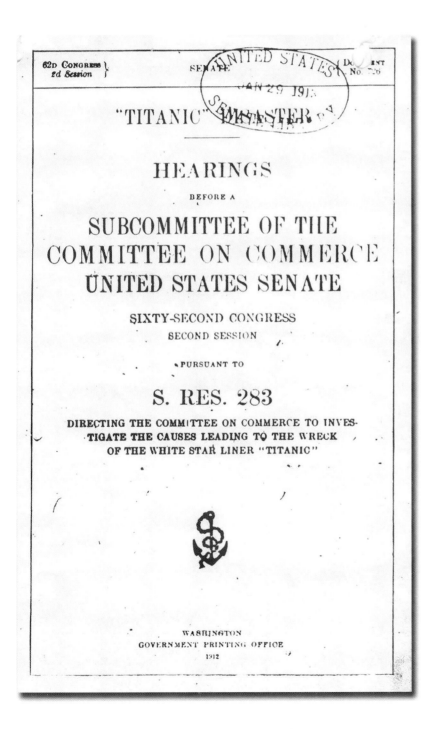

The U.S. inquiry into the sinking of the Titanic blamed the captain, Edward J. Smith, who went down with the ship, and the captain of the SS Californian, which failed to respond to distress signals sent from the stricken liner. It also reported numerous safety deficiencies and recommended legislation to remedy them.

Transcript of THE INQUIRY INTO THE SINKING OF RMS *TITANIC*

❝ RECOMMENDATIONS

The committee finds that this accident clearly indicates the necessity of additional legislation to secure safety of life at sea . . .

The committee recommends that sections 4481 and 4488, Revised Statutes, be so amended as to definitely require sufficient lifeboats to accommodate every passenger and every member of the crew . . .

Not less than four members of the crew, skilled in handling boats, should be assigned to every boat. All members of the crew assigned to lifeboats should be drilled in lowering and rowing the boats, not less than twice each month and the fact of such drill or practice should be noted in the log.

The committee recommends the assignment of passengers and crew to lifeboats before sailing; that occupants of certain groups of staterooms and the stewards of such groups of rooms be assigned to certain boats most conveniently located with reference to the rooms in question; the assignment of boats and the shortest route from stateroom to boat to be posted in every stateroom.

The committee recommends that every ocean steamship carrying 100 or more passengers be required to carry 2 electric searchlights.

The committee finds that this catastrophe makes glaringly apparent the necessity for regulation of radiotelegraphy. There must be an operator on duty at all times, day and night, to insure the immediate receipt of all distress, warning, or other important calls. Direct communication either by clear-speaking telephone, voice tube, or messenger must be provided between the wireless room and the bridge, so that the operator does not have to leave his station. There must be definite legislation to prevent interference by amateurs, and to secure secrecy of radiograms or wireless messages. There must be some source of auxiliary power, either storage battery or oil engine, to insure the operation of the wireless installation until the wireless room is submerged.

The committee recommends that the firing of rockets or candles on the high seas for any other purpose than as a signal of distress be made a misdemeanor.

The committee recommends that the following additional structural requirements be required as regards ocean-going passenger steamers the construction of which is begun after this date:

All steel ocean and coastwise seagoing ships carrying 100 or more passengers should have a watertight skin inboard of the outside plating, . . . and this construction should extend from the forward collision bulkhead over not less than two-thirds of the length of the ship.

All steel ocean and coastwise seagoing ships carrying 100 or more passengers should have bulkheads so spaced that any two adjacent compartments of the ship may be flooded without destroying the flotability or stability of the ship . . . ❞

Arthur Zimmermann
(1864–1940), German
foreign minister
(1916–17)

The

ZIMMERMANN TELEGRAM

From the German Foreign Minister, Arthur
Zimmermann, to the German Ambassador in
Mexico, Heinrich von Eckhardt

January 9, 1917

GERMANY'S DECISION TO restart unrestricted submarine warfare, announced in the Zimmermann telegram, could be seen as one of the most stupendous political miscalculations of World War I. It was in Germany's interest for the United States to remain neutral. Germany could not hope to win the war if pitted against the colossal wealth and resources, and apparently unlimited manpower, of the U.S. President Woodrow Wilson wanted to maintain U.S. neutrality and the policy of non-interference in European affairs, but faced with attacks on American ships and the possibility of neighboring Mexico becoming involved, he saw no other choice than to declare war on Germany. So why did Germany seal its fate in this way?

■ *President Woodrow Wilson, who was re-elected in 1916 with the slogan "He kept us out of the war," finally took the United States into World War I in 1917 when American shipping came under U-boat attack and the Zimmermann telegram revealed Germany's plan to involve Mexico in a war against the United States.*

Britain's interception and decoding of the Zimmermann telegram in January 1917 is a classic spy story. Unfortunately, President Woodrow Wilson did not approve of spying, which he saw as the sign of a dangerous autocracy, so Britain had to cover its tracks from both the Germans and the Americans. Woodrow Wilson had given Germany access to the U.S. diplomatic telegraph between Germany and Washington. The British tapped into the Zimmermann telegram on this route. Realizing its huge importance, a British agent was sent to intercept a coded copy sent from the German ambassador in Washington to his counterpart in Mexico. This copy, decrypted using a codebook captured from a German agent in the Middle East, was then shown to the American ambassador in Britain, Walter Page, who sent it two days later to President Wilson.

At the beginning of the war in Europe, Woodrow Wilson had offered to act as a mediator, and had called on all Americans to remain neutral in thought as well as deed. Although the U.S. had close ties with Britain and France, there were also a great many German- and Austrian-born citizens in the country, and U.S. foreign policy since the Monroe Doctrine had been to remain neutral in the arguments between the old world's imperial powers. Wilson refused to build up the army, arguing that it would be provocative to do so. In 1915, the Germans sank the British ship, RMS *Lusitania*, with the loss of 128 lives. Despite the anti-German feeling this aroused, Woodrow Wilson was re-elected by a narrow majority in 1916 precisely because he had not taken the U.S. to war. War in fact threatened in two different regions: as well as the war in Europe, the U.S. faced the threat of insurgency from Mexico, where the revolutionary Pancho Villa was making cross-border raids into the U.S. However, in his acceptance speech in 1916, Wilson warned that the U.S. would retaliate if directly attacked or if its citizens were killed.

It would, therefore, seem madness on Germany's part to provoke the U.S. by attacking its shipping or encouraging Mexico to attack. However, Germany's position in 1917 was becoming desperate, owing largely to the British blockade of German ports. President Wilson had objected to Britain's blockade affecting neutral shipping, but had objected much more strongly to Germany's sinking of shipping bound for Allied ports, which was costing lives. Neutrality had also not prevented the U.S. from sending millions of dollars worth of arms shipments to Britain and

France, while American bankers loaned the Allies over $2 billion. A clue to Zimmermann's thinking came in the last line of his telegram: that unrestricted submarine warfare would compel England to make peace in a few months. If the allies were cut off from their resources in the U.S., and if the U.S. were distracted by an attack from Mexico and the possibility of attack by Japan, Germany might have a chance of ending the war on its own terms. Zimmermann was mistaken, both about Mexico's willingness and ability to attack the United States, and the U.S. response.

The Zimmermann telegram revealed that Germany was about to restart unrestricted submarine warfare and, in the event of the United States entering the war, it offered money and support for Mexico to retake territories from the U.S. The discovery of this telegram was instrumental in bringing the United States into World War I. The original of the deciphered telegram was discovered at GCHQ, the British intelligence agency, in 2005.

The contents of the telegram, once it was proved to be genuine, convinced President Wilson that the U.S. must enter the war. Wilson addressed Congress on April 2, 1917. He condemned Germany's methods, and characterized the Allied cause as "championing the rights of mankind," in order to keep "a world safe for democracy." Wilson hoped World War I would be "the war to end all wars," and that it would establish a basis for world peace. Although an Allied victory was now inevitable, his optimisim was not to be justified.

Transcript of THE ZIMMERMANN TELEGRAM

'MOST SECRET

For Your Excellency's personal information and to be handed on to the Imperial Minister in Mexico.

We intend to begin unrestricted submarine warfare on the first of February. We shall endeavor in spite of this to keep the United States neutral. In the event of this not succeeding, we make Mexico a proposal of an alliance on the following basis: Make war together, make peace together, generous financial support, and an understanding on our part that Mexico is to reconquer the lost territory in Texas, New Mexico, and Arizona. The settlement detail is left to you.

You will inform the President [of Mexico] of the above most secretly as soon as the outbreak of war with the United States is certain and add the suggestion that he should, on his own initiative, invite Japan to immediate adherence and at the same time mediate between Japan and ourselves.

Please call the President's attention to the fact that the unrestricted employment of our submarines now offers the prospect of compelling England to make peace within a few months. Acknowledge receipt.

ZIMMERMANN '

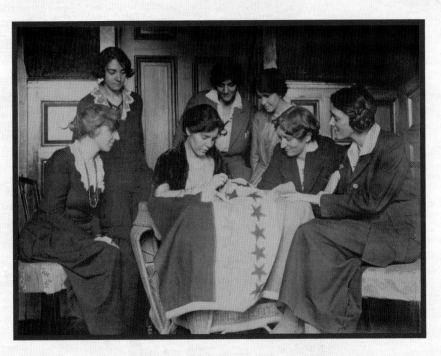

LEADING SUFFRAGETTE ALICE PAUL (1885–1977) SEWING
STARS ON THE SUFFRAGE FLAG AS OTHER WOMEN LOOK ON

The

19th
AMENDMENT

to the U.S. Constitution:
women's right to vote

AUGUST 18, 1920

THE ABSURDITY AND injustice of a democratic country denying half its population a voice in government was publicly exposed at the first Women's Rights Convention in New York in 1848. It was a further 72 years before Congress relented. After one of the longest sustained political campaigns in history, the 19th Amendment to the Constitution, granting women the right to vote, was passed in 1920. Very few of the original campaigners lived to see the day of victory.

■ *Alice Paul (1885–1977) participated in the British suffrage campaign for four years, and applied many of their strategies to the American campaign, including mass demonstrations, picketing, starting fires, and hunger striking. President Woodrow Wilson was repelled by the activities of her National Woman's Party, but eventually gave his support to the campaign for women's votes.*

The women's suffrage movement in the United States arose directly out of the movement for the abolition of slavery. When two American delegates, Elizabeth Cady Stanton and Lucretia Mott, both Quakers, were refused a platform to speak at an anti-slavery convention in London because they were women, they decided to apply their energy and commitment to the issue of equality for women. They organized the first Women's Rights Convention in Seneca Falls, New York, in 1848, where they drew up the *Declaration of Sentiments*, a comprehensive and damning list of the inequalities suffered by women in marriage, work, religion, education, and civil rights.

The *Declaration* laid down the means by which women would fight: "We shall employ agents, circulate tracts, petition the state and national legislatures, and endeavor to enlist the pulpit and the press in our behalf." The American campaign for women's suffrage was generally far less militant than the British suffragettes of the early 1900s, although some later campaigners, such as Harriet Stanton Blatch (Elizabeth Cady Stanton's daughter) and Alice Paul, knew British activists, and Paul was even imprisoned in Britain. Both women returned to the U.S. to start their own parties, respectively, the Equality League of Self-Supporting Women and the National Woman's Party, both of which adopted the more aggressive techniques of the British campaigners. Mostly, however, the earlier members of the U.S. movement threw themselves into an extensive publicity and lobbying campaign.

One tactic was to challenge the legality of denying women the vote. After the 14th Amendment was passed in 1868, suffragists tried to test whether voting was a "privilege" of U.S. citizenship. Susan B. Anthony, a tireless campaigner, was prosecuted for voting illegally in the 1872 election. Although the judge directed the jury to find her guilty, having written his speech before the trial, Anthony gave a speech in her defense that was a model of great suffrage oratory: "It is a downright mockery to talk to women of their enjoyment of the blessings of liberty while they are denied the only means of serving them provided by this democratic-republican government—the ballot." She refused to pay her fine.

HIS MOTHER'S VOICE
Twenty-four-year-old Harry Burns, who cast the deciding vote in Tennessee that led to the 19th Amendment being ratified, is said to have had a letter in his pocket from his mother saying, "Don't forget to be a good boy and help Mrs. Catt put the 'Rat' in Ratification," and "Vote for suffrage."

Abolitionists and suffragists initially worked together, but many in the National Woman's Suffrage Association felt betrayed by the "precedence" given to black men over women in the 15th Amendment. A more disturbing split came later when the "Jim Crow" laws (requiring racial segregation in all public facilities) were passed in Southern states. To keep the white suffragists' support, the newly formed National American Woman's Suffrage Association (NAWSA) refused to take a position on segregation, alienating black supporters, who set up their own suffrage societies to address their particular social, economic, and cultural needs, especially the campaign against lynching.

Another tactic was to lobby for women's suffrage laws to be passed in individual states. In 1890 Wyoming joined the Union as a state that allowed women to vote. However, by 1900 only three other states—Utah, Colorado, and Idaho—had given women the vote. In 1912, Theodore Roosevelt's Progressive Party was the first national party to support women's suffrage.

By 1916, almost all the major suffrage associations were systematically lobbying the federal government for constitutional amendment. Alice Paul's Silent Sentinels protested outside the White House continuously for 30 months between January 1917 and June 1919, despite imprisonment and brutal treatment by the authorities. President Woodrow Wilson was initially amused by the demonstration and chose to ignore it. However, the women's demands, and growing public support, made the issue of women's

---

H. J. Res. 1.

5

Sixty-sixth Congress of the United States of America;

At the First Session,

Begun and held at the City of Washington on Monday, the nineteenth day of May, one thousand nine hundred and nineteen.

JOINT RESOLUTION

Proposing an amendment to the Constitution extending the right of suffrage to women.

Resolved by the Senate and House of Representatives of the United States of America in Congress assembled (two-thirds of each House concurring therein), That the following article is proposed as an amendment to the Constitution, which shall be valid to all intents and purposes as part of the Constitution when ratified by the legislatures of three-fourths of the several States.

"ARTICLE ———.

"The right of citizens of the United States to vote shall not be denied or abridged by the United States or by any State on account of sex.

"Congress shall have power to enforce this article by appropriate legislation."

F. H. Gillett

Speaker of the House of Representatives.

Thos. R. Marshall

Vice President of the United States and President of the Senate.

The 19th Amendment, giving women the right to vote, was initially proposed in 1878 and introduced in every session of Congress for the next 41 years before it was finally ratified in August 1920.

rights unavoidable, and in 1918 Wilson publicly asserted his support for the campaign. Anti-suffragists were boycotted in the Senate elections in 1918, and by June 1919 Congress had approved the Amendment. In 1920, Tennessee, the necessary 36th state, ratified the Amendment and women finally won the right to vote throughout the U.S.

Transcript of THE 19TH AMENDMENT TO THE U.S. CONSTITUTION

'Sixty-sixth Congress of the United States of America; At the First Session,

Begun and held at the City of Washington on Monday, the nineteenth day of May, one thousand nine hundred and nineteen.

JOINT RESOLUTION

Proposing an amendment to the Constitution extending the right of suffrage to women.

Resolved by the Senate and House of Representatives of the United States of America in Congress assembled (two-thirds of each House concurring therein), That the following article is proposed as an amendment to the Constitution, which shall be valid to all intents and purposes as part of the Constitution when ratified by the legislature of three-fourths of the several States.

"ARTICLE ————.

"The right of citizens of the United States to vote shall not be denied or abridged by the United States or by any State on account of sex.

Congress shall have power to enforce this article by appropriate legislation." '

U.S. Federal Agents pouring 900 gallons of high-quality
wine into the gutter in front of the Federal Building,
Los Angeles, 1920

The National

PROHIBITION ACT

January 16, 1920

GREAT AMERICAN DOCUMENTS

THE NATIONAL PROHIBITION ACT of 1920 has become one of the most notorious pieces of legislation in U.S. history. This is largely because it encouraged precisely what it set out to restrict—the consumption of alcohol and the criminal behavior associated with it. Feelings had not always run high about alcohol in America. The Pilgrim Fathers brought more beer than water with them on the *Mayflower*: it was safer to drink, and socially and medicinally acceptable. The consumption of alcohol was only condemned in excess, and was easily controlled in close-knit, rural societies.

■ *The initial fall in the consumption of alcohol at the beginning of prohibition was not followed by the social improvements campaigners had anticipated. People turned to bootleg drink, or to drugs like opium and cocaine, which became a huge problem in their turn. Crime rocketed, courts and prisons could not cope, and government spending was hit by reduced tax revenue.*

The first temperance societies were set up by farmers in the late 1700s to encourage moderation. As society fragmented and drinking became a more individual, masculine activity, alcohol was often blamed for new social ills, such as unemployment, poverty, and crime. By 1810 there were at least 2,000 distilleries throughout the U.S., and whiskey was soon cheaper than beer, wine, coffee, tea—or milk. The grog shop and saloon replaced the more social tavern. Alcohol was blamed for ruining marriages and families, with men drinking the family's money, losing their jobs, and becoming violent. In 1826, the American Temperance Society campaigned for voluntary abstinence. With 1,500,000 members "taking the pledge" in the first ten years, it appeared to be successful, but the movement stalled during the Civil War.

In the 1870s, the Woman's Christian Temperance Union, supported by religious groups like the Methodists, campaigned for the preservation of the family and improvements in social morality. Despite its name, it called for abstinence supported by legal enforcement—prohibition, not temperance—and took its campaign into saloons and classrooms across America.

Many states and counties enacted prohibition laws at this time. Business leaders, who believed that production would increase if workers were denied access to alcohol, also supported the movement. Campaigners began to aim for federal prohibition. Wayne B. Wheeler, the counsel for the Anti-Saloon League, one of the most powerful and influential men in the country, pioneered "pressure politics," whereby candidates were ruthlessly questioned and lobbied about prohibition, turning many elections into single-issue debates. John D. Rockefeller, Jr. donated over $350,000 to the League.

World War I gave a boost to the campaign, as emergency restrictions on the use of grain prohibited alcohol production. Anti-German feeling also led to a boycott of brewers of German origin. The Senate and the House of Representatives supported the 18th Amendment, which banned the manufacture, sale, and transportation of intoxicating liquor, and was ratified in just 13 months. In 1920 the National Prohibition Act was passed. Religious and medicinal use of alcohol was highly regulated, but consumption in private homes was never prohibited, though how private stocks were to be legally

"THE REAL MCCOY"

There was a real McCoy—William S. McCoy—a teetotal smuggler who became famous and very rich from his reputation for supplying good, high-quality liquor, albeit illegally. "The real McCoy" became a catchphrase, used to distinguish good liquor from bad. The latter—which was often all the poor could afford—caused alcohol poisoning, which could be fatal.

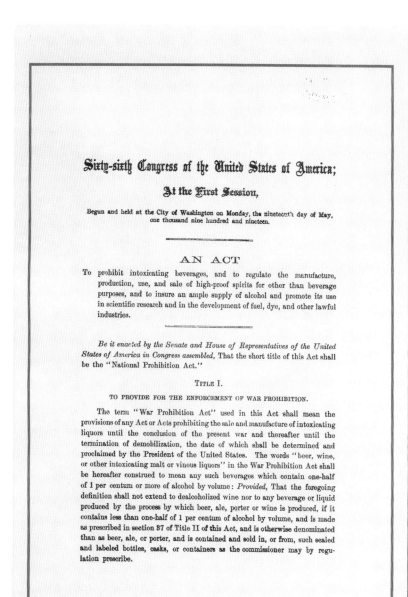

Sixty-sixth Congress of the United States of America;

At the First Session,

Begun and held at the City of Washington on Monday, the nineteenth day of May, one thousand nine hundred and nineteen.

AN ACT

To prohibit intoxicating beverages, and to regulate the manufacture, production, use, and sale of high-proof spirits for other than beverage purposes, and to insure an ample supply of alcohol and promote its use in scientific research and in the development of fuel, dye, and other lawful industries.

Be it enacted by the Senate and House of Representatives of the United States of America in Congress assembled, That the short title of this Act shall be the "National Prohibition Act."

TITLE I.

TO PROVIDE FOR THE ENFORCEMENT OF WAR PROHIBITION.

The term "War Prohibition Act" used in this Act shall mean the provisions of any Act or Acts prohibiting the sale and manufacture of intoxicating liquors until the conclusion of the present war and thereafter until the termination of demobilization, the date of which shall be determined and proclaimed by the President of the United States. The words "beer, wine, or other intoxicating malt or vinous liquors" in the War Prohibition Act shall be hereafter construed to mean any such beverages which contain one-half of 1 per centum or more of alcohol by volume: *Provided,* That the foregoing definition shall not extend to dealcoholized wine nor to any beverage or liquid produced by the process by which beer, ale, porter or wine is produced, if it contains less than one-half of 1 per centum of alcohol by volume, and is made as prescribed in section 37 of Title II of this Act, and is otherwise denominated than as beer, ale, or porter, and is contained and sold in, or from, such sealed and labeled bottles, casks, or containers as the commissioner may by regulation prescribe.

The National Prohibition Act was necessary to define the terms used in the 18th Amendment, and set out the details relating to the enforcement of the Amendment in law.

replenished posed an interesting dilemma.

People were so convinced that this act would provide a cure-all for society's ills that some communities even sold their jails. Official statistics appeared to show the act was working: alcohol consumption fell by 30 percent; there were fewer arrests for drunkenness; black market prices put illegal alcohol out of reach of the average worker; and consumption of hard liquor went down by 50 percent. However, the real story that lay beyond official statistics was very different. Bootlegging—the illegal production and distribution of liquor—became a large-scale operation run by organized crime. There was open warfare among rival gangs, and civic authorities and law enforcement agents became involved in corruption. Profits from bootlegging were invested in legal and illegal businesses. By 1925 there were between 30,000 and 100,000 illegal drinking clubs ("speakeasies") in New York alone.

Such huge interference in the lives of ordinary, generally law-abiding citizens had the effect of promoting lawbreaking as a way of life. The use of legislation to control moral issues in this way was increasingly questioned. In 1933, the first year of President Franklin D. Roosevelt's administration, the 18th Amendment was repealed by the 21st, ratified on December 5. The National Prohibition Act was automatically repealed with it.

Transcript of THE NATIONAL PROHIBITION ACT

' Be it Enacted. . . . That the short title of this Act shall be the "National Prohibition Act."

TITLE II.

PROHIBITION OF INTOXICATING BEVERAGES.

SEC. 3. No person shall on or after the date when the eighteenth amendment to the Constitution of the United States goes into effect, manufacture, sell, barter, transport, import, export, deliver, furnish or possess any intoxicating liquor except as authorized in this Act, and all the provisions of this shall be liberally construed to the end that the use of intoxicating liquor as a beverage may be prevented.

> "No person shall on or after the date when the eighteenth amendment to the Constitution of the United States goes into effect, manufacture, sell, barter, transport, import, export, deliver, furnish or possess any intoxicating liquor except as authorized in this Act."

Liquor . . . for non-beverage purposes and wine for sacramental purposes may be manufactured, purchased, sold, bartered, transported, imported, exported, delivered, furnished, and possessed, but only as herein provided, and the commissioner may, upon application, issue permits therefor . . . Provided, That nothing in this Act shall prohibit the purchase and sale of warehouse receipts covering distilled spirits on deposit in Government bonded warehouses, and no special tax liability shall attach to the business of purchasing and selling such warehouse receipts . . .

SEC. 6. No one shall manufacture, sell, purchase, transport, or prescribe any liquor without first obtaining a permit from the commissioner so to do, except that a person may, without a permit, purchase and use liquor for medicinal purposes when prescribed by a physician as herein provided, and except that any person who in the opinion of the commissioner is conducting a bona fide hospital or sanatorium engaged in the treatment of persons suffering from alcoholism, may, under such rules, regulations, and conditions as the commissioner shall prescribe, purchase and use, in accordance with the methods in use in such institution, liquor, to be administered to the patients of such institution under the direction of a duly qualified physician employed by such institution.

All permits to manufacture, prescribe, sell, or transport liquor, may be issued for one year, and shall expire on the 31st day of December next succeeding the issuance thereof: . . . Permits to purchase liquor shall specify the quantity and kind to be purchased and the purpose for which it is to be used . . .

Nothing in this title shall be held to apply to the manufacture, sale, transportation, importation, possession, or distribution of wine for sacramental purposes, or like religious rites, except section 6 (save as the same requires a permit to purchase) and section 10 hereof, and the provisions of this Act prescribing penalties for the violation of either of said sections. No person to whom a permit may be issued to manufacture, transport, import, or sell wines for sacramental purposes or like religious rites shall sell, barter, exchange, or furnish any such to any person not a rabbi, minister of the gospel, priest, or an officer duly authorized for the purpose by any church or congregation, nor to any such except upon an application duly subscribed by him, which application, authenticated as regulations may prescribe, shall be filed and preserved by the seller. The head of any conference or diocese or other ecclesiastical jurisdiction may designate any rabbi, minister, or priest to supervise the manufacture of wine to be used for the purposes and rites in this section mentioned, and the person so designated may, in the discretion of the commissioner, be granted a permit to supervise such manufacture.

> "Any person who manufactures or sells liquor in violation of this title shall for a first offense be fined not more than $1,000, or imprisoned not exceeding six months . . ."

SEC. 7. No one but a physician holding a permit to prescribe liquor shall issue any prescription for liquor. And no physician shall prescribe liquor unless after careful physical examination of the person for whose use such prescription is sought, or if such examination is found impracticable, then upon the best information obtainable, he in good faith believes that the use of such liquor as a medicine by such person is necessary and will afford relief to him from some known ailment. Not more than a pint of spiritous liquor to be taken internally shall be prescribed for use by the same person within any period of ten days and no prescription shall be filled more than once . . .

SEC. 18. It shall be unlawful to advertise, manufacture, sell, or possess for sale any utensil, contrivance, machine, preparation, compound, tablet, substance, formula direction, recipe advertised, designed, or intended for use in the unlawful manufacture of intoxicating liquor . . .

SEC. 21. Any room, house, building, boat, vehicle, structure, or place where intoxicating liquor is manufactured, sold, kept, or bartered in violation of this title, and all intoxicating liquor and property kept and used in maintaining the same, is hereby declared to be a common nuisance, and any person who maintains such a common nuisance shall be guilty of a misdemeanor and upon conviction thereof shall be fined not more than $1,000 or be imprisoned for not more than one year, or both . . .

SEC. 25. It shall be unlawful to have or possess any liquor or property designed for the manufacture of liquor intended for use in violating this title or which has been so used, and no property rights shall exist in any such liquor or property . . .

SEC. 29. Any person who manufactures or sells liquor in violation of this title shall for a first offense be fined not more than $1,000, or imprisoned not exceeding six months, and for a second or subsequent offense shall be fined not less than $200 nor more than $2,000 and be imprisoned not less than one month nor more than five years.

Any person violating the provisions of any permit, or who makes any false record, report, or affidavit required by this title, or violates any of the provisions of this title, for which offense a special penalty is not prescribed, shall be fined for a first offense not more than $500; for a second offense not less than $100 nor more than $1,000, or be imprisoned not more than ninety days; for any subsequent offense he shall be fined not less than $500 and be imprisoned not less than three months nor more than two years . . .

> "But it shall not be unlawful to possess liquors in one's private dwelling while the same is occupied and used by him as his dwelling only . . . and such liquor need not be reported."

SEC. 33. After February 1, 1920, the possession of liquors by any person not legally permitted under this title to possess liquor shall be prima facie evidence that such liquor is kept for the purpose of being sold, bartered, exchanged, given away, furnished, or otherwise disposed of in violation of the Provisions of this title . . . But it shall not be unlawful to possess liquors in one's private dwelling while the same is occupied and used by him as his dwelling only and such liquor need not be reported, provided such liquors are for use only for the personal consumption of the owner thereof and his family residing in such dwelling and of his bona fide guests when entertained by him therein; and the burden, of proof shall be upon the possessor in any action concerning the same to prove that such liquor was lawfully acquired, possessed, and used.

CROWDS IN WALL STREET, NEW YORK, ON THE
MORNING AFTER THE STOCK MARKET COLLAPSED
ON BLACK THURSDAY, OCTOBER 24, 1929

The
WALL STREET CRASH

BLACK THURSDAY, OCTOBER 24, 1929

THE WALL STREET Crash of 1929 was the most dramatic stock-market failure in history, affecting more people worldwide for longer than any other, before or since. The crash wiped out huge fortunes in days or, in some cases, hours, and bankrupted millions of small investors, leaving them in desperate straits with debts that could not be paid. President Herbert Hoover believed in "rugged individualism," and made it clear that no one could expect help from the government.

In his study The Great Crash: 1929, *the economist John Kenneth Galbraith stated: "No one was responsible for the great Wall Street crash. No one engineered the speculation that preceded it. Both were the product of the free choice and decisions of thousands of individuals. The latter were not led to the slaughter. They were impelled to it by the seminal lunacy which has always seized people who are seized in turn with the notion that they can become very rich."*

In 1920s America—the Jazz Age—times were very good for a small number of people. There was money to spend and luxuries, like automobiles, to spend it on. But not everyone was doing well, and the great wealth of the U.S. was in many ways an illusion. Most people were poor, especially farmers and African Americans, and around 60 percent of Americans lived on less than $2,000 a year. A good deal of consumer spending was built on credit. Many ordinary people borrowed to buy stock and then used that stock as collateral for their borrowing—around 300 million shares were carried "on margin" like this. If share prices fell, they would be unable to repay their original loans. Much apparent wealth therefore depended on borrowing that could only be sustained as long as share prices continued to rise.

The Wall Street Crash did not come out of the blue. In 1925, the respected *New York Times* financial correspondent, Alexander Noyes, had voiced fears that the market could not keep rising indefinitely. There were warnings in the shape of strange changes in the market on September 3, 1929; and on October 4, the market dipped sharply but rose again. These warnings went unheeded.

There were various reasons for the eventual crash in late October: a recession had started in the summer; the level of borrowing could not be sustained by the banks; and the Federal Reserve raised the discount rate from five to six percent. Then, once the selling started, plummeting confidence meant that it could not be stopped. The dream was over. Most of the smaller investors were wiped out on the first day of the crash: October 24, Black Thursday—when selling of a record 12.9 million shares overwhelmed the New York stock exchange. Some of the major banks and investment companies tried to halt the slide by buying great blocks of shares, a tactic that had worked previously, but this provided only temporary relief. After a relatively stable Friday and Saturday, panic selling began again the following Monday, reaching its peak on October 29, Black Tuesday, when more than 16 million shares were traded and most of the large investors saw their great fortunes disappear literally before their eyes. On October 30, the *New York Times* described Wall Street as "a street of vanished hopes, of curiously silent apprehension and of a sort of paralyzed hypnosis." The market rose again early in 1930, but crashed once more to reach an all-time low in 1932. It did not reach its peak again until November 1954.

Many banks were forced to close. Consumer spending plummeted, bankrupting many businesses, and factories

"NAMELESS, UNREASONING, UNJUSTIFIED TERROR"

With these words in his inaugural speech in 1933, the new President, Franklin D. Roosevelt, identified and challenged the nation's loss of confidence in the wake of the crash and gave America the courage—and means—to pull itself back together: "The only thing we have to fear is fear itself."

STAGE   BROADWAY   SCREEN

VARIETY

PRICE 25¢·

Published Weekly at 154 West 46th St., New York, N. Y., by Variety, Inc. Annual subscription, $10. Single copies, 25 cents.
Entered as second-class matter December 22, 1905, at the Post Office at New York, N. Y., under the act of March 3, 1879.

VOL. XCVII. No. 3   NEW YORK, WEDNESDAY, OCTOBER 30, 1929   88 PAGES

WALL ST. LAYS AN EGG

Going Dumb Is Deadly to Hostess In Her Serious Dance Hall Profesh

A hostess at Roseland has her problems. The paid steppers consider their work a definite profession calling for specialized technique and high-power salesmanship.

"You see, you gotta sell your personality," said one. "Each one of we girls has our own clientele to cater to. It's just like selling dresses in a store—you have to know what to sell each particular customer.

"Some want to dance, some want to kid, some want to get soupy, and others are just 'misunderstood husbands'."

Girls applying for hostess jobs at Roseland must be 21 or older. They must work five nights a week. They

Hunk on Winchell

When the Walter Winchells moved into 204 West 55th street, late last week, June, that's Mrs. Winchell, selected a special room as Walter's exclusive sleep den for his late hour nights. She shushed the Winchell kidlets when her husband dove in at his usual eight o'clock the first morning.

At noon, Walter's midnight, his sound proof room was penetra d by so many high C's he awoke with but four hours of dreams and a week

DROP IN STOCKS ROPES SHOWMEN

Many Weep and Call Off Christmas Orders — Legit Shows Hit

MERGERS HALTED

The most dramatic event in the financial history of America is the collapse of the New York Stock Market. The stage was Wall Street, but the onlookers covered the country. Estimates are that

Kidding Kissers in Talkers Burns Up Fans of Screen's Best Lovers

Talker Crashes Olympus

Paris, Oct. 29.
Fox "Follies" and the Fox Movietone newsreel are running this week in Athens, Greece, the first sound pictures heard in the birthplace of world culture, and in all Greece, for that matter.

Several weeks ago, Variety's Cairo correspondent cabled that a cinema had been wired in Alexandria, Cleopatra's home town

Boys who used to whistle and girls who used to giggle when love scenes were flashed on the screen are in action again. A couple of years ago they began to take the love stuff seriously and desisted. but the talkers are reviving the ha ha for film osculators.

Heavy loving lovers of silent picture days accustomed to charming audiences into spasms of silent ecstasy when kissing the leading lady are getting the bird instead of the heartbeat. The sound accompaniment is making it tough.

Such a picture romancer as John Gilbert is getting laughs in place

Variety reports the last desperate days of the Wall Street Crash, October 30, 1929. Although newspapers were already reporting hopes of a turn-round, it would take a quarter of a century before the market fully recovered.

closed because there was no demand for their goods. As unemployment increased to 12 million, the situation worsened. There was no social security to fall back on, and many relied on charitable handouts—the food handout was nicknamed "Hoover-stew" after the President, who believed that "It is not the function of the government to relieve individuals of their responsibilities to their neighbors, or to relieve private institutions of their responsibilities to the public." The Smoot-Hawley Tariff Act (1930) raised tariffs on foreign imports to record levels, initially to protect U.S. farm produce from cheap foreign imports. However, many countries responded by imposing their own tariffs on American goods. The result was that many U.S. farmers lost their livelihood and were evicted from their land. The annual suicide rate climbed to 23,000, the highest ever recorded.

The Wall Street Crash and the Great Depression that followed affected countries all over the world, many weakened by war, who had invested in or had trade links with the U.S. The Weimar government in Germany was one of the most seriously affected. The resulting financial crisis was a major factor in Adolf Hitler's rise to power.

Only with President Franklin D. Roosevelt's New Deal in 1932 did government intervention help to turn the country around and free it from its paralysis.

Vital supplies are handed out to a line of impoverished
New York citizens during the Great Depression

THE SOCIAL
SECURITY
ACT

August 14, 1935

THE SOCIAL SECURITY ACT, 1935, is one of the most significant pieces of legislation ever passed. Despite its limitations and faults, it was a sign to millions that the government was no longer prepared to turn a blind eye to people facing destitution because of old age, unemployment, or disability. One of its most important effects was to validate the view that welfare support was the right of working people and those in need—part of a larger social framework in which everyone was interdependent.

■ *Life in the U.S. was desperately hard in the Great Depression. Charities and voluntary organizations could not cope with the extent of the suffering: some people literally starved to death, and many more clung onto life in unimaginable circumstances. Fifty percent of the country's senior citizens lived in poverty.*

The act was initiated under President Franklin D. Roosevelt's New Deal, and was one of several pieces of social legislation aimed at boosting earning power, which in turn was intended to help the economy recover from the Great Depression. The act also went some way to relieving hardship and fear of the future.

The Depression spread in the 1930s. There were food and rent riots in several cities in 1931, and across the country large groups of dispossessed people were homeless and sleeping rough. When Franklin D. Roosevelt became president in 1932, pronouncing confidently, "the only thing we have to fear is fear itself," many put their hope in the promises of his reforming New Deal.

It was going to be difficult for the government to match peoples' expectations, when many politicians, including some Democrats, were opposed to state welfare. A flurry of new social-welfare legislation—such as the 1933 National Industrial Recovery Act (setting minimum wages and maximum working hours) and the Works Progress Administration (a national relief agency)—was the first real sign that the changes being made would make a difference in people's lives. Some high-profile appointments of women with backgrounds in social reform and the civil rights movement brought an awareness of gender and race to the New Deal.

In 1933, Dr. Francis Townsend, a physician in his sixties who had lost his practice during the Depression, proposed a scheme in which the federal government would pay every person aged over 60 a $200 monthly pension, funded through federal tax on commercial transactions. He worked to obtain Congressional support for his Townsend Plan, and by 1935 his lobbying organization of Townsend Clubs had over two million members.

Roosevelt charged Frances Perkins, Secretary of Labor, with drawing up an old-age insurance program to provide workers with pensions on retirement. Its terms were not as generous as the Townsend Plan, but because so many more people needed help, the federal scheme was expanded. The Social Security Act was drafted by Edwin E. Witte and the Committee on Economic Security, and

THE FIRST RECIPIENT
On January 31, 1940, Ida May Fuller of Brattleboro, Vermont, was the first person to be paid a monthly security pension—$22.54—under the provision of the Social Security Act, 1935. Miss Fuller had paid Social Security for only three years before her retirement, but was still entitled to a pension. She received her first check at age 66 and continued to receive monthly payments until her death aged 100. For her three years' contribution, at a total of $24.75, she was paid over $22,000.

gave benefits to people aged 65 and over. It also provided funds for the unemployed, people with disabilities, maternal and child welfare "especially in rural areas and areas suffering severe economic stress," vocational rehabilitation, and public health services. It was ultimately to be funded by employee and employer tax contributions.

Many were excluded from the original legislation, and the act had critics who found it either inadequate or overgenerous. Despite warnings in the act that "the funds must be available in all political subdivisions of the State and mandatory" to all U.S. citizens, some white administrators, especially in the South, restricted payments to black families. However, the act generally achieved what it set out to do, and remains the basis for much present-day social-security legislation.

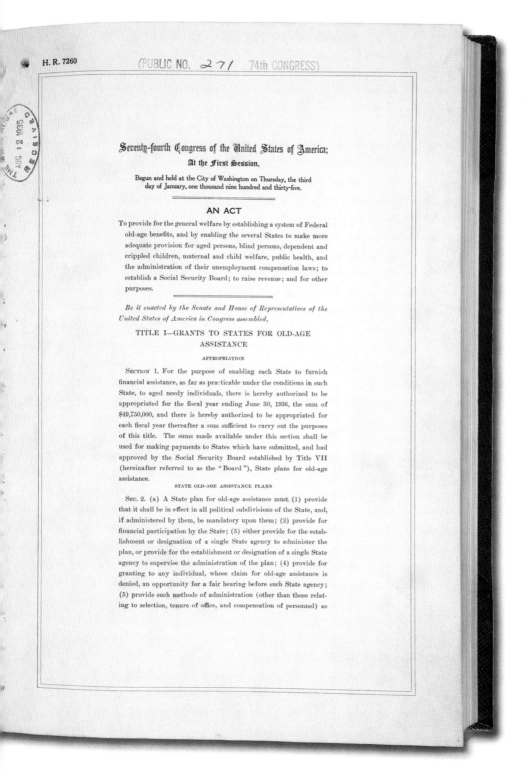

The Social Security Act, 1935, was the first nationally coordinated federal legislation dealing with old-age pensions and offering support for the unemployed, the disabled, children in need, public-health work, maternity care, and vocational rehabilitation.

Transcript of THE SOCIAL SECURITY ACT

'AN ACT to provide for the general welfare by establishing a system of Federal old-age benefits, and by enabling the several States to make more adequate provision for aged persons, blind persons, dependent and crippled children, maternal and child welfare, public health, and the administration of their unemployment compensation laws; to establish a Social Security Board; to raise revenue; and for other purposes.

Be it enacted by the Senate and House of Representatives of the United States of America in Congress assembled,

TITLE I–GRANTS TO STATES FOR OLD-AGE ASSISTANCE

APPROPRIATION

SECTION 1. For the purpose of enabling each State to furnish financial assistance, as far as practicable under the conditions in such State, to aged needy individuals, there is hereby authorized to be appropriated for the fiscal year ended June 30, 1936, the sum of $49,750,000, and there is hereby authorized to be appropriated for each fiscal year thereafter a sum sufficient to carry out the purposes of this title. The sums made available under this section shall be used for making payments to States which have submitted, and had approved by the Social Security Board established by Title VII (hereinafter referred to as the Board), State plans for old-age assistance. . .

OLD-AGE BENEFIT PAYMENTS

> "Every qualified individual . . . shall be entitled to receive, with respect to the period beginning on the date he attains the age of sixty-five . . . and ending on the date of his death, an old-age benefit."

SEC. 202. (a) Every qualified individual (as defined in section 210) shall be entitled to receive, with respect to the period beginning on the date he attains the age of sixty-five, or on January 1, 1942, whichever is the later, and ending on the date of his death, an old-age benefit (payable as nearly as practicable in equal monthly installments)

TITLE III–GRANTS TO STATES FOR UNEMPLOYMENT COMPENSATION ADMINISTRATION APPROPRIATION

SECTION 301. For the purpose of assisting the States in the administration of their unemployment compensation laws, there is hereby authorized to be appropriated, for the fiscal year ending June 30, 1936, the sum of $4,000,000, and for each fiscal year thereafter the sum of $49,000,000, to be used as hereinafter provided. . .

TITLE IV–GRANTS TO STATES FOR AID TO DEPENDENT CHILDREN APPROPRIATION

SECTION 401. For the purpose of enabling each State to furnish financial assistance, as far as practicable under the conditions in such State, to needy dependent children, there is hereby authorized to be appropriated for the fiscal year ending June 30, 1936, the sum of $24,750,000, and there is hereby authorized to be appropriated for each fiscal year thereafter a sum sufficient to carry out the purposes of this title. The sums made available under this section shall be used for making payments to States which have submitted, and had approved by the Board, State plans for aid to dependent children. . .

TITLE V–GRANTS TO STATES FOR MATERNAL AND CHILD WELFARE

PART 1-MATERNAL AND CHILD HEALTH SERVICES

APPROPRIATION

SECTION 501. For the purpose of enabling each State to extend and improve, as far as practicable under the conditions in such State, services for promoting the health of mothers and children, especially in rural areas and in areas suffering from severe economic distress, there is hereby authorized to be appropriated for each fiscal year, beginning with the fiscal year ending June 30, 1936, the sum of $3,800,000. The sums made available under this section shall be used for making payments to States which have submitted, and had approved by the Chief of the Children's Bureau, State plans for such services. . .

> "For the purpose of enabling each State to extend and improve . . . services for promoting the health of mothers and children . . . there is hereby authorized . . . for each fiscal year . . . the sum of $3,800,000."

PART 2-SERVICES FOR CRIPPLED CHILDREN

APPROPRIATION

SEC. 511. For the purpose of enabling each State to extend and improve (especially in rural areas and in areas suffering from severe economic distress), as far as practicable under the conditions in such State, services for locating crippled children and for providing medical, surgical, corrective, and other services and care, and facilities for diagnosis, hospitalization, and aftercare, for children who are crippled or who are suffering from conditions which lead to crippling, there is hereby authorized to be appropriated for each fiscal year beginning with the fiscal year ending June 30, 1936, the sum of $2,850,000. The sums made available under this section shall be used for making payments to States which have submitted, and had approved by the Chief of the Children's Bureau, State plans for such services . . .

PART 3–CHILD WELFARE SERVICES

SEC. 521. (a) For the purpose of enabling the United States, through the Children's Bureau, to cooperate with State public-welfare agencies establishing, extending, and strengthening, especially in predominantly rural areas, public-welfare services (hereinafter in this section referred to as child-welfare services) for the protection and care of homeless, dependent, and neglected children, and children in danger of becoming delinquent, there is hereby authorized to be appropriated for each fiscal year, beginning with the year ending June 30, 1936, the sum of $1,500,000 . . .

PART 4–VOCATIONAL REHABILITATION

SEC. 531. (a) In order to enable the United States to cooperate with the States and Hawaii in extending and strengthening their programs of vocational rehabilitation of the physically disabled, and to continue to carry out the provisions and purposes of the Act entitled An Act to provide for the promotion of vocational rehabilitation of persons disabled in industry or otherwise and their return to civil employment, approved June 2, 1920, as amended (U.S.C., title 29, ch. 4; U.S.C., Supp. VII title 29, secs. 31, 32, 34, 35, 37, 39, and 40), there is hereby authorized to be appropriated for the fiscal years ending June 30, 1936, and June 30, 1937, the sum of $841,000 for each such fiscal year in addition to the amount of the existing authorization, and for each fiscal year thereafter the sum of $1,938,000 . . .

TITLE X–GRANTS TO STATES FOR AID TO THE BLIND APPROPRIATION

SECTION 1001. For the purpose of enabling each State to furnish financial assistance, as far as practicable under the conditions in such State, to needy individuals who are blind, there is hereby authorized to be appropriated for the fiscal year ending June 30, 1936, the sum of $3,000,000, and there is hereby authorized to be appropriated for each fiscal year thereafter a sum sufficient to carry out the purposes of this title. The sums made available under this section shall be used for making payments to States which have submitted, and had approved by the Social Security Board, State plans for aid to the blind.

Albert Einstein (1879–1955)
developed the theory of relativity
and was rewarded with the
Nobel Prize in 1921

The

EINSTEIN–SZILÁRD LETTER

to President Franklin D. Roosevelt

August 2, 1939

THE LATE 1930S saw Adolf Hitler's Third Reich expand across Europe. Political opponents and people the Nazis deemed *Untermensch* (subhuman) were rounded up, forced to work as slave labor, and murdered. Hitler made it clear that nothing was to stand in the way of German domination. The Hungarian physicist Léo Szilárd had been a student in Germany before fleeing the Nazis in 1933, and knew the potential for Nazi researchers to create a nuclear bomb. In 1939 he persuaded his old teacher, Albert Einstein, that they must write a letter to pressure President Franklin D. Roosevelt to invest in nuclear research.

■ *Albert Einstein (1879–1955) was passionate about science and politics. The FBI file on the pioneering physicist ran to nearly 1,500 pages. A Jew born in Germany, Einstein fled the country after the Nazi Party came to power in 1933 and moved to the United States.*

Einstein and Szilárd collaborated on their letter to Roosevelt in the summer of 1939. Their letter explained the potentially destructive power of a nuclear bomb, and advised the President that America should "speed up the experimental work" in nuclear physics. By the time the letter reached Roosevelt, Hitler's army had invaded Poland, and Britain and France had declared war on Germany.

Roosevelt agreed that action should be taken. An Advisory Committee on Uranium (the key element involved in sustaining a nuclear chain reaction) was set up, and a budget of $6,000 set aside for neutron experiments.

From then on, atomic research became increasingly distanced from the scientists who had campaigned for it. On December 6, 1941, one day before the Japanese air force attacked the U.S. naval fleet at Pearl Harbor, the American government authorized the nuclear research team to develop a nuclear bomb. Known as the Manhattan Project, and led by the American physicist J. Robert Oppenheimer, the team made spectacular advances. In May 1945 Hitler, who had never made a successful atomic bomb, was defeated. The Allied victory in Europe removed the original purpose for the research proposed in the Einstein-Szilárd letter—to match or pre-empt the enemy's nuclear advances. The government, however, saw that the bomb the Manhattan Project was developing could be used to bring a swift end to the war with Japan.

Szilárd was horrified. In May 1945, he and two other scientists, Harold Urey and Walter Bartky, met with Secretary of State James F. Byrnes, to argue against using the atomic bomb against Japan. In July 1945, Szilárd started a petition asking the new President, Harold S. Truman, to view the effects of the bomb before dropping it on people. He was convinced that use of the atomic bomb would make the world more unstable and would not bring peace: "We might start an atomic arms race between America and Russia which might end with the destruction of both countries."

In June 1945 a group of scientists, led by the Nobel Prize-winning physicist James Franck,

PHYSICS AND SOCIALISM
Although recognized as a brilliant scientist, Albert Einstein was viewed with great suspicion by the American government. He was a socialist and member of the National Association for the Advancement of Colored People, and with his friend, the actor and civil-rights activist Paul Robeson, he was co-chair of the American Crusade to End Lynching. He once described racism as "America's worst disease."

The Einstein-Szilárd letter, written on August 2, 1939, was presented to President Roosevelt by his unofficial adviser, Alexander Sachs, on October 11. It called on the U.S. government to invest in atomic research, as the authors believed the Nazis were trying to develop a nuclear weapon.

> Albert Einstein
> Old Grove Rd.
> Nassau Point
> Peconic, Long Island
>
> August 2nd, 1939
>
> F.D. Roosevelt,
> President of the United States,
> White House
> Washington, D.C.
>
> Sir:
>
>   Some recent work by E.Fermi and L. Szilard, which has been com-
> municated to me in manuscript, leads me to expect that the element uran-
> ium may be turned into a new and important source of energy in the im-
> mediate future. Certain aspects of the situation which has arisen seem
> to call for watchfulness and, if necessary, quick action on the part
> of the Administration. I believe therefore that it is my duty to bring
> to your attention the following facts and recommendations:
>
>   In the course of the last four months it has been made probable -
> through the work of Joliot in France as well as Fermi and Szilard in
> America - that it may become possible to set up a nuclear chain reaction
> in a large mass of uranium,by which vast amounts of power and large quant-
> ities of new radium-like elements would be generated. Now it appears
> almost certain that this could be achieved in the immediate future.
>
>   This new phenomenon would also lead to the construction of bombs,
> and it is conceivable - though much less certain - that extremely power-
> ful bombs of a new type may thus be constructed. A single bomb of this
> type, carried by boat and exploded in a port, might very well destroy
> the whole port together with some of the surrounding territory. However,
> such bombs might very well prove to be too heavy for transportation by
> air.
>
>   ab4a01

warned that the use of the bomb "would sacrifice public support throughout the world, precipitate the race for armaments, and prejudice the possibility of reaching an international agreement on the future control of such weapons." His words, with hindsight, seem prophetic: within a few years British statesman Sir Winston Churchill was describing the "iron curtain" that had dropped between the ex-allies. The Cold War—an aggressive arms race between the Soviet Union and the United States—was to define four and a half post-war decades.

The first atomic bomb was dropped on the Japanese port of Hiroshima on August 6, 1945. Einstein believed it was dropped because of "a desire to end the war in the Pacific by any means before Russia's participation," and there is evidence

-2-

The United States has only very poor ores of uranium in moderate quantities. There is some good ore in Canada and the former Czechoslovakia, while the most important source of uranium is Belgian Congo.

In view of this situation you may think it desirable to have some permanent contact maintained between the Administration and the group of physicists working on chain reactions in America. One possible way of achieving this might be for you to entrust with this task a person who has your confidence and who could perhaps serve in an inofficial capacity. His task might comprise the following:

a) to approach Government Departments, keep them informed of the further development, and put forward recommendations for Government action, giving particular attention to the problem of securing a supply of uranium ore for the United States;

b) to speed up the experimental work,which is at present being carried on within the limits of the budgets of University laboratories, by providing funds, if such funds be required, through his contacts with private persons who are willing to make contributions for this cause, and perhaps also by obtaining the co-operation of industrial laboratories which have the necessary equipment.

I understand that Germany has actually stopped the sale of uranium from the Czechoslovakian mines which she has taken over. That she should have taken such early action might perhaps be understood on the ground that the son of the German Under-Secretary of State, von Weizsäcker, is attached to the Kaiser-Wilhelm-Institut in Berlin where some of the American work on uranium is now being repeated.

Yours very truly,

A. Einstein

(Albert Einstein)

a64a02

that President Truman was anticipating Soviet intervention in Japan. Four days before Hiroshima, members of the Japanese government had called for discussions about the surrender of the Japanese army. James F. Byrnes told Truman that "the bomb might well put us in a position to dictate our own terms at the end of the war." At this stage, while only the U.S. had the bomb, it was a powerful political bargaining tool. On August 9, when Soviet forces invaded Japanese-occupied Manchuria, it seemed Truman's fears may well have been justified. Soon, as the scientists had predicted, there was a race across the world to acquire the devastating weapon.

For the rest of their lives, the two scientists who had lobbied for the development of the bomb campaigned for nuclear disarmament. Charges of mass murder, and use of the nuclear threat to dominate the planet, could now be laid not against the Nazis, as everyone had feared in 1939, but against the government of the United States. In the 1960s, Szilárd and other scientists formed an organization calling for the abolition of nuclear weapons, the Council for a Livable World. Just days before his death in 1955, Einstein collaborated with the British pacifist Bertrand Russell on the Russell-Einstein Manifesto, which urged nations to seek peaceful resolutions to conflict and not to resort to nuclear warfare.

The battleships USS *West Virginia* (foreground) and *Tennessee* burning after the Japanese attack on Pearl Harbor

PEARL HARBOR

President Franklin D. Roosevelt's address to Congress

December 8, 1941

ON THE MORNING of Sunday December 7, 1941, more than 200 Japanese aircraft bombed the U.S. naval base at Pearl Harbor in Hawaii. Within two hours they had destroyed 188 aircraft, sunk or damaged eight battleships, and killed or wounded more than 3,500 Americans. There was outrage at the surprise attack since Japan had not declared war on America—in fact, diplomatic discussions were still being conducted. The Japanese attack, although hugely destructive, failed in its aim of destroying the U.S. fleet of aircraft carriers, as these were out of the harbor that morning. The day after the attack, President Franklin D. Roosevelt delivered his famous speech to Congress, and the United States entered World War II.

The Japanese attack on Pearl Harbor lasted 90 minutes. Although U.S. forces were caught unawares, with only skeleton crews at most posts, enough anti-aircraft resistance was organized against the second wave of bombing, an hour after the first, to deter the Japanese from a planned third wave. Two-thirds of Japanese losses occurred during the second part of the attack.

Before December 1941, the U.S. had avoided direct involvement in the war, although Congress had supplied Britain and the Soviet Union with weapons to fight Hitler in Europe and signed the Atlantic Charter condemning Nazi tyranny. Relations between the U.S. and Japan had been steadily deteriorating in the previous decade, and the Japanese invasion of China in 1937 had worried the government sufficiently for them to strengthen the U.S. fleet stationed at Pearl Harbor.

In September 1940 the U.S. banned the export of scrap iron and steel to Japan, the day before Japan strengthened its membership of the Axis by declaring a ten-year alliance with Germany and Italy. When Japan took military control of French colonies in Indo-China in July 1941, the U.S., Britain, and the Netherlands responded by putting an embargo on exports to Japan, reducing oil supplies by 90 percent. In October that year, the Japanese Prime Minister, Prince Konoye, who had been negotiating a peaceful settlement with the United States, was replaced by General Hideki Tojo, who was determined to end American and British influence in Asia. On December 6, President Roosevelt asked the Japanese Emperor, Hirohito, to intervene personally to prevent war. Face-to-face diplomatic negotiations also continued in Washington in a determined effort to avoid conflict.

Unknown to Washington, on November 26 a secret Japanese taskforce, commanded by Vice Admiral Chuichi Nagumo, set sail from Japan and headed southeastward across the Pacific. At 7.53 a.m. on December 7, a wave of Japanese bombers struck Pearl Harbor, targeting airfields and the larger U.S. ships, followed swiftly by a second wave from a different direction. Most U.S. planes were destroyed on the ground in the first minutes of the attack. With no U.S. fighters to contend with, the Japanese then bombed the fleet moored in the harbor. Although American losses were great, the three aircraft carriers that were at sea, 20 cruisers, 65 destroyers, oil storage tanks, and repair yards were for the most part undamaged.

The Japanese had achieved maximum surprise by attacking on a Sunday when many of the ships were not fully manned. Furthermore, although Tokyo sent a formal declaration of war to the Japanese embassy in Washington on the morning of the attack, only a few diplomats were there to decode, type, and deliver the message to the U.S. government—by which time Pearl Harbor was already being bombed. Subsequent Congressional investigations also revealed that a U.S. army

peace in the Pacific.   Indeed, one hour af

GREAT AMERICAN DOCUMENTS

adrons had commenced bombing in Oahu, the

or to the United States and his collea

TO THE CONGRESS OF THE UNITED STATES:

Yesterday, December 7, 1941 -- a date which will
live in infamy -- the United States of America was suddenly
and deliberately attacked by naval and air forces of the
Empire of Japan.

The United States was at peace with *that* nation and,
at the solicitation of Japan, was still in conversation with
its Government and its Emperor looking toward the maintenance
of peace in the Pacific.   Indeed, one hour after Japanese air
squadrons had commenced bombing in Oahu, the Japanese Ambassador to the United States and his colleague delivered to the
Secretary of State a formal reply to a recent American message.
While this reply stated that it seemed useless to continue the
existing diplomatic negotiations, it contained no threat or
hint of war or armed attack.

It will be recorded that the distance of Hawaii from
Japan makes it obvious that the attack was deliberately planned
many days or even weeks ago.   During the intervening time the
Japanese Government has deliberately sought to deceive the
United States by false statements and expressions of hope for
continued peace.

The attack yesterday on the Hawaiian Islands has
caused severe damage to American naval and military forces.
Very many American lives have been lost.   In addition American
ships have been *reported* torpedoed on the high seas between San Francisco
and Honolulu.

- 3 -

With confidence in our armed forces -- with the
unbounding determination of our people -- we will gain the
inevitable triumph -- so help us God.

I ask that the Congress declare that since the unprovoked and dastardly attack by Japan on Sunday, December
seventh, a state of war has existed between the United States
and the Japanese Empire.

Franklin D Roosevelt

THE WHITE HOUSE,
December 8, 1941.

*After delivering his speech to Congress and returning
to the White House, President Roosevelt discovered
that he had left behind the draft he read from as he
spoke. He wrote to his son that the speech should be
traced and kept, like all other speeches, because "this
particular one is just about the equal in importance
to the first inaugural address." Believed to have been
lost for over 40 years, the document was discovered in
the Senate records in 1984. The final version, with
the changes made by Roosevelt as he spoke, is in the
Roosevelt Library in Hyde Park, New York.*

officer who had picked up the approach of the Japanese aircraft on his radar was told to ignore it, since a flight of U.S. B-17 bombers was expected at the time.

President Roosevelt received news of the attack just after lunch on 7 December. One of his top aides present could not believe the report, but Roosevelt was unsurprised, commenting, "The very time they were discussing peace in the Pacific, they were plotting to overthrow it." For the rest of the day he drafted and redrafted his short address to Congress. This was not just an announcement of a national tragedy but also a psychological preparation for his audience, who would be asked to accept entry into a war that would bring privation and loss of life. Roosevelt gave his six-minute speech to a joint session of Congress and a nationwide radio audience. Even as he delivered it, he made spontaneous changes to enhance its impact. His speech became a historical and oratorical landmark.

On December 8, the United States declared war against Japan, and on December 11, Germany and Italy declared war against the U.S. As the war progressed, the U.S. supplied huge numbers of soldiers, large quantities of weapons and vital supplies to the Allies, and joined forces with Britain and the Soviet Union to form a Grand Alliance dedicated to securing unconditional surrender by the Axis powers.

The elimination of the U.S. Pacific Fleet's battleships meant the navy had to rely on aircraft carriers and submarines. This strategy proved to be highly effective, successfully halting and eventually reversing the Japanese advance, most notably at the battles of Coral Sea and Midway in 1942.

Transcript of PRESIDENT FRANKLIN D. ROOSEVELT'S ADDRESS TO CONGRESS

'Mr. Vice President, Mr. Speaker, Members of the Senate, and of the House of Representatives:

Yesterday, December 7th, 1941—a date which will live in infamy—the United States of America was suddenly and deliberately attacked by naval and air forces of the Empire of Japan.

> "A date which will live in infamy."

The United States was at peace with that nation and, at the solicitation of Japan, was still in conversation with its government and its emperor looking toward the maintenance of peace in the Pacific. Indeed, one hour after Japanese air squadrons had commenced bombing in the American island of Oahu, the Japanese ambassador to the United States and his colleagues delivered to our Secretary of State a formal reply to a recent American message. And while this reply stated that it seemed useless to continue the existing diplomatic negotiations, it contained no threat or hint of war or of armed attack.

peace in the Pacific.   Indeed, one hour af

GREAT AMERICAN DOCUMENTS

adrons had commenced bombing in Oahu, the

or to the United States and his collea

It will be recorded that the distance of Hawaii from Japan makes it obvious that the attack was deliberately planned many days or even weeks ago. During the intervening time, the Japanese government has deliberately sought to deceive the United States by false statements and expressions of hope for continued peace.

"The American people in their righteous might will win through to absolute victory."

The attack yesterday on the Hawaiian islands has caused severe damage to American naval and military forces. I regret to tell you that very many American lives have been lost. In addition, American ships have been reported torpedoed on the high seas between San Francisco and Honolulu.

Yesterday, the Japanese government also launched an attack against Malaya. Last night, Japanese forces attacked Hong Kong. Last night, Japanese forces attacked Guam. Last night, Japanese forces attacked the Philippine Islands. Last night, the Japanese attacked Wake Island. And this morning, the Japanese attacked Midway Island. Japan has, therefore, undertaken a surprise offensive extending throughout the Pacific area.

The facts of yesterday and today speak for themselves. The people of the United States have already formed their opinions and well understand the implications to the very life and safety of our nation. As commander in chief of the Army and Navy, I have directed that all measures be taken for our defense.

"Since the unprovoked and dastardly attack by Japan on Sunday, December 7th, 1941, a state of war has existed between the United States and the Japanese empire."

But always will our whole nation remember the character of the onslaught against us. No matter how long it may take us to overcome this premeditated invasion, the American people in their righteous might will win through to absolute victory. I believe that I interpret the will of the Congress and of the people when I assert that we will not only defend ourselves to the uttermost, but will make it very certain that this form of treachery shall never again endanger us.

Hostilities exist. There is no blinking at the fact that our people, our territory, and our interests are in grave danger. With confidence in our armed forces, with the unbounding determination of our people, we will gain the inevitable triumph—so help us God.

I ask that the Congress declare that since the unprovoked and dastardly attack by Japan on Sunday, December 7th, 1941, a state of war has existed between the United States and the Japanese empire.

VIEW OF HIROSHIMA SHOWING THE DEVASTATION FOLLOWING
THE ATOMIC BOMBING ON AUGUST 6, 1945

The
BOMBING
OF
HIROSHIMA, JAPAN

TELEGRAM FROM SECRETARY OF WAR HENRY STIMSON
TO PRESIDENT HARRY S. TRUMAN

AUGUST 6, 1945

WHEN THE UNITED STATES entered the war in 1941, President Franklin D. Roosevelt established the Manhattan Project. This top-secret project, involving an international team of physicists, was intended to harness nuclear energy for military purposes. By the time the first atomic bomb was tested on July 16, 1945 the Allies had pushed the Japanese back across the Pacific. However, despite heavy bombing of Tokyo in March 1945, causing the deaths of 83,000 civilians, the Japanese fought on, refusing to surrender. President Harry S. Truman decided to shock Japan into submission and bring a swift end to the war. Two atomic bombs were dropped in August 1945, and Japan surrendered unconditionally on September 2.

■ *The atomic bomb that struck Hiroshima on August 6, 1945, was nicknamed "Little Boy." It exploded 2,000 feet above the ground, creating an area of total destruction one mile in radius. Ninety percent of the city's buildings were destroyed. Three days later, another bomb, "Fat Man," similarly devastated Nagasaki. A further seven atomic weapons had been prepared for deployment against Japan.*

When Harry S. Truman unexpectedly became President in April 1945 following the sudden death of President Roosevelt, he had been Vice-President for 52 days, and had met Roosevelt only twice. Truman's diary records how he was gradually informed about the top-secret atomic bomb project by Secretary of War Henry Stimson early in April. By April 25, Stimson was telling Truman: "Within four months we shall in all probability have completed the most terrible weapon ever known in human history, one bomb of which could destroy a whole city."

In July the bomb was ready for testing. When it was detonated in the New Mexican desert, observers were stunned by its power. A blinding flash of light and a wave of heat that turned the desert sand to glass was followed by a deafening roar as the shock wave shot outward from the point of detonation. A mushroom-shaped cloud rose high into the sky. Military representative General Leslie Groves commented, "The war's over. One or two of those things and Japan will be finished."

At the time, President Truman was attending the Potsdam Conference with British Prime Minister Sir Winston Churchill and Soviet leader Josef Stalin. On hearing of the test, Truman recorded in his diary on July 25 that the bomb would be used against Japan between that date and August 10. He also noted that he had told "Secretary of War, Mr. Stimson to use it so that military objectives and soldiers are the target and not women and children."

On July 26 the Potsdam Declaration warned the Japanese government to surrender unconditionally or face "prompt and utter destruction." Aware that Japan considered unconditional surrender a great dishonor, the ultimatum stated that while Japanese war criminals would be punished and Japan be required to pay reparations, "we do not intend that the Japanese shall be enslaved as a race nor destroyed as a nation." The Japanese issued a statement two days later that appeared to reject the surrender demand.

"THIS BARBAROUS WEAPON"

Questioned in 1947 over the American decision to drop the bomb, Henry Stimson justified the action, calculating that over a million American lives had been saved as a result. Others disagreed. Another of President Truman's advisers in 1945 was Admiral William D. Leahy. In 1950 he commented: "In my opinion the use of this barbarous weapon at Hiroshima and Nagasaki was of no material assistance in our war against Japan. The Japanese were already defeated and were ready to surrender because of the effective sea blockade and the successful bombing with conventional weapons."

Shortly after this rejection, Truman authorized the dropping of the bomb. Planned for August 3, the operation was postponed until August 6 because of bad weather. At 8:15 a.m. that day Colonel Paul Tibbets and his crew flew a B-29 bomber, the *Enola Gay*, above Hiroshima, carrying a uranium-235 bomb with an explosive power 2,000 times greater than the blast of any previous conventional bomb.

The bomb took 53 seconds to fall, and as the shock wave rocked the plane, Tibbets cried, "My God, what have we done?" The ensuing mushroom cloud was visible 360 miles away. Five square miles of buildings were completely flattened, almost 60 percent of the city destroyed, and more than 66,000 men, women, and children reduced to vapor in the first seconds following the explosion. Within five days, more than 138,661 people had died, a figure that rose to 140,000 by the end of 1945.

On August 8, the Soviet Union declared war on Japan. Now worried about Soviet intentions in the Pacific area, and with no news of surrender by the Japanese government, Truman authorized the dropping of a second bomb, which fell on the city of Nagasaki on August 9, creating an even more powerful explosion. About one-third of the city was reduced to rubble and some 70,000 people killed, most of them civilians. On August 13, Japanese physicists reported very high levels of radioactivity at the epicentre of the Hiroshima bomb blast.

On August 14, Emperor Hirohito overruled his military advisers and accepted the Allied demand for surrender, provided he remained Emperor. He then broke imperial tradition by broadcasting a speech to his people announcing Japan's surrender, stating, "The enemy has begun to employ a new and most cruel bomb, the power of which to damage is indeed incalculable, taking the toll of many innocent lives." On September 2, Japan formally surrendered to the Allies aboard the U.S.S. *Missouri*.

DECLASSIFIED
E.O. 11652, Sec. 3(E) and 5(D) or (E)
OSD letter, May 3, 1972
By _____ NARS Date 9-29-75

WHITE HOUSE
MAP ROOM

6 August 1945

FROM: THE SECRETARY OF WAR
TO : THE PRESIDENT

NR : 335

Big bomb dropped on Hiroshima 5 August at 7:15 P.M. Washington time. First reports indicate complete success which was even more conspicuous than earlier test.

STIMSON

REC'D 061500Z

This telegram to President Harry S. Truman from Henry Stimson, Secretary of War, confirmed the dropping of the atomic bomb on the Japanese city of Hiroshima. The "earlier test" he refers to was the trial detonation of the bomb in the New Mexico desert in July 1945.

General Alfred Jodl signs the surrender on behalf of Germany at Reims on May 7, 1945.

The

SURRENDER OF GERMANY

in World War II at Reims, France

May 7, 1945

THE REIMS SURRENDER document was one of several drawn up during May 1945. Fighting in Italy had been ended by a document signed on May 2, and on May 4 another was signed at the British commander's headquarters on Lüneburg Heath, marking the surrender of German forces in northwestern Europe. After Reims, the Soviet chief of staff, General Alexei Antonov, was concerned that continued fighting in the east between Germany and the U.S.S.R. made the Reims surrender look like a separate peace. At Russian insistence, the Reims surrender document—slightly, but not significantly, modified—was signed again in Berlin on May 8. This day became known as V.E. (Victory in Europe) Day.

General Alfred Jodl represented Hitler's successor, Admiral Karl Dönitz, at the signing of the surrender documents at Reims, France, on May 7, 1945. He was arrested and charged with crimes against humanity at the International Military Tribunal at Nuremburg. Jodl was found guilty and sentenced to death. With ten other leading Nazis, he was hanged at Nuremburg on October 16, 1946.

The end of the war came swiftly for Germany as the country's cities suffered massive attacks from U.S. and British bombers and the Allied armies closed in all around. The capital, Berlin, fell to the Soviets in early May. After the suicide of Adolf Hitler in an underground bunker in Berlin in late April 1945, the leadership of the German Reich passed to his chosen successor, Admiral Karl Dönitz. The peace overtures Dönitz sent to the British Field Marshal Bernard Montgomery at Lüneburg Heath on May 3 were refused because the terms were too limited.

On May 4 Admiral Hans-Georg von Friedeburg, acting on behalf of Dönitz, went again to Montgomery's headquarters, this time with authority to surrender all German forces in northern Germany, Holland, Denmark, and Schleswig-Holstein. Montgomery accepted this offer on May 5 and ordered his troops to cease fire.

The Reims signing took place two days later at the Supreme Headquarters, Allied Expeditionary Force (SHAEF). The leader of the Allied delegation was U.S. Lieutenant General Walter Bedell Smith, SHAEF chief of staff—acting for General Dwight D. Eisenhower, who refused to meet the Germans until the surrender was accomplished.

As the war in Europe drew to its chaotic close, the killing did not stop immediately. The chief concern for most of the defeated German people was now avoiding the attentions of the Soviet Red Army. Elsewhere in Europe and America, the ending of the war was cause for great celebration. Festivities were held in every Allied city still standing. There were street parties in Britain and France, a huge fireworks display in Moscow, and in New York ticker-tape streamers added to the party atmosphere as massive crowds lined Wall Street. However, it was to be another three months before the war in other parts of the globe finally ended, following the dropping of two atomic bombs in August 1945 and the surrender of Japan in September.

COUNTING THE HUMAN COST

The worldwide cost of World War II in human lives was vast, with an estimated 55 million people losing their lives in battle or on the home front. There were 20 million deaths in the U.S.S.R., and Poland lost one-fifth of its entire pre-war population. Six million Jews lost their lives in the Holocaust. The United States lost 400,000 soldiers, Britain 380,000 and France 212,000. German losses in fighting reached 5.5 million and two million Japanese servicemen died.

The unconditional surrender by Germany at the end of World War II took place on May 7, 1945, in Reims, northern France, attended by four representatives of the Allied forces and three German officers authorized to sign for Germany.

Transcript of THE GERMAN ACT OF MILITARY SURRENDER

'ACT OF MILITARY SURRENDER

We the undersigned, acting by authority of the German High Command, hereby surrender unconditionally to the Supreme Commander, Allied Expeditionary Forces and simultaneously to the Soviet High Command all forces on land, sea and in the air who are at this date under German control.

The German High Command will at once issue orders to all German military, naval and air authorities and to all forces under German control to cease active operations at 2301 hours Central European time on 8 May and to remain in the positions occupied at that time. No ship, vessel, or aircraft is to be scuttled, or any damage done to their hull, machinery or equipment.

> "This act of military surrender is without prejudice to, and will be superseded by any general instrument of surrender imposed by, or on behalf of the United Nations . . ."

The German High Command will at once issue to the appropriate commander, and ensure the carrying out of any further orders issued by the Supreme Commander, Allied Expeditionary Force and by the Soviet High Command.

This act of military surrender is without prejudice to, and will be superseded by any general instrument of surrender imposed by, or on behalf of the United Nations and applicable to GERMANY and the German armed forces as a whole.

In the event of the German High Command or any of the forces under their control failing to act in accordance with this Act of Surrender, the Supreme Commander, Allied Expeditionary Force and the Soviet High Command will take such punitive or other action as they deem appropriate.

Signed at REIMS at 0241 on the 7th day of May, 1945. France

On behalf of the German High Command.

JODL

IN THE PRESENCE OF

On behalf of the Supreme Commander,
Allied Expeditionary Force.
W. B. SMITH

On behalf of the Soviet High Command.
SOUSLOPAROV

F. SEVEZ
Major General, French Army (Witness)'

GENERAL DOUGLAS MACARTHUR, SUPREME ALLIED
COMMANDER, LOOKS ON AS THE JAPANESE SURRENDER
TREATY IS SIGNED ON SEPTEMBER 2, 1945

The

SURRENDER
OF JAPAN

IN WORLD WAR II

TOKYO BAY, SEPTEMBER 2, 1945

THE JAPANESE MADE considerable headway after their attack on Pearl Harbor in December 1941. Their conquest of Hong Kong, Burma, the Philippines, Malaya, and Borneo swiftly followed. However, the war began to drain the country's economy, and Japan was gradually driven back across the Pacific by U.S. forces. The Japanese mainland was then subjected to heavy bombing, which razed Tokyo to the ground and killed scores of thousands. The dropping of two atomic bombs on the cities of Hiroshima and Nagasaki, and the Soviet Union's simultaneous declaration of war, led Japan to accept surrender terms on August 14. The only condition Japan applied in accepting the terms of the surrender was that the Emperor's position as ruler should be maintained. The Allies granted this, subjecting the Emperor only to the Supreme Commander's directives.

■ *Even after the destruction of Hiroshima and Nagasaki, the six-man Japanese Supreme Council was divided about the question of surrender. With three members advocating it, and three opposing, there was deadlock, reflected in the views of the Japanese cabinet. At midnight on August 9, 1945—the day the second atomic bomb was dropped—an Imperial council was convened and after the personal intervention of Emperor Hirohito, who urged surrender, the objectors capitulated.*

President Harry S. Truman ordered General Douglas MacArthur, Supreme Commander of the Allied forces in the Pacific, to accept Japan's formal surrender on the U.S. navy's flagship, U.S.S. *Missouri,* in the presence of 50 Allied generals and other officials.

The first signatory of the document was the Japanese Foreign Minister, Mamoru Shigemitsu, on behalf of the Emperor and his government. He was followed by General Yoshijiro Umezu, on behalf of the Imperial General Headquarters. The document was then signed by General MacArthur and other representatives of the Allies. Under the terms of the document Japan agreed to end all hostilities, release all prisoners of war, and obey the terms of the Potsdam Declaration, which limited its sovereignty to the four main islands that make up Japan. Half an hour after the signing, a convoy of 42 U.S. ships entered Tokyo Bay and landed 13,000 American troops. The Allies had celebrated victory over Japan on August 15, 1945 and that date, as well as September 2, are both known as V.J. Day. It has been estimated that the Japanese were responsible for the deaths of 30 million people, including 23 million Chinese, during the 1930s and 1940s. The death rate among Allied prisoners of war held by the Japanese was nearly 30 percent, compared with four percent among those held by the Germans.

Japan signed a separate surrender with China at a ceremony in Nanking on 9 September 1945, the final formal surrender of World War II. Shortly after this, Emperor Hirohito offered to take responsibility for Japanese war atrocities, but he was never tried for war crimes. Instead, the Americans used him to help push through democratic reforms that transformed Japanese politics.

> **THE THIRTY YEARS WAR**
> *Hiroo Onoda, a Japanese army intelligence officer stationed on Lubang Island in the Philippines in 1945, remained hidden in the jungle there until 1974, refusing to accept that the war was over and that Japan had surrendered. He was eventually persuaded of the truth when the authorities traced his former commanding officer and sent him to Lubang formally to order Onoda's surrender. His gun was still in perfect working order.*

INSTRUMENT OF SURRENDER

e, acting by command of and in behalf of the Emperor of Japan, the Japanese Government and the Japanese Imperial General Headquarters, hereby accept the provisions set forth in the declaration issued by the heads of the Governments of the United States, China and Great Britain on 26 July 1945, at Potsdam, and subsequently adhered to by the Union of Soviet Socialist Republics, which four powers are hereafter referred to as the Allied Powers.

We hereby proclaim the unconditional surrender to the Allied Powers of the Japanese Imperial General Headquarters and of all Japanese armed forces and all armed forces under Japanese control wherever situated.

We hereby command all Japanese forces wherever situated and the Japanese people to cease hostilities forthwith, to preserve and save from damage all ships, aircraft, and military and civil property and to comply with all requirements which may be imposed by the Supreme Commander for the Allied Powers or by agencies of the Japanese Government at his direction.

We hereby command the Japanese Imperial General Headquarters to issue at once orders to the Commanders of all Japanese forces and all forces under Japanese control wherever situated to surrender unconditionally themselves and all forces under their control.

We hereby command all civil, military and naval officials to obey and enforce all proclamations, orders and directives deemed by the Supreme Commander for the Allied Powers to be proper to effectuate this surrender and issued by him or under his authority and we direct all such officials to remain at their posts and to continue to perform their non-combatant duties unless specifically relieved by him or under his authority.

We hereby undertake for the Emperor, the Japanese Government and their successors to carry out the provisions of the Potsdam Declaration in good faith, and to issue whatever orders and take whatever action may be required by the Supreme Commander for the Allied Powers or by any other designated representative of the Allied Powers for the purpose of giving effect to that Declaration.

We hereby command the Japanese Imperial Government and the Japanese Imperial General Headquarters at once to liberate all allied prisoners of war and civilian internees now under Japanese control and to provide for their protection, care, maintenance and immediate transportation to places as directed.

The authority of the Emperor and the Japanese Government to rule the state shall be subject to the Supreme Commander for the Allied Powers who will take such steps as he deems proper to effectuate these terms of surrender.

Signed at TOKYO BAY, JAPAN at _____ on the SECOND day of SEPTEMBER, 1945.

重光 葵

By Command and in behalf of the Emperor of Japan and the Japanese Government.

梅津美治郎

By Command and in behalf of the Japanese Imperial General Headquarters.

Accepted at TOKYO BAY, JAPAN at _____ on the SECOND day of SEPTEMBER, 1945, for the United States, Republic of China, United Kingdom and the Union of Soviet Socialist Republics, and in the interests of the other United Nations at war with Japan.

Douglas MacArthur
Supreme Commander for the Allied Powers.

C.W. Nimitz
United States Representative

Republic of China Representative

Bruce Fraser
United Kingdom Representative

Union of Soviet Socialist Republics Representative

T.A. Blamey
Commonwealth of Australia Representative

Dominion of Canada Representative

Provisional Government of the French Republic Representative

Kingdom of the Netherlands Representative

Dominion of New Zealand Representative

The formal surrender of Japan in World War II took place on board the U.S.S. Missouri in Tokyo Bay on September 2, 1945. This document was the penultimate surrender between the various countries that had been involved in the war, which had lasted six years and cost millions of lives.

Transcript of THE JAPANESE ACT OF MILITARY SURRENDER

❝ INSTRUMENT OF SURRENDER

We, acting by command of and in behalf of the Emperor of Japan, the Japanese Government and the Japanese Imperial General Headquarters, hereby accept the provisions set forth in the declaration issued by the heads of the Governments of the United States, China, and Great Britain on 26 July 1945 at Potsdam, and subsequently adhered to by the Union of Soviet Socialist Republics, which four powers are hereafter referred to as the Allied Powers.

We hereby proclaim the unconditional surrender to the Allied Powers of the Japanese Imperial General Headquarters and of all Japanese armed forces and all armed forces under the Japanese control wherever situated.

> "We hereby proclaim the unconditional surrender to the Allied Powers of the Japanese Imperial General Headquarters and of all Japanese armed forces and all armed forces under the Japanese control wherever situated."

We hereby command all Japanese forces wherever situated and the Japanese people to cease hostilities forthwith, to preserve and save from damage all ships, aircraft, and military and civil property and to comply with all requirements which may be imposed by the Supreme Commander for the Allied Powers or by agencies of the Japanese Government at his direction.

We hereby command the Japanese Imperial Headquarters to issue at once orders to the Commanders of all Japanese forces and all forces under Japanese control wherever situated to surrender unconditionally themselves and all forces under their control.

We hereby command all civil, military and naval officials to obey and enforce all proclamations, and orders and directives deemed by the Supreme Commander for the Allied Powers to be proper to effectuate this surrender and issued by him or under his authority and we direct all such officials to remain at their posts and to continue to perform their non-combatant duties unless specifically relieved by him or under his authority.

We hereby undertake for the Emperor, the Japanese Government and their successors to carry out the provisions of the Potsdam Declaration in good faith, and to issue whatever orders and take whatever actions may be required by the Supreme Commander for the Allied Powers or by any other designated representative of the Allied Powers for the purpose of giving effect to that Declaration.

We hereby command the Japanese Imperial Government and the Japanese Imperial General Headquarters at once to liberate all allied prisoners of war and civilian internees now under Japanese control and to provide for their protection, care, maintenance and immediate transportation to places as directed.

The authority of the Emperor and the Japanese Government to rule the state shall be subject to the Supreme Commander for the Allied Powers who will take such steps as he deems proper to effectuate these terms of surrender.

Signed at TOKYO BAY, JAPAN at 0904 on the SECOND day of SEPTEMBER, 1945

MAMORU SHIGEMITSU
By Command and on behalf of the Emperor
of Japan and the Japanese Government

YOSHIJIRO UMEZU
By Command and on behalf of the Japanese
Imperial General Headquarters

Accepted at TOKYO BAY, JAPAN at 0903 on the SECOND day of SEPTEMBER, 1945, for the United States, Republic of China, United Kingdom and the Union of Soviet Socialist Republics, and in the interests of the other United Nations at war with Japan.

DOUGLAS MACARTHUR
Supreme Commander for the Allied
Powers

C. W. NIMITZ
United States Representative

HSU YUNG-CH'ANG
Republic of China Representative

BRUCE FRASER
United Kingdom Representative

KUZMA DEREVYANKO
Union of Soviet Socialist
Republics Representative

THOMAS BLAMEY
Commonwealth of Australia
Representative

L. MOORE COSGRAVE
Dominion of Canada Representative

JACQUES LE CLERC
Provisional Government of the French
Republic Representative

C. E. L. HELFRICH
Kingdom of the Netherlands
Representative

LEONARD M. ISITT
Dominion of New Zealand
Representative

U.S. Secretary of State Edward Stettinius signs
the United Nations Charter for the U.S. while
President Harry S. Truman and others look on

The

UNITED
NATIONS
CHARTER

June 26, 1945

DURING WORLD WAR II the Allied nations had agreed to create a new international organization to replace the failed League of Nations, set up by the Treaty of Versailles in 1919. The United States had never ratified the League, which had become discredited in the 1930s after failing to take action over Japanese aggression in China and Italy's invasion of Ethiopia. As early as 1941 representatives of Britain had met with those of France and many other exiled governments then situated in London to discuss joint aims, and in the same year Britain and the U.S. agreed the Atlantic Charter, whose principles influenced those of the United Nations Charter. The phrase "united nations" was first used by President Franklin D. Roosevelt in the "Declaration by United Nations" (1942), when representatives of 26 nations pledged to continue fighting the Axis powers together.

■ *There are 192 member states of the United Nations, and a number of General Assembly observers—representatives who have the right to speak at meetings but cannot vote on resolutions. Observers range from the Holy See to various inter-governmental and non-governmental organizations, like the Palestine Liberation Organization and the International Committee of the Red Cross.*

In many ways, the organization finally established in 1945 built on the precedent of the League of Nations. However, the intentions expressed in the United Nations Charter far outreached those of the League, which was concerned with maintaining the status quo after World War I. The U.N.'s goals included avoiding future wars, recognizing basic human rights, and promoting better standards of living the world over.

The San Francisco Conference in April–June 1945 was the final outcome of several stages in the creation of the new United Nations. The basic principles were developed at the Dumbarton Oaks Conference in 1944, attended by representatives from the United States, Britain, the Soviet Union, and China. Although it was agreed that the organization's major role was maintaining international peace and security, difficult issues remained and had to be addressed at the Yalta Conference in early 1945. The debate reached fruition at the San Francisco Conference, where leading roles were taken by ministers from the so-called "Big Four" nations: U.S. Secretary of State Edward Stettinius, British Foreign Secretary Anthony Eden, Soviet Foreign Minister Vyacheslav Molotov, and Chinese Minister of Foreign Affairs T.V. Soong.

The conference was dominated by discussion of the extent of the Big Four's powers, since they were permanent members of the U.N.'s peacekeeping Security Council. Smaller or less powerful nations failed to reduce these powers, and the Big Four (later the Big Five, with the inclusion of France) retained their supremacy.

The conference ended with the signing of the United Nations Charter by 50 nations on June 26, 1945.

Modeled on the U.S. Constitution, the Charter pledged to maintain world peace and security, and to let the residents of colonial areas "gradually develop their free political institutions." The Charter details the various U.N. institutions and their powers, including the Security Council and the International Court of Justice.

The two main bodies of the United Nations are the General Assembly, composed of all member nations, and the Security Council, the main body responsible for

LEADING THE WORLD'S NATIONS
The head of the U.N. is the Secretary General, proposed by the Security Council and elected by the Assembly for a five-year term. Since 1946 there have been nine: four from Europe, two each from Africa and Asia, and one from South America. The composition of U.N. membership is reflected in the election of succeeding Secretaries: Kofi Annan of Ghana was succeeded in 2007 by Ban Ki-moon of South Korea.

CHARTER OF THE UNITED NATIONS

WE THE PEOPLES OF THE UNITED NATIONS DETERMINED

> to save succeeding generations from the scourge of war, which twice in our lifetime has brought untold sorrow to mankind, and

> to reaffirm faith in fundamental human rights, in the dignity and worth of the human person, in the equal rights of men and women and of nations large and small, and

> to establish conditions under which justice and respect for the obligations arising from treaties and other sources of international law can be maintained, and

> to promote social progress and better standards of life in larger freedom,

AND FOR THESE ENDS

> to practice tolerance and live together in peace with one another as good neighbors, and

> to unite our strength to maintain international peace and security, and

> to ensure, by the acceptance of principles and the institution of methods, that armed force shall not be used, save in the common interest, and

> to employ international machinery for the promotion of the economic and social advancement of all peoples,

HAVE RESOLVED TO COMBINE OUR EFFORTS TO ACCOMPLISH THESE AIMS.

Accordingly, our respective Governments, through representatives assembled in the city of San Francisco, who have exhibited their full powers found to be in good and due form, have agreed to the present Charter of the United Nations and do hereby establish an international organization to be known as the United Nations.

Meeting at the United Nations Conference on International Organization in San Francisco in 1945, the representatives of 50 countries drew up the U.N. Charter. The United Nations organization began officially on 24 October 1945—United Nations Day—following the Charter's ratification by the five founding members and most other countries.

save succeeding generations from the scourge of war, which

me has brought untold sorrow to mankind, and

GREAT AMERICAN DOCUMENTS

reaffirm faith in fundamental human rights, in the dignity

uman person, in the equal rights of men and women and of

mall, and

establish conditions under which justice and respect for

ensuring peace, whose decisions are binding on all member states. The U.N. also includes special agencies like the World Health Organization (WHO), UNICEF, and UNESCO, which have improved the lives of millions throughout the world.

The U.N. is not a form of world government, nor is it a superstate. All members are sovereign and equal, and the Charter states that the U.N. must not intervene in the internal affairs of any country, except to maintain or restore peace. Keeping the peace, however, has often meant going to war. The U.N. authorized military interventions in the Korean War (1950–3), and in Operation Desert Storm in 1990, after Iraq invaded Kuwait, and U.N. peacekeeping forces have been deployed in numerous conflict zones, from East Timor to the former Yugoslavia.

The U.N. did not, however, intervene, in world crises like the Hungarian uprising in 1956, the Cuban Missile Crisis in 1962, the Vietnam War (1959–75) or the Falklands War in 1982. This was either because the Security Council and the General Assembly could not agree on the extent of U.N. involvement, or because the great powers simply ignored them. The joint U.S.–U.K. invasion of Iraq in 2003 was made without U.N. Security Council approval, and later criticized by Secretary General Kofi Annan, who said it "did not conform with the U.N. Charter."

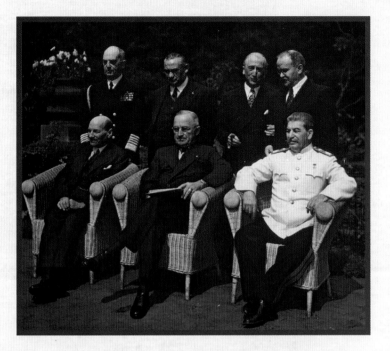

The "big three." Seated, left to right:
British Prime Minister Clement Attlee,
U.S. President Harry S. Truman, and
Soviet leader Josef Stalin

The

TRUMAN DOCTRINE

The containment of Communist expansion

March 12, 1947

WHEN BRITAIN ANNOUNCED in February 1947 that it could no longer financially support the Greek government's war with Communist insurgents, there was great concern that Greece and its neighbor Turkey might fall to the Soviets, and that Communist influence would spread through the Middle East and Asia. Congress swiftly agreed to provide aid, and President Harry S. Truman stressed the severity of the crisis in an address to Congress and a radio broadcast on March 12. The subsequent allocation of $400 million to Greece and Turkey helped thwart Soviet ambitions in these countries.

Political commentators disagree about whether the Truman Doctrine extended the principles of the Monroe Doctrine, which had defined U.S. foreign policy since 1823, or overturned it completely. The Monroe Doctrine vowed to defend the United States from foreign intervention; Truman enlarged that theater to countries in the world that had asked for U.S. protection.

Following the defeat of Hitler and the Japanese in World War II, friendly co-operation between the former Allies soon disintegrated as their opposing political interests re-emerged. The Truman administration grew increasingly worried by the Soviet threat to the West, although some consider that they overestimated the power of the U.S.S.R., which was still suffering severely from damage inflicted during the war. With a strong Soviet military presence in Eastern Europe, American protests about the U.S.S.R.'s conduct there were ineffective. However, Soviet support for the Communist-led uprising in Greece created a turning point in U.S. foreign policy, which resulted in détente being replaced by a new policy of active containment of Communist expansion.

Greece was embroiled in a bitter civil war between government forces and the mainly Communist National Liberation Front. Greece and Turkey were strategically vital—and vulnerable—Western outposts on the southern flank of the U.S.S.R., and the Greek economy was near collapse. Under-Secretary of State Dean Acheson outlined the dangers of the situation to Congress and State Department officials using what later became known as the "domino theory:" should Greece and Turkey fall to the Soviets then, as a direct consequence, many neighboring countries would do the same.

Less than three weeks after the British announcement, Truman proposed a new departure for the U.S.: a policy of actively supporting free peoples against armed repression, mainly through economic and military aid. Truman argued that "totalitarian regimes" represented a threat to international peace, as well as the national security of the United States. By May 22, Truman had been empowered to sign the Greek-Turkish Aid Act. Not only did his new policy, which rapidly became known as the Truman Doctrine, assist both Greece and Turkey with grants, it also promised future economic and military aid to other nations threatened "by armed minorities or by outside pressure." The Truman Doctrine heralded the start of more than four decades of Cold War with the U.S.S.R.

The new policy of containment was effective in Greece and Turkey. It was later supported economically in Western Europe by aid under the Marshall Plan (see page 187), and in military terms through the founding of the North Atlantic Treaty Organization in 1949.

THE SAVIOR OF WESTERN CIVILIZATION?

While dining with President Truman in Washington in January 1950, former British Prime Minister and wartime leader Sir Winston Churchill referred to their first meeting, at the Potsdam Conference just after the death of Truman's predecessor, Franklin D. Roosevelt: "I must confess, sir, I held you in very low regard then. I loathed your taking the place of Franklin Roosevelt. I misjudged you badly. Since that time, you more than any other man, have saved Western civilization."

The Truman Doctrine had other consequences in Europe. The United States gave financial support to governments with powerful Communist movements, such as Italy and France, in order to keep Communist groups out of government. The Doctrine was also applied in South Korea, where the U.S. military intervened after an attack by North Korea in 1950.

However, as the Truman administration itself had recognized, it was not possible to achieve all the Doctrine implied.

In 1950, under the terms of the Doctrine, the U.S. supplied equipment and military advisers to the French, to help them fight Ho Chi Minh's anti-colonial revolutionaries in France's territories in Vietnam. This initial involvement eventually drew the U.S. into the costly and ultimately futile Vietnam War.

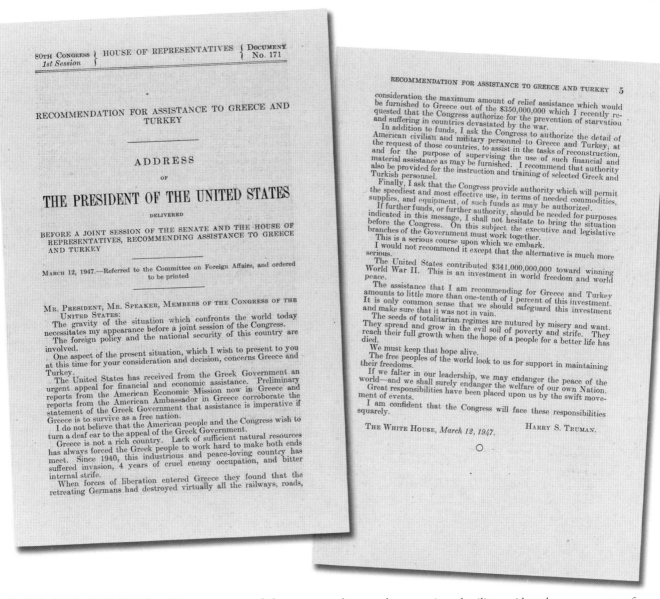

On March 12, 1947, President Truman announced the urgent need to supply economic and military aid to the governments of Greece and Turkey to combat Soviet expansion in the Mediterranean. This action effectively signaled the beginning of the Cold War between America and the U.S.S.R.

Transcript of THE TRUMAN DOCTRINE

' Mr. President, Mr. Speaker, Members of the Congress of the United States:

. . . One of the primary objectives of the foreign policy of the United States is the creation of conditions in which we and other nations will be able to work out a way of life free from coercion. This was a fundamental issue in the war with Germany and Japan. Our victory was won over countries which sought to impose their will, and their way of life, upon other nations.

To ensure the peaceful development of nations, free from coercion, the United States has taken a leading part in establishing the United Nations. The United Nations is designed to make possible lasting freedom and independence for all its members. We shall not realize our objectives, however, unless we are willing to help free peoples to maintain their free institutions and their national integrity against aggressive movements that seek to impose upon them totalitarian regimes. This is no more than a frank recognition that totalitarian regimes imposed on free peoples, by direct or indirect aggression, undermine the foundations of international peace and hence the security of the United States.

The peoples of a number of countries of the world have recently had totalitarian regimes forced upon them against their will. The Government of the United States has made frequent protests against coercion and intimidation, in violation of the Yalta agreement, in Poland, Rumania, and Bulgaria. I must also state that in a number of other countries there have been similar developments.

At the present moment in world history nearly every nation must choose between alternative ways of life. The choice is too often not a free one.

> "I believe that it must be the policy of the United States to support free peoples who are resisting attempted subjugation by armed minorities or by outside pressures."

One way of life is based upon the will of the majority, and is distinguished by free institutions, representative government, free elections, guarantees of individual liberty, freedom of speech and religion, and freedom from political oppression.

The second way of life is based upon the will of a minority forcibly imposed upon the majority. It relies upon terror and oppression, a controlled press and radio; fixed elections, and the suppression of personal freedoms.

I believe that it must be the policy of the United States to support free peoples who are resisting attempted subjugation by armed minorities or by outside pressures.

I believe that we must assist free peoples to work out their own destinies in their own way.

I believe that our help should be primarily through economic and financial aid which is essential to economic stability and orderly political processes.

The world is not static, and the status quo is not sacred. But we cannot allow changes in the status quo in violation of the Charter of the United Nations by such methods as coercion, or by such subterfuges as political infiltration. In helping free and independent nations to maintain their freedom, the United States will be giving effect to the principles of the Charter of the United Nations.

> "It would be an unspeakable tragedy if these countries, which have struggled so long against overwhelming odds, should lose that victory for which they sacrificed so much."

It is necessary only to glance at a map to realize that the survival and integrity of the Greek nation are of grave importance in a much wider situation. If Greece should fall under the control of an armed minority, the effect upon its neighbor, Turkey, would be immediate and serious. Confusion and disorder might well spread throughout the entire Middle East.

Moreover, the disappearance of Greece as an independent state would have a profound effect upon those countries in Europe whose peoples are struggling against great difficulties to maintain their freedoms and their independence while they repair the damages of war.

It would be an unspeakable tragedy if these countries, which have struggled so long against overwhelming odds, should lose that victory for which they sacrificed so much. Collapse of free institutions and loss of independence would be disastrous not only for them but for the world. Discouragement and possibly failure would quickly be the lot of neighboring peoples striving to maintain their freedom and independence.

Should we fail to aid Greece and Turkey in this fateful hour, the effect will be far reaching to the West as well as to the East.

We must take immediate and resolute action.

I therefore ask the Congress to provide authority for assistance to Greece and Turkey in the amount of $400,000,000 for the period ending June 30, 1948. In requesting these funds, I have taken into consideration the maximum amount of relief assistance which would be furnished to Greece out of the $350,000,000 which I recently requested that the Congress authorize for the prevention of starvation and suffering in countries devastated by the war.

In addition to funds, I ask the Congress to authorize the detail of American civilian and military personnel to Greece and Turkey, at the request of those countries, to assist in the tasks of reconstruction, and for the purpose of supervising the use of such financial and material assistance as may be furnished. I recommend that authority also be provided for the instruction and training of selected Greek and Turkish personnel . . .

This is a serious course upon which we embark.

> "If we falter in our leadership, we may endanger the peace of the world—and we shall surely endanger the welfare of our own nation."

I would not recommend it except that the alternative is much more serious. The United States contributed $341,000,000,000 toward winning World War II. This is an investment in world freedom and world peace.

The assistance that I am recommending for Greece and Turkey amounts to little more than 1 tenth of 1 percent of this investment. It is only common sense that we should safeguard this investment and make sure that it was not in vain.

The seeds of totalitarian regimes are nurtured by misery and want. They spread and grow in the evil soil of poverty and strife. They reach their full growth when the hope of a people for a better life has died. We must keep that hope alive.

The free peoples of the world look to us for support in maintaining their freedoms.

If we falter in our leadership, we may endanger the peace of the world—and we shall surely endanger the welfare of our own nation.

Great responsibilities have been placed upon us by the swift movement of events.

I am confident that the Congress will face these responsibilities squarely.

A POSTER ADVERTISING AID FOR
EUROPE UNDER THE MARSHALL
PLAN

The

MARSHALL PLAN

THE ECONOMIC CO-OPERATION ACT

APRIL 3, 1948

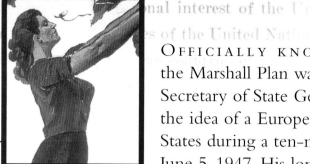

OFFICIALLY KNOWN AS the European Recovery Program, the Marshall Plan was so called because it was the brainchild of Secretary of State George C. Marshall. Marshall first proposed the idea of a European self-help program financed by the United States during a ten-minute address at Harvard University on June 5, 1947. His long-term aim was to bring about conditions that would enable democracy to thrive as Europe struggled to recover after World War II. In the words of British statesman Sir Winston Churchill, Europe at that time was "a rubble heap, a charnel house, a breeding ground of pestilence and hate."

In 1953 George Marshall was awarded the Nobel Peace Prize for his plan to provide economic aid to Europe. However, economist John Kenneth Galbraith maintained: "It was Harry Truman who had responsibility for giving the project substance." Truman himself described the Truman Doctrine and the Marshall Plan as "two halves of the same walnut."

Although European countries received over $5 billion in loans and grants after the war, this money was quickly swallowed up. A massive program of long-term support was clearly necessary to bring about the reconstruction of European nations so that they could once again become self-sufficient, as well as viable trading partners of the United States.

In his speech Marshall outlined how Europe's need for foreign food and goods over the coming years would far exceed her ability to pay for them. He described the implications of this in economic, social, and political terms, emphasizing both the humanitarian and political reasons for the U.S. to help Europe and also the benefits it would bring to the American economy.

Marshall attached three conditions to the plan: aid must be systematic, not piecemeal; the countries of Europe must work out their needs and plans together; and public opinion must back up the policy. Aid would be offered to most European countries, even those occupied by the U.S.S.R. The European nations would be invited to outline their own requirements so that material and financial aid could be used most effectively.

Marshall's ideas were greeted enthusiastically in some quarters, particularly by British Foreign Secretary Ernest Bevin, who invited his French and Soviet counterparts George Bidault and Vyacheslav Molotov to join him in responding. Molotov refused, regarding the plan as a violation of other nations' sovereignty.

HUMANITARIAN AID OR POLITICAL WEAPON?

In a speech given in September 1946, Andrei Vyshinsky, Soviet spokesman at the United Nations, argued that the Marshall Plan "conflicts sharply with the . . . resolution of December 11, 1946, which declares that relief supplies to other countries 'should at no time be used as a political weapon' . . . The implementation of the Marshall Plan will mean placing European countries under the economic and political control of the United States."

Stalin also saw the plan as a trick, and the U.S.S.R. later prevented countries under its control, such as Czechoslovakia, from participating—thus limiting the application of the plan to Western and Southern Europe.

In July 1947 the representatives of 16 nations met in Paris and established a temporary Committee of European Economic Cooperation. By mid-September they had drafted an initial four-year recovery plan. The committee was replaced in 1948 by the more permanent body, the Organization for European Economic Cooperation (OEEC).

The first ships carrying direct aid to Europe left within two weeks of the passing of the Economic Co-operation Act in April 1948. They carried loads as diverse as wheat, powdered eggs, and tractors. Aid was mostly given as grants or loans to help support industry and agriculture, although Marshall aid also financed some huge projects, including land reclamation in Italy and the Netherlands, and a hydroelectric scheme in Austria. The program supplied $13.5 billion in aid, five percent of U.S. national income. The U.S. economy also benefited, as markets for American goods began to recover.

By 1950 trade in Western Europe had returned to its pre-war volume, and by 1951 European industrial output was 43 percent more than before the war. One long-term effect of the creation of the OEEC was a reduction in the barriers that had previously hampered European trade. The plan also led to much stronger transatlantic ties as the two regions were now joined in a common commitment to democracy—a way of life that was being suppressed in Eastern Europe.

[PUBLIC LAW _472_]
[CHAPTER _169_]

S. 2202

THE WHITE HOUSE
APR 3 - 1948
RECEIVED

DEPARTMENT OF STATE
RECEIVED
APR 3 1948
PS
LAWS BRANCH

Eightieth Congress of the United States of America

At the Second Session

Begun and held at the City of Washington on Tuesday, the sixth day of January, one thousand nine hundred and forty-eight

AN ACT

To promote world peace and the general welfare, national interest, and foreign policy of the United States through economic, financial, and other measures necessary to the maintenance of conditions abroad in which free institutions may survive and consistent with the maintenance of the strength and stability of the United States.

Be it enacted by the Senate and House of Representatives of the United States of America in Congress assembled, That this Act may be cited as the "Foreign Assistance Act of 1948".

TITLE I

SEC. 101. This title may be cited as the "Economic Cooperation Act of 1948".

FINDINGS AND DECLARATION OF POLICY

SEC. 102. (a) Recognizing the intimate economic and other relationships between the United States and the nations of Europe, and recognizing that disruption following in the wake of war is not contained by national frontiers, the Congress finds that the existing situation in Europe endangers the establishment of a lasting peace, the general welfare and national interest of the United States, and the attainment of the objectives of the United Nations. The restoration or maintenance in European countries of principles of individual liberty, free institutions, and genuine independence rests largely upon the establishment of sound economic conditions, stable international economic relationships, and the achievement by the countries of Europe of a healthy economy independent of extraordinary outside assistance. The accomplishment of these objectives calls for a plan of European recovery, open to all such nations which cooperate in such plan, based upon a strong production effort, the expansion of foreign trade, the creation and maintenance of internal financial stability, and the development of economic cooperation, including all possible steps to establish and maintain equitable rates of exchange and to bring about the progressive elimination of trade barriers. Mindful of the advantages which the United States has enjoyed through the existence of a large domestic market with no internal trade barriers, and believing that similar advantages can accrue to the countries of Europe, it is declared to be the policy of the people of the United States to encourage these

The Economic Co-operation Act (1948) enshrined the Marshall Plan in law. The economic and technical assistance given to European countries after World War II restored Western Europe economically, and also prevented Communism from establishing a stronger foothold in Europe.

Transcript of GEORGE C. MARSHALL'S SPEECH AT HARVARD, JUNE 5, 1947

'I need not tell you gentlemen that the world situation is very serious. That must be apparent to all intelligent people. I think one difficulty is that the problem is one of such enormous complexity that the very mass of facts presented to the public by press and radio make it exceedingly difficult for the man in the street to reach a clear appraisement of the situation. Furthermore, the people of this country are distant from the troubled areas of the earth and it is hard for them to comprehend the plight and consequent reaction of the long-suffering peoples, and the effect of those reactions on their governments in connection with our efforts to promote peace in the world.

In considering the requirements for the rehabilitation of Europe the physical loss of life, the visible destruction of cities, factories, mines, and railroads was correctly estimated, but it has become obvious during recent months that this visible destruction was probably less serious than the dislocation of the entire fabric of European economy. For the past ten years conditions have been highly abnormal. The feverish maintenance of the war effort engulfed all aspects of national economics. Machinery has fallen into disrepair or is entirely obsolete. Under the arbitrary and destructive Nazi rule, virtually every possible enterprise was geared into the German war machine. Long-standing commercial ties, private institutions, banks, insurance companies and shipping companies disappeared, through the loss of capital, absorption through nationalization or by simple destruction. In many countries, confidence in the local currency has been severely shaken. The breakdown of the business structure of Europe during the war was complete. Recovery has been seriously retarded by the fact that two years after the close of hostilities a peace settlement with Germany and Austria has not been agreed upon. But even given a more prompt solution of these difficult problems, the rehabilitation of the economic structure of Europe quite evidently will require a much longer time and greater effort than had been foreseen.

> "...the rehabilitation of the economic structure of Europe quite evidently will require a much longer time and greater effort than had been foreseen."

There is a phase of this matter which is both interesting and serious. The farmer has always produced the foodstuffs to exchange with the city dweller for the other necessities of life. This division of labor is the basis of modern civilization. At the present time it is threatened with breakdown. The town and city industries are not producing adequate goods to exchange with the food-producing farmer. Raw materials and fuel are in short supply. Machinery is lacking or worn out. The farmer or the peasant cannot find the goods for sale which he desires to purchase. So the sale of his farm produce for money which he cannot use seems to him unprofitable transaction. He, therefore, has withdrawn many fields from crop cultivation and is using them for grazing. He feeds more grain to stock and finds for himself and his family an ample supply of food, however short he may be on clothing and the other ordinary gadgets of civilization. Meanwhile people in the cities are short of food and fuel. So the governments are forced to use their foreign money and credits to procure these necessities abroad. This process exhausts funds which are urgently needed for reconstruction. Thus a very serious situation is rapidly developing which bodes no good for the world. The modern system of the division of labor upon which the exchange of products is based is in danger of breaking down.

The truth of the matter is that Europe's requirements for the next three or four years of foreign food and other essential products—principally from America—are so much greater than her present ability to pay that she must have substantial additional help, or face economic, social, and political deterioration of a very grave character.

The remedy lies in breaking the vicious circle and restoring the confidence of the European people in the economic future of their own countries and of Europe as a whole. The manufacturer and the farmer throughout wide areas must be able and willing to exchange their products for currencies the continuing value of which is not open to question.

"Our policy is directed not against any country or doctrine but against hunger, poverty, desperation, and chaos."

Aside from the demoralizing effect on the world at large and the possibilities of disturbances arising as a result of the desperation of the people concerned, the consequences to the economy of the United States should be apparent to all. It is logical that the United States should do whatever it is able to do to assist in the return of normal economic health in the world, without which there can be no political stability and no assured peace. Our policy is directed not against any country or doctrine but against hunger, poverty, desperation, and chaos. Its purpose should be the revival of working economy in the world so as to permit the emergence of political and social conditions in which free institutions can exist. Such assistance, I am convinced, must not be on a piecemeal basis as various crises develop. Any assistance that this Government may render in the future should provide a cure rather than a mere palliative. Any government that is willing to assist in the task of recovery will find full cooperation, I am sure, on the part of the United States Government. Any government which maneuvers to block the recovery of other countries cannot expect help from us. Furthermore, governments, political parties, or groups which seek to perpetuate human misery in order to profit therefrom politically or otherwise will encounter the opposition of the United States.

It is already evident that, before the United States Government can proceed much further in its efforts to alleviate the situation and help start the European world on its way to recovery, there must be some agreement among the countries of Europe as to the requirements of the situation and the part those countries themselves will take in order to give proper effect to whatever action might be undertaken by this Government. It would be neither fitting nor efficacious for this Government to undertake to draw up unilaterally a program designed to place Europe on its feet economically. This is the business of the Europeans. The initiative, I think, must come from Europe. The role of this country should consist of friendly aid in the drafting of a European program so far as it may be practical for us to do so. The program should be a joint one, agreed to by a number, if not all European nations.

An essential part of any successful action on the part of the United States is an understanding on the part of the people of America of the character of the problem and the remedies to be applied. Political passion and prejudice should have no part. With foresight, and a willingness on the part of our people to face up to the vast responsibilities which history has clearly placed upon our country, the difficulties I have outlined can and will be overcome.

SENATOR JOSEPH McCARTHY AT THE OPENING OF
HEARINGS INTO HIS DISPUTE WITH THE ARMY, 1954

STATE RESOLUTION 301

CENSURE OF SENATOR JOSEPH McCARTHY

DECEMBER 2, 1954

FOR FOUR YEARS in the early 1950s America's growing fears about Communist infiltration were fueled by the efforts of a relatively obscure Senator from Wisconsin, Joseph McCarthy. The "McCarthy era" began with a speech given by the Senator at a Republican Women's Club in Wheeling, West Virginia, on February 9, 1950, in which he first spoke about "enemies from within." During his address, McCarthy claimed to have a list of 205 Communist Party adherents in the Truman administration State Department. Although he never backed up his claims with hard evidence, McCarthy stirred the fears of many Americans and received huge press coverage. From then on he conducted a crusade to unearth Communists in every walk of life, his name becoming synonymous with the use of reckless smear tactics to destroy someone's political and personal reputation.

Joseph McCarthy's anti-Communist crusade is frequently confused with the House Un-American Activities Committee (1938–75), a subcommittee of the House of Representatives that investigated accusations of subversion and became infamous for its persecution of prominent Hollywood figures. As a Senator, McCarthy had nothing to do with the HUAC.

Anti-Communist feeling in the West after World War II intensified with the explosion of the first Soviet atomic bomb and Communist victory in China in 1949, and U.S. entry into the Korean War the following year. It was the "red scare" then gripping the country that enabled McCarthy to establish his extraordinary period of tyranny in American public life.

The fifth child of devout Catholic parents, McCarthy was a painfully shy and unpopular child, over-protected by his mother. After training as an engineer he turned to law. In 1939 he became a state circuit judge, the youngest in Wisconsin's history. Two years later he served in the South Pacific in the Marine Corps, although he later exaggerated his war record.

In 1946, McCarthy won the Republican senatorial nomination in Wisconsin, and during his first three years in the Senate he was in demand as a public speaker. A popular guest at Washington cocktail parties, he was considered charming and friendly in social circles. However, his political colleagues soon became aware of his other characteristics: resourcefulness, relentless energy, a refusal ever to back down, personal vengefulness, a flair for self-dramatization, and total amorality. McCarthy soon found a cause to feed his large appetite for self-promotion: Communist infiltration of the government.

After the Wheeling speech, McCarthy repeatedly altered the tally of the number of people he claimed were on his list. However, his accusations triggered a Senate subcommittee investigation, chaired by Millard Tydings. McCarthy was unable to prove his charges, and the Tydings Committee produced a majority report dismissing his claims as "a fraud and a hoax." At the time, Senator Margaret Chase Smith of Maine, and six fellow Republicans, also issued a "declaration of conscience," stating that because of McCarthy's tactics, the Senate had been "debased to the level of a forum for hate and character assassination."

[Insert No. 2 on page 1 of 8.

ITALIC

Sec. 2. The Senator from Wisc

ducting a senatorial inquiry intemp

executive hearings in which he denc

the executive branch of the Governm

an officer of the United States Arr

his superior officers and for resp

executive directives, thereby tend

which must be maintained between t

branches in our system of governme

denunciation of General Zwicker b

of a Senate subcommittee and cens

But McCarthy had strong public support and continued to attack, ruthlessly destroying the reputation and careers of his political opponents, including Millard Tydings. In September 1950, against the wishes of President Truman, Congress passed an act requiring American Communist organizations to name their members on a government register. A ban on visas for visitors from "totalitarian states" followed, and several states passed their own laws requiring job applicants to sign anti-Communist affidavits.

McCarthy famously defamed the Roosevelt and Truman administrations as "20 years of treason." However, in 1952, following the Republicans' electoral triumph,

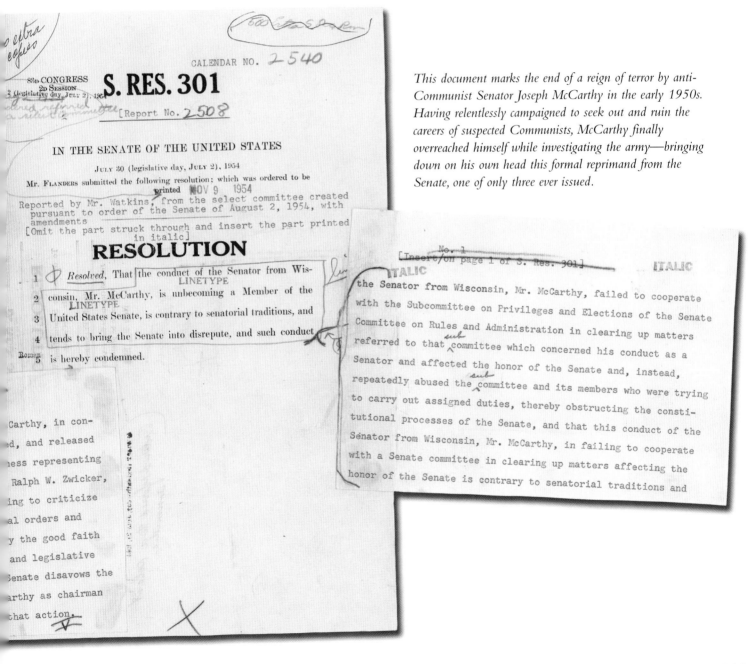

This document marks the end of a reign of terror by anti-Communist Senator Joseph McCarthy in the early 1950s. Having relentlessly campaigned to seek out and ruin the careers of suspected Communists, McCarthy finally overreached himself while investigating the army—bringing down on his own head this formal reprimand from the Senate, one of only three ever issued.

McCarthy was appointed as chair of the Senate Permanent Subcommittee on Investigations, through which he continued to make accusations of Communist influence in government, even though the government was now Republican. President Dwight D. Eisenhower privately loathed McCarthy but never acted overtly to remove him, thus enhancing the Senator's perceived invincibility. However, by this time McCarthy's methods were attracting considerable criticism from other Senators, and the Permanent Subcommittee's work was generally labeled a witch-hunt.

As Committee chair, McCarthy launched 157 enquiries, most notably into the official broadcasting service, Voice of America, and the Army Signal Corps, but failed to unearth any cases of subversive activity. He also came into open conflict with the army, leading to a televised hearing in January 1954 that lasted over a month. But it was the sight of McCarthy's brutal style of interrogation that eventually turned the public against him. Although many Americans were happy to see suspected Communists cleared out of government, they disliked the sight of army personnel subjected to McCarthy's hectoring cross-examination, damaging innuendo, and personal disrespect.

PROTESTING TOO MUCH?

One of the most damaging appearances by McCarthy was on a popular television show See It Now, *hosted by journalist Edward R. Murrow, in which the Senator made histrionic accusations, and attacked Murrow himself. In 2005, an Oscar-nominated film about Murrow was released. Test audiences at* Good Night and Good Luck *complained that the actor portraying McCarthy overacted, not realizing that the director, George Clooney, had used archive footage of McCarthy himself.*

During the rest of 1954 McCarthy's conduct was subjected to a Senate debate, initiated by Republican Senators Ralph Flanders, Arthur Watkins, and Margaret Chase Smith. In December 1954, McCarthy was formally condemned on a vote of 67 to 22 for conduct "contrary to Senate traditions." There was no penalty for the reprimand, but McCarthy's fall from grace was punishment enough.

From then on McCarthy was largely ignored by his colleagues and by the media. Denied the headlines he craved he swiftly declined both physically and emotionally. Always a heavy drinker, McCarthy died of cirrhosis of the liver in 1957, aged 48. He was given a state funeral attended by many Senators, and thousands of people viewed his body in Washington.

Many of McCarthy's allegations were later shown to be invented or inaccurate. But this was small consolation to the thousands of Americans, both well known and anonymous, who were blacklisted and never worked again—the lives of some so devastated that they were driven to suicide.

Transcript of STATE RESOLUTION 301: CENSURE OF SENATOR JOSEPH McCARTHY

'Resolved, That the Senator from Wisconsin, Mr. McCarthy, failed to cooperate with the Subcommittee on Privileges and Elections of the Senate Committee on Rules and Administration in clearing up matters referred to that subcommittee which concerned his conduct as a Senator and affected the honor of the Senate and, instead, repeatedly abused the subcommittee and its members who were trying to carry out assigned duties, thereby obstructing the constitutional processes of the Senate, and that this conduct of the Senator from Wisconsin, Mr. McCarthy, is contrary to senatorial traditions and is hereby condemned.

Sec 2. The Senator from Wisconsin, Mr. McCarthy, in writing to the chairman of the Select Committee to Study Censure Charges (Mr. Watkins) after the Select Committee had issued its report and before the report was presented to the Senate charging three members of the Select Committee with "deliberate deception" and "fraud" for failure to disqualify themselves; in stating to the press on November 4, 1954, that the special Senate session that was to begin November 8, 1954, was a "lynch-party"; in repeatedly describing this special Senate session as a "lynch bee" in a nationwide television and radio show on November 7, 1954; in stating to the public press on November 13, 1954, that the chairman of the Select Committee (Mr. Watkins) was guilty of "the most unusual, most cowardly things I've ever heard of" and stating further: "I expected he would be afraid to answer the questions, but didn't think he'd be stupid enough to make a public statement"; and in characterizing the said committee as the "unwitting handmaiden," "involuntary agent" and "attorneys-in-fact" of the Communist Party and in charging that the said committee in writing its report "imitated Communist methods—that it distorted, misrepresented, and omitted in its effort to manufacture a plausible rationalization" in support of its recommendations to the Senate, which characterizations and charges were contained in a statement released to the press and inserted in the Congressional Record of November 10, 1954, acted contrary to senatorial ethics and tended to bring the Senate into dishonor and disrepute, to obstruct the constitutional processes of the Senate, and to impair its dignity; and such conduct is hereby condemned. '

> "[The] conduct of the Senator from Wisconsin, Mr. McCarthy, is contrary to senatorial traditions and is hereby condemned."

Elizabeth Eckford, one of the Little Rock
Nine, surrounded by a hostile white mob

Executive Order 10730

DESEGREGATION

OF

CENTRAL HIGH SCHOOL

Little Rock, Arkansas

September 23, 1957

IN 1954, a controversial U.S. Supreme Court ruling found separate educational facilities for black and white Americans to be unequal and, therefore, unconstitutional. Arkansas was one of only two Southern states that actually started to comply with the ruling. Although the school board in the Arkansas city of Little Rock decided unanimously to enroll African American students in 1957, State Governor Orval Faubus feared that civil unrest would follow. He therefore ordered state troops to surround the school on the night before the school year began to stop nine black students entering the following day. To uphold federal law, President Dwight D. Eisenhower ordered the deployment of 1,200 paratroopers to enable the black children to attend in the face of a hostile white mob.

In 1999, President Bill Clinton awarded the Little Rock Nine, as the first black students at Central High School became known, with the Congressional Medal. The Nine endured continual abuse and harassment during their year at the school, despite the initial presence of federal troops and the high profile their case had in the media.

In spite of the constitutional amendments that had freed them from slavery and enfranchised them, from the 1870s onwards, many African Americans were second-class citizens in their own country because of segregation laws passed in the Southern states. Although President Harry S. Truman's Committee on Civil Rights had issued a denunciation of racial segregation in 1947, and it had been banned in the armed forces, most African Americans still lived segregated lives.

The mid-1950s saw some significant changes. The Supreme Court order in 1954 resulted from the *Brown v. Board of Education of Topeka* case, when a group of parents in Kansas took legal action after their children were excluded from the nearest available school and obliged to go to a segregated black school some distance from their homes. The order was treated differently in different states. By Fall 1957, only 684 of the 3,000 southern school districts had started to integrate. Arkansas, however, was regarded as one of the more progressive states. Its law school had been integrated since 1949, as had seven of its eight universities, together with public transport and public amenities like the zoo, library, and parks. The Little Rock school board's decision to desegregate its public schools seemed in keeping with this trend.

It was therefore a surprise when the Governor of Arkansas, Orval Faubus, considered a liberal, ordered the posting of National Guardsmen outside Central High School on the night before integration was to take effect. Faubus claimed violent protesters were headed in convoys toward Little Rock. Although officially enrolled, no African American children were allowed into the school when the new trimester began as scheduled on September 5.

On September 20, an injunction was issued against Governor Faubus' attempts to prevent integration. Three days later the National Guardsmen left and the nine children were theoretically able to enter the school. However, a hostile mob of about 1,000 whites gathered

A QUESTIONABLE VICTORY
Forty years after Brown v. Board of Education of Topeka, *segregation remained an issue in U.S. schools. Studies carried out in the late 1990s showed that, despite government measures to assist integration, 70 percent of black students attended all-black schools, and the average white student attended a school where more than 80 percent of the school population was white.*

outside the school and by noon the city authorities had decided that all the children in school should leave. The National Association for the Advancement of Colored People (NAACP) announced that the black children would not attend the school unless there was presidential assurance that they would be protected from the mob.

Eisenhower responded to the crisis by issuing an executive order, commenting, "Mob rule cannot be allowed to override the decisions of our courts." On September 25, under the protection of federal paratroopers, the nine black pupils entered the school and the mob dispersed. The paratroopers stayed for a month, but tension remained high in the school for the rest of the year, at the end of which Central High School, and several other schools in the South, closed rather than confront the issue of integration. Central High did not reopen for another two years.

EXECUTIVE ORDER

PROVIDING ASSISTANCE FOR THE REMOVAL OF AN OBSTRUCTION

OF JUSTICE WITHIN THE STATE OF ARKANSAS

WHEREAS on September 23, 1957, I issued Proclamation No.

3204 reading in part as follows:

"WHEREAS certain persons in the State of Arkansas, individually and in unlawful assemblages, combinations, and conspiracies, have wilfully obstructed the enforcement of orders of the United States District Court for the Eastern District of Arkansas with respect to matters relating to enrollment and attendance at public schools, particularly at Central High School, located in Little Rock School District, Little Rock, Arkansas; and

"WHEREAS such wilful obstruction of justice hinders the execution of the laws of that state and of the United States, and makes it impracticable to enforce such laws by the ordinary course of judicial proceedings; and

"WHEREAS such obstruction of justice constitutes a denial of the equal protection of the laws secured by the Constitution of the United States and impedes the course of justice under those laws:

"NOW, THEREFORE, I, DWIGHT D. EISENHOWER, President of the United States, under and by virtue of the authority vested in me by the Constitution and statutes of the United States, including Chapter 15 of Title 10 of the United States Code, particularly sections 332, 333 and 334 thereof, do command all persons engaged in such obstruction of justice to cease and desist therefrom, and to disperse forthwith;" and

WHEREAS the command contained in that Proclamation has not

been obeyed and wilful obstruction of enforcement of said court orders

still exists and threatens to continue:

Signed on September 23, 1957, by President Dwight D. Eisenhower, Executive Order 10730 empowered federal troops to maintain peace at Little Rock, Arkansas, while nine African American students attempted to attend its high school, in keeping with the 1954 ruling that U.S. public schools should be desegregated. This order overruled the actions of Arkansas State Governor Orval Faubus.

Transcript of EXECUTIVE ORDER 10730: DESEGREGATION OF CENTRAL HIGH SCHOOL, LITTLE ROCK

EXECUTIVE ORDER 10730

PROVIDING ASSISTANCE FOR THE REMOVAL OF AN OBSTRUCTION OF JUSTICE WITHIN THE STATE OF ARKANSAS

WHEREAS on September 23, 1957, I issued Proclamation No. 3204 reading in part as follows:

"WHEREAS certain persons in the state of Arkansas, individually and in unlawful assemblages, combinations, and conspiracies, have willfully obstructed the enforcement of orders of the United States District Court for the Eastern District of Arkansas with respect to matters relating to enrollment and attendance at public schools, particularly at Central High School, located in Little Rock School District, Little Rock, Arkansas; and

"WHEREAS such willful obstruction of justice hinders the execution of the laws of that State and of the United States, and makes it impracticable to enforce such laws by the ordinary course of judicial proceedings; and

"WHEREAS such obstruction of justice constitutes a denial of the equal protection of the laws secured by the Constitution of the United States and impedes the course of justice under those laws:

"NOW, THEREFORE, I, DWIGHT D. EISENHOWER, President of the United States, under and by virtue of the authority vested in me by the Constitution and Statutes of the United States, including Chapter 15 of Title 10 of the United States Code, particularly sections 332, 333 and 334 thereof, do command all persons engaged in such obstruction of justice to cease and desist therefrom, and to disperse forthwith;" and

WHEREAS the command contained in that Proclamation has not been obeyed and willful obstruction of enforcement of said court orders still exists and threatens to continue:

NOW, THEREFORE, by virtue of the authority vested in me by the Constitution and Statutes of the United States, including Chapter 15 of Title 10, particularly sections 332, 333 and 334 thereof, and section 301 of Title 3 of the United States Code, It is hereby ordered as follows:

SECTION 1. I hereby authorize and direct the Secretary of Defense to order into the active military service of the United States as he may deem appropriate to carry out the purposes of this Order, any or all of the units of the National Guard of the United States and of the Air National Guard of the United States within the State of Arkansas to serve in the active military service of the United States for an indefinite period and until relieved by appropriate orders.

SEC. 2. The Secretary of Defense is authorized and directed to take all appropriate steps to enforce any orders of the United States District Court for the Eastern District of Arkansas for the removal of obstruction of justice in the State of Arkansas with respect to matters relating to enrollment and attendance at public schools in the Little Rock School District, Little Rock, Arkansas. In carrying out the provisions of this section, the Secretary of Defense is authorized to use the units, and members thereof, ordered into the active military service of the United States pursuant to Section 1 of this Order.

SEC. 3. In furtherance of the enforcement of the aforementioned orders of the United States District Court for the Eastern District of Arkansas, the Secretary of Defense is authorized to use such of the armed forces of the United States as he may deem necessary.

SEC. 4. The Secretary of Defense is authorized to delegate to the Secretary of the Army or the Secretary of the Air Force, or both, any of the authority conferred upon him by this Order.

DWIGHT D. EISENHOWER
THE WHITE HOUSE,
September 24, 1957.

John F. Kennedy (1917–63), 35th
President of the United States,
making his inaugural speech

The inaugural address of

PRESIDENT JOHN F. KENNEDY

January 20, 1961

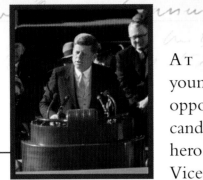

AT THE AGE of 43, Democrat John F. Kennedy was one of the youngest men, and the first Catholic, to become President. His opponent in the campaign was the equally youthful Republican candidate Richard M. Nixon, who, like Kennedy, was a naval war hero and moreover had been President Dwight D. Eisenhower's Vice-President for eight years. Nixon began the campaign as by far the stronger candidate, but despite his inexperience, and the vigorous anti-Catholic propaganda produced by his opponents, Kennedy won by one of the narrowest margins ever recorded in a Presidential election.

■ *John F. Kennedy was an admirer of political oratory, and some of his own speeches are considered among the greatest in U.S. history. He worked on his inaugural address with speechwriter Ted Sorensen— his collaborator on his Pulitzer Prize-winning* book Profiles in Courage *—for two months, making changes right up to delivery.*

Kennedy's inaugural speech expressed the young President's vision of an America that would uphold human rights, reject tyranny, and help the poor. A patriotic man, Kennedy believed that American ideals could liberate the planet. Yet the 1960s were one of the most menacing decades of the Cold War, as the U.S.S.R. also sought to increase its influence across the globe. In the end, Kennedy's desire to assert U.S. dominance in foreign affairs conflicted with his idealistic vision of a world without tyranny, poverty, or war. He became locked in growing military and propagandist competition with Moscow.

One area in which rivalry was most fierce was the space race. Kennedy's interest in space exploration was driven by the fact that the Soviets were stealing America's thunder in the race to put a man in space, despite superior U.S. rocket technology. In 1957, the U.S.S.R. launched *Sputnik 1*, the first man-made satellite to orbit the earth, and in 1961 the Russian cosmonaut Yuri Gagarin became the first person in space, beating U.S. astronaut John Glenn by a year.

However, there was a more sinister and serious side to the competition between the United States and the U.S.S.R. In August 1961, Soviet leader Nikita Khrushchev ordered the construction of the ultimate symbol of the Cold War: the Berlin Wall, which divided the city of Berlin into two, Communist East Berlin and "free" West Berlin. In response, Kennedy expanded American military power, and when the Soviet Union resumed atmospheric testing of nuclear weapons in 1962, Kennedy did the same, despite an election pledge not to do so.

In the same year, the Cuban Missile Crisis (see page 209) caused fear around the world that nuclear warfare was about to break out. War was only averted by intensive diplomacy on both sides. Kennedy concluded afterwards, "It is insane that two men, sitting on opposite sides of the world, should be able to decide to bring an end to civilization." In July 1963 he reintroduced the ban on atmospheric testing of nuclear weapons, and on August 6, the governments of the United States, Britain, and the U.S.S.R. signed the Limited Nuclear Test Ban Treaty, which called on all parties concerned to try to work for an end to the arms race. Kennedy began to abandon his patriotic rhetoric, saying in August 1963: "We all inhabit this small planet. We all breathe the same air. We all cherish our children's future, and we are all mortal."

Nevertheless, for Kennedy, the issue of America's sphere of influence remained crucial. One initiative he used to enhance U.S. influence was the Peace Corps, which he inaugurated in 1961. The Peace Corps sent young volunteers to do practical and professional work in developing countries, strengthening the relationships between those countries and the U.S.A. More controversially, he supplied 18,000 military advisers to South Vietnam, and gave tacit support to the overthrow of South Vietnamese President Ngo Dinh Diem in November 1963. That same month, Kennedy was assassinated in Dallas, Texas. The President who had spoken so eloquently about the need for peace in his inaugural address less than three years earlier had hugely escalated his country's involvement in a long and bloody war in Southeast Asia.

President Kennedy's inaugural speech conveyed a sense of youthful optimism. His memorable exhortation—"Ask not what your country can do for you—ask what you can do for your country"—reflected his belief in active citizenship, both nationally and globally.

Transcript of THE INAUGURAL SPEECH OF PRESIDENT JOHN F. KENNEDY

'*Vice President Johnson, Mr. Speaker, Mr. Chief Justice, President Eisenhower, Vice President Nixon, President Truman, Reverend Clergy, fellow citizens:*

We observe today not a victory of party but a celebration of freedom—symbolizing an end as well as a beginning—signifying renewal as well as change. For I have sworn before you and Almighty God the same solemn oath our forebears prescribed nearly a century and three-quarters ago.

The world is very different now. For man holds in his mortal hands the power to abolish all forms of human poverty and all forms of human life. And yet the same revolutionary beliefs for which our forebears fought are still at issue around the globe—the belief that the rights of man come not from the generosity of the state but from the hand of God.

> "... the torch has been passed to a new generation of Americans—born in this century, tempered by war, disciplined by a hard and bitter peace, proud of our ancient heritage."

We dare not forget today that we are the heirs of that first revolution. Let the word go forth from this time and place, to friend and foe alike, that the torch has been passed to a new generation of Americans—born in this century, tempered by war, disciplined by a hard and bitter peace, proud of our ancient heritage—and unwilling to witness or permit the slow undoing of those human rights to which this nation has always been committed, and to which we are committed today at home and around the world.

Let every nation know, whether it wishes us well or ill, that we shall pay any price, bear any burden, meet any hardship, support any friend, oppose any foe to assure the survival and the success of liberty.

This much we pledge—and more.

To those old allies whose cultural and spiritual origins we share, we pledge the loyalty of faithful friends. United there is little we cannot do in a host of cooperative ventures. Divided there is little we can do—for we dare not meet a powerful challenge at odds and split asunder.

To those new states whom we welcome to the ranks of the free, we pledge our word that one form of colonial control shall not have passed away merely to be replaced by a far more iron tyranny. We shall not always expect to find them supporting our view. But we shall always hope to find them strongly supporting their own freedom—and to remember that, in the past, those who foolishly sought power by riding the back of the tiger ended up inside ...

To that world assembly of sovereign states, the United Nations, our last best hope in an age where the instruments of war have far outpaced the instruments of peace, we renew our pledge of support—to prevent it from becoming merely a forum for invective—to strengthen its shield of the new and the weak—and to enlarge the area in which its writ may run.

Finally, to those nations who would make themselves our adversary, we offer not a pledge but a request: that both sides begin anew the quest for peace, before the dark powers of destruction unleashed by science engulf all humanity in planned or accidental self-destruction.

We dare not tempt them with weakness. For only when our arms are sufficient beyond doubt can we be certain beyond doubt that they will never be employed.

> "Let us never negotiate out of fear. But let us never fear to negotiate."

But neither can two great and powerful groups of nations take comfort from our present course—both sides overburdened by the cost of modern weapons, both rightly alarmed by the steady spread of the deadly atom, yet both racing to alter that uncertain balance of terror that stays the hand of mankind's final war.

So let us begin anew—remembering on both sides that civility is not a sign of weakness, and sincerity is always subject to proof. Let us never negotiate out of fear. But let us never fear to negotiate.

Let both sides explore what problems unite us instead of belaboring those problems which divide us.

Let both sides, for the first time, formulate serious and precise proposals for the inspection and control of arms—and bring the absolute power to destroy other nations under the absolute control of all nations.

Let both sides seek to invoke the wonders of science instead of its terrors. Together let us explore the stars, conquer the deserts, eradicate disease, tap the ocean depths and encourage the arts and commerce.

Let both sides unite to heed in all corners of the earth the command of Isaiah—to "undo the heavy burdens . . . (and) let the oppressed go free."

And if a beachhead of cooperation may push back the jungle of suspicion, let both sides join in creating a new endeavor, not a new balance of power, but a new world of law, where the strong are just and the weak secure and the peace preserved.

All this will not be finished in the first one hundred days. Nor will it be finished in the first one thousand days, nor in the life of this Administration, nor even perhaps in our lifetime on this planet. But let us begin.

In your hands, my fellow citizens, more than mine, will rest the final success or failure of our course. Since this country was founded, each generation of Americans has been summoned to give testimony to its national loyalty. The graves of young Americans who answered the call to service surround the globe.

Now the trumpet summons us again—not as a call to bear arms, though arms we need—not as a call to battle, though embattled we are—but a call to bear the burden of a long twilight struggle, year in and year out, "rejoicing in hope, patient in tribulation"—a struggle against the common enemies of man: tyranny, poverty, disease and war itself.

Can we forge against these enemies a grand and global alliance, North and South, East and West, that can assure a more fruitful life for all mankind? Will you join in that historic effort?

> "And so, my fellow Americans: ask not what your country can do for you—ask what you can do for your country. My fellow citizens of the world: ask not what America will do for you, but what together we can do for the freedom of man."

In the long history of the world, only a few generations have been granted the role of defending freedom in its hour of maximum danger. I do not shrink from this responsibility—I welcome it. I do not believe that any of us would exchange places with any other people or any other generation. The energy, the faith, the devotion which we bring to this endeavor will light our country and all who serve it—and the glow from that fire can truly light the world.

And so, my fellow Americans: ask not what your country can do for you— ask what you can do for your country.

My fellow citizens of the world: ask not what America will do for you, but what together we can do for the freedom of man.

Finally, whether you are citizens of America or citizens of the world, ask of us here the same high standards of strength and sacrifice which we ask of you. With a good conscience our only sure reward, with history the final judge of our deeds, let us go forth to lead the land we love, asking His blessing and His help, but knowing that here on earth God's work must truly be our own.

CUBAN SOLDIERS STAND BY ON THE HAVANA WATERFRONT IN
RESPONSE TO A WARNING OF INVASION BY THE UNITED STATES

The

CUBAN MISSILE CRISIS

LETTER FROM SOVIET LEADER NIKITA KHRUSHCHEV TO
PRESIDENT JOHN F. KENNEDY

OCTOBER 24, 1962

BY 1962, THE UNITED STATES had a hostile relationship with Cuba. The year before, President John F. Kennedy had authorized an attempt by Cuban exiles, trained by the U.S. military, to overthrow the revolutionary Cuban leader, Fidel Castro. The operation, at the Bay of Pigs in Cuba, was a failure but it pushed Castro further into the Communist camp. Castro wanted a strong ally against any further attempt at invasion. At the same time, the Soviet Union wanted a missile base closer to the U.S. so that they could match the U.S.'s ability to reach targets within the U.S.S.R. from bases in Turkey.

■ *Fidel Castro had good reason to think that the U.S. would attempt to invade Cuba again after the Bay of Pigs fiasco. In 1962, with no attempt at subtlety, an American military exercise involved the invasion of an island in the Caribbean, whose leader was given the name "Ortsac"—Castro spelled backwards.*

The first evidence that the Soviet Union might be about to use Cuba as a base for nuclear warheads was discovered on October 14, 1962 in photographs taken by an American U-2 spy plane. They showed what appeared to be preparations for a missile site near San Cristobal. Two days later, the photographs were shown to Kennedy, who decided not to make an immediate public response. Instead, he met secretly with the Executive Committee of the National Security Council—ExComm—to discuss U.S. options in response to such a provocative Soviet move. The committee's conversations were recorded: some members argued that the U.S. should launch an air strike, but Kennedy was reluctant, maintaining that this would alienate international opinion.

At first the Soviet Foreign Minister, Andrei Gromyko, denied that Soviet weapons were being deployed on the island. Kennedy was unconvinced and, on October 22, he went on national television to warn that the U.S. would hold the U.S.S.R. responsible for any attack that came from Cuba. He announced that America would blockade the island to prevent Soviet ships unloading weaponry. Kennedy knew he was taking a massive gamble, telling his advisers, "What we are doing is throwing down a card on the table in a game which we don't know the ending of." The crucial question was whether the Soviet ships would turn back and risk losing face or whether they would persist in landing the weapons on Cuba.

On October 24, Kennedy received a letter from the Soviet leader Nikita Khrushchev. It gave the impression that the Soviet ships would not be turning back. Khrushchev accused the U.S. government of "propelling humankind into the abyss of a world nuclear missile war." His tone was aggressive and he blamed U.S. foreign policy for the crisis: "The actions of the U.S.A. in relation to Cuba are outright piracy. This, if you will, is the madness of a degenerating imperialism." According to his brother, Robert, whose support and advice John Kennedy relied on heavily during the crisis, the President was anxious not to respond with similar threats: "I don't want to put him in a corner from which he cannot escape."

By October 26, Kennedy was instructing the State Department to plan for a government of Cuba after an American invasion. However, Khrushchev produced an offer. If the Americans would promise not to invade Cuba, the

THE VOCABULARY OF CRISIS
Kennedy referred to the naval blockade of Cuba as "quarantine," using an expression coined by President Roosevelt during World War II, when proposing the containment of aggressor nations. The blockade was in international waters, and Kennedy was concerned that it might be interpreted as an act of war, if sufficient care was not taken to use the correct terminology in referring to it.

As Soviet ships carrying nuclear weapons to Cuba drew ever closer to the American naval blockade, Soviet leader Nikita Khrushchev and President Kennedy began a fraught correspondence to negotiate their way around a nuclear confrontation.

missile sites could be dismantled and Cuba would not be used as a Soviet base. The next day, however, the situation became very bleak. A U.S. plane was shot down over Cuba and Khrushchev wrote again, adding the withdrawal of American missiles from Turkey to his demands.

In a simple but brilliantly effective move to defuse the escalating tension, Kennedy decided to respond publicly to Khrushchev's first offer, and make no reference to the Soviet leader's later, more aggressive demands. Privately, the President sent Robert Kennedy to the Soviet embassy and, in response to Khrushchev's second letter, agreed that the U.S. missile sites in Turkey would be dismantled in six months' time. The tactic worked. On Sunday October 28, Khrushchev announced on Radio Moscow that the missile sites on Cuba were being dismantled in response to an American promise not to invade the country. By common agreement, the two leaders' behind-the-scenes accord was kept entirely secret for decades afterwards.

Both felt that they could never again go so close to the edge of the abyss. Recognizing that slow communications had been a contributory factor to the tensions and brinkmanship of the crisis (it took 12 hours to transmit and translate each of Khrushchev's letters), a telephone hotline was set up between the Kremlin and the White House. The following year, both the U.S. and Soviet governments were signatories to the first Nuclear Test Ban Treaty, a move to limit the arms race. Nevertheless, the specter of mutually assured destruction haunted peoples' imaginations for many years following the Cuban Missile Crisis.

Transcript of KHRUSHCHEV'S LETTER TO PRESIDENT KENNEDY

Dear Mr. President,

. . . Imagine, Mr. President, what if we were to present to you such an ultimatum as you have presented to us by your actions. How would you react to it? I think you would be outraged at such a move on our part. And this we would understand.

Having presented these conditions to us, Mr. President, you have thrown down the gauntlet. Who asked you to do this? By what right have you done this? Our ties with the Republic of Cuba, as well as our relations with other nations, regardless of their political system, concern only the two countries between which these relations exist. And, if it were a matter of quarantine as mentioned in your letter, then, as is customary in international practice, it can be established only by states agreeing between themselves, and not by some third party. Quarantines exist, for example, on agricultural goods and products. However, in this case we are not talking about quarantines, but rather about much more serious matters, and you yourself understand this. You, Mr. President, are not declaring a quarantine, but rather issuing an ultimatum, and you are threatening that if we do not obey your orders, you will then use force. Think about what you are saying! And you want to persuade me to agree to this! What does it mean to agree to these demands? It would mean for us to conduct our relations with other countries not by reason, but by yielding to tyranny. You are not appealing to reason; you want to intimidate us.

> "This, if you will, is the madness of a degenerating imperialism."

No, Mr. President, I cannot agree to this, and I think that deep inside, you will admit that I am right. I am convinced that if you were in my place you would do the same.

. . . This Organization [of American States] has no authority or grounds whatsoever to pass resolutions like those of which you speak in your letter. Therefore, we do not accept these resolutions. International law exists, generally accepted standards of conduct exist. We firmly adhere to the principles of international law and strictly observe the standards regulating navigation on the open sea, in international waters. We observe these standards and enjoy the rights recognized by all nations.

You want to force us to renounce the rights enjoyed by every sovereign state; you are attempting to legislate questions of international law; you are violating the generally accepted standards of this law. All this is due not only to hatred for the Cuban people and their government, but also for reasons having to do with the election campaign in the U.S.A. What morals, what laws can justify such an approach by the American government to international affairs? Such morals and laws are not to be found, because the actions of the U.S.A. in relation to Cuba are outright piracy. This, if you will, is the madness of a degenerating imperialism. Unfortunately, people of all nations, and not least the American people themselves, could suffer heavily from madness such as this, since with the appearance of modern types of weapons, the U.S.A. has completely lost its former inaccessibility.

Therefore, Mr. President, if you weigh the present situation with a cool head without giving way to passion, you will understand that the Soviet Union cannot afford not to decline the despotic demands of the U.S.A. When you lay conditions such as these before us, try to put yourself in our situation and consider how the U.S.A. would react to such conditions. I have no doubt that if anyone attempted to dictate similar conditions to you—the U.S.A., you would reject such an attempt. And we likewise say—no.

"With the appearance of modern types of weapons, the U.S.A. has completely lost its former inaccessibility."

The Soviet government considers the violation of the freedom of navigation in international waters and air space to constitute an act of aggression propelling humankind into the abyss of a world nuclear-missile war. Therefore, the Soviet government cannot instruct captains of Soviet ships bound for Cuba to observe orders of American naval forces blockading this island. Our instructions to Soviet sailors are to observe strictly the generally accepted standards of navigation in international waters and not retreat one step from them. And, if the American side violates these rights, it must be aware of the responsibility it will bear for this act.

To be sure, we will not remain mere observers of pirate actions by American ships in the open sea. We will then be forced on our part to take those measures we deem necessary and sufficient to defend our rights. To this end we have all that is necessary.

Respectfully,
N. KHRUSHCHEV
Moscow
24 October 1962

John F. Kennedy's accused assassin
Lee Harvey Oswald is escorted in the
Dallas Police Department hallway

Report of the President's
Commission on the

ASSASSINATION OF PRESIDENT KENNEDY

The Warren Commission Report

1964

WITH NEW PRESIDENTIAL elections approaching, President John F. Kennedy undertook a whirlwind tour of the country. In less than a week in September 1963 he spoke in nine different states. On November 22, he was in Dallas, traveling in an open limousine with his wife, Jacqueline, the Governor of Texas, John Connally, Mrs Connally, and the head of the Secret Service at the White House. They were followed by Secret Service agents, Vice-President Lyndon B. Johnson, and Senator Ralph Yarborough in two further cars. As the motorcade rounded a corner into Dealey Plaza, shots rang out. The President and Governor Connally were clearly injured. Their car accelerated toward Parkland Memorial Hospital where Kennedy was pronounced dead shortly afterwards.

After two days of questioning by Dallas police, the man accused of assassinating the President, Lee Harvey Oswald, was shot and fatally wounded as he was transferred to jail. He died two days later. His murder was the first homicide to be seen on television, shocking the millions around the world who saw it.

Three quarters of an hour after Kennedy was assassinated, a policeman was shot dead while trying to detain Lee Harvey Oswald in downtown Dallas. Oswald was later arrested, and as world news cameras broadcast his removal to jail he, too, was murdered by a restaurant owner called Jack Ruby.

Kennedy's successor, Lyndon B. Johnson, set up a Commission to investigate the circumstances of President Kennedy's assassination. The Commission was made up of leading establishment figures and chaired by the Chief Justice, Earl Warren. The Commission report was critical of the fact that 24-year-old Oswald, the subject of an F.B.I. file before the shooting, was able to get so close to the President. Its recommendations included that security should be improved; that the work of the Secret Service should be supervised by the cabinet committee; that an automatic data-processing machine should be used to monitor people more closely; that the President's doctor should be with him when he traveled; and that the assassination of the President or Vice-President should be made a federal offense.

The report also adopted the "lone gunman theory," concluding that Oswald had fired three shots at the President and that he had acted alone. This was later disputed in 1979 by the House Select Committee on Assassinations, which revealed that there was taped evidence of four shots, one of which appeared to come from a different direction. Oswald, they concluded, fired three of the shots, but the fourth shot came from behind a picket fence on a grassy knoll in Dealey Plaza. It has been argued that the sound quality of the tapes makes this evidence extremely unreliable.

Nevertheless, many people have never felt that the Commission's report closed the case. For those who believe that Kennedy's murder was a conspiracy by his enemies to silence him, the assassination has never been fully explained.

The conspiracy theory was fed by the fact that Kennedy had plenty of enemies—people who thought he went too far, and those who feared he

THE ASSASSINATION OF *John F. Kennedy has become an almost iconic cultural point of reference. At the time, the U.S. Ambassador to the United Nations, Adlai Stevenson, said, "all of us . . . will bear the grief of his death until the day of ours." Millions of people around the world remember where they were when they heard the news of his assassination, as if it were an event of personal, as well as political, significance.*

on the known facts of the assassination, the Marine marksmanship experts, Major Anderson and Sergeant Zahm, concurred in the opinion that Oswald had the capability to fire three shots, with two hits, within 4.8 and 5.6 seconds. Concerning the shot which struck the President in the back of the neck, Sergeant Zahm testified: "With the equipment he [Oswald] had and with his ability I consider it a very easy shot." Having fired this shot the assassin was then required to hit the target one more time within a space of from 4.8 to 5.6 seconds. On the basis of Oswald's training and the accuracy of the weapon as established by the tests, the Commission concluded that Oswald was capable of accomplishing this second hit even if there was an intervening shot which missed. The probability of hitting the President a second time would have been markedly increased if, in fact, he had missed either the first or third shots thereby leaving a time span of 4.8 to 5.6 seconds between the two shots which struck their mark. The Commission agrees with the testimony of Marine marksmanship expert Zahm that it was "an easy shot" to hit some part of the President's body, and that the range where the rifleman would be expected to hit would include the President's head.

CONCLUSION

On the basis of the evidence reviewed in this chapter, the Commission has found that Lee Harvey Oswald (1) owned and possessed the rifle used to kill President Kennedy and wound Governor Connally, (2) brought this rifle into the Depository Building on the morning of the assassination, (3) was present, at the time of the assassination, at the window from which the shots were fired, (4) killed Dallas Police Officer J. D. Tippit in an apparent attempt to escape, (5) resisted arrest by drawing a fully loaded pistol and attempting to shoot another police officer, (6) lied to the police after his arrest concerning important substantive matters, (7) attempted, in April 1963, to kill Maj. Gen. Edwin A. Walker, and (8) possessed the capability with a rifle which would have enabled him to commit the assassination. On the basis of these findings the Commission has concluded that Lee Harvey Oswald was the assassin of President Kennedy.

183

OPPOSITE:
Following the assassination of President Kennedy, his successor, President Lyndon B. Johnson, set up an investigative commission into the circumstances of the shooting, how it might have been prevented, and how the safety of the President could be protected in future. The 300,000-word commission report is popularly known as the Warren Report after its chairman, Chief Justice Earl Warren.

would not go far enough. Kennedy had affronted traditionalists when he had received leaders of the civil rights movement when they marched on Washington in August 1963. On the other hand, he had intervened in Cuba and Vietnam in his short Presidency and many considered him an aggressive imperialist. Black radical leader Malcolm X said that Kennedy's assassination was "chickens coming home to roost," adding that, for someone with a rural background, "chickens coming home to roost never made me sad. It only made me glad."

But for most, John Kennedy's death was a national tragedy that inspired mourning on a huge scale. His funeral was a state occasion, with 800,000 people on the streets of Washington. His youth and the manner of his death contributed to a poignant and widespread sense of loss. This was reinforced when civil rights leader Martin Luther King, Jr., was shot in April 1968, and when the President's younger brother, Senator Robert Kennedy, was assassinated three months later. Speaking in 1979, President Jimmy Carter described the sense of dislocation: "We were sure that ours was a nation of the ballot, not the bullet, until the murders of John Kennedy, Robert Kennedy, and Martin Luther King, Jr."

Transcript of THE WARREN COMMISSION REPORT

'On the basis of the evidence reviewed in this chapter, the Commission has found that Lee Harvey Oswald (1) owned and possessed the rifle used to kill President Kennedy and wound Governor Connally, (2) brought this rifle into the Depository Building on the morning of the assassination, (3) was present, at the time of the assassination, at the window from which the shots were fired, (4) killed Dallas Police Officer J. D. Tippit in an apparent attempt to escape, (5) resisted arrest by drawing a fully loaded pistol and attempting to shoot another police officer, (6) lied to the police after his arrest concerning important substantive matters, (7) attempted, in April 1963, to kill Maj. Gen. Edwin A. Walker, and (8) possessed the capability with a rifle which would have enabled him to commit the assassination. On the basis of these findings the Commission has concluded that Lee Harvey Oswald was the assassin of President Kennedy.'

NEIL ARMSTRONG, THE FIRST MAN ON THE MOON,
IS REFLECTED IN THE HELMET OF HIS FELLOW
ASTRONAUT, BUZZ ALDRIN, AS HE PHOTOGRAPHS
HIM ON THE LUNAR SURFACE

The plaque commemorating the

FIRST MANNED LUNAR LANDING

JULY 20, 1969

It is sometimes asked why the first step on the Moon was regarded as so significant when it appears to have had so little lasting consequence for anyone on Earth. The consequences of earlier exploration—like the moment when the Pilgrim Fathers first set foot on American soil—are there for all to see. Although there have been important technological advances as a result of the space program, the real significance of the event lies elsewhere. It represents the ultimate human challenge—greater than circumnavigating the world, reaching the summit of Everest, or getting to the South Pole. Many human challenges have an element of nationalistic competition, and nowhere was this more evident than in the space race between the U.S.A. and U.S.S.R.

"It suddenly struck me that that tiny pea, pretty and blue, was the Earth. I put up my thumb and shut one eye, and my thumb blotted out the planet Earth. I didn't feel like a giant. I felt very, very small."
—Neil Armstrong, 1969

By the end of the 1950s, the two nations were waging what President Dwight D. Eisenhower called "total cold war," that is, a war on all fronts—technological, scientific, military, and ideological—but without a shot being fired. A series of events, including the launch of the first artificial satellite, *Sputnik 1*, by the U.S.S.R. in 1957, cosmonaut Yuri Gagarin becoming the first human in space, and the Bay of Pigs fiasco—both in April 1961—left President John F. Kennedy feeling that the United States needed to do something spectacular so as not to appear to be falling behind. On May 25, 1961, before a special joint session of Congress, Kennedy announced his ambition to send a man safely to the Moon before the end of the decade. Although, at the time, the U.S. space program was nowhere near achieving this goal, Kennedy had been assured that it could be done by the National Aeronautics and Space Administration (NASA), the federal agency set up in 1958 with the aim of exploring space.

The Apollo manned space program, initiated by President Eisenhower, was put into accelerated development. Its earliest trial was marked by tragedy when the three astronauts on board *Apollo 1* died during a launch pad fire in 1967. The first manned Apollo craft to orbit the moon was *Apollo 8*, in December 1968, only seven months before the actual Moon landing. Then, on July 16, 1969, *Apollo 11* was launched from the Kennedy Space Center in Florida with three astronauts, commander Neil Armstrong, command module pilot Michael Collins, and lunar module pilot Edwin "Buzz" Aldrin on board. On July 20, on the far side of the Moon, the lunar module *Eagle* separated from the command module *Columbia* and began to descend toward the lunar surface.

After several unusual "program alarms," Armstrong took manual control of the module and guided it down to the Moon's surface. Six and a half hours after landing, an estimated 600 million people around the world watched as Armstrong

PLANS FOR DISASTER
In a grim reminder that failure of the Moon landing had to be contemplated, a speech was prepared for President Nixon to broadcast to the nation in the event of the Apollo 11 astronauts being stranded on the Moon. Following this address, radio communications with the Moon would have been cut off and the astronauts left alone to die. A clergyman would have commended their souls to "the deepest of the deep," as in a burial at sea.

This commemorative plaque was fixed to the leg of the lunar module descent stage ladder, which was left behind in the Sea of Tranquillity. It was signed by President Richard M. Nixon and the three astronauts of the Apollo 11 *spacecraft, Neil A. Armstrong, Edwin E. "Buzz" Aldrin, Jr., and Michael Collins.*

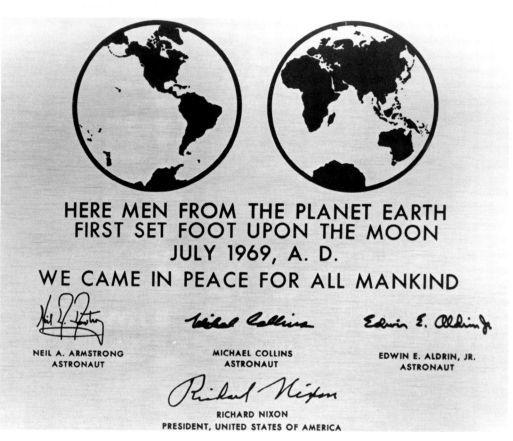

HERE MEN FROM THE PLANET EARTH
FIRST SET FOOT UPON THE MOON
JULY 1969, A. D.
WE CAME IN PEACE FOR ALL MANKIND

NEIL A. ARMSTRONG
ASTRONAUT

MICHAEL COLLINS
ASTRONAUT

EDWIN E. ALDRIN, JR.
ASTRONAUT

RICHARD NIXON
PRESIDENT, UNITED STATES OF AMERICA

descended a short ladder to the Moon's surface. His words as he put his foot to the ground—"That's one small step for man, one giant leap for mankind"—instantly became some of the most famous in history, even if his grammar was disputed. Aldrin joined him on the lunar surface and the first Moon walk began.

Armstrong and Aldrin gathered around 48 lb of lunar surface material and spent some two and a half hours outside their module. They did tests, took photographs, and set up an American flag. After seven hours' rest in the lunar module, *Eagle* lifted off from the Moon's surface, leaving behind the descent ladder with a commemorative plaque fixed to its leg.

There were five further Moon landings, when astronauts drove vehicles on the surface, and even played golf, but none were as memorable as the first. The last manned mission to the Moon was *Apollo 17* in 1972.

The space race itself is traditionally seen as ending with the Apollo-Soyuz Test Project (ASTP) in July 1975, when an Apollo craft and the Soviet ship *Soyuz 19* docked in Earth orbit. The three astronauts and two cosmonauts opened a hatch between the two craft, shook hands, exchanged gifts, visited each others' ships, and then spent almost two days together, practicing docking maneuvers.

In 2000, work began on the International Space Station, a joint project funded by NASA, the Russian Federal Space Agency, and space agencies in Japan, Canada, and Europe. The station has been permanently manned ever since. It has hosted astronauts from 12 countries and has also welcomed a handful of space tourists.

President Richard Nixon shakes hands with Soviet leader Leonid Brezhnev after the signing of the SALT treaty

The

ANTI-BALLISTIC MISSILE TREATY

May 26, 1972

By THE 1970s, the United States and the U.S.S.R. had enough nuclear weapons to devastate the planet. Neither side could use the threat of a nuclear strike, previously the ultimate sanction, against the other: their destructive power was matched. As both sides in the Cold War began to develop defensive systems against nuclear attack, the great fear was that nuclear war might be launched in the belief that a counter-strike by the other side could be repulsed by anti-ballistic missiles. In November 1969 the two great powers began Strategic Arms Limitation Talks (SALT 1).

In the early 1970s, the U.S.S.R. was at the height of its power. While the U.S. struggled to rebuild morale after defeat in Vietnam and the Watergate scandal, the U.S.S.R. was extending its influence in Asia and Africa. The Cold War entered a period of détente rather than confrontation.

The SALT 1 talks produced the Anti-Ballistic Missile (ABM) Treaty, signed in Moscow on May 26, 1972. The Senate ratified it on August 3, and it came into force on October 3. The Soviet Foreign Minister, Andrei Gromyko, described it as "a significant achievement in restraining the arms race." The treaty did not ban nuclear weapons but it did codify the United States' relationship with the U.S.S.R., and it put limits on what had become, in the absurd logic of the Cold War, an aggressive defensive policy.

The treaty proceeded "from the premise that nuclear war would have devastating consequences for all mankind," and aimed at initiating a wider disarmament process: "to achieve at the earliest possible date the cessation of the nuclear arms race and to take effective measures toward reductions in strategic arms, nuclear disarmament and general and complete disarmament." Subsequent administrations have been challenged by their attempts to rearm and yet conform with the rubric of the treaty.

The treaty could not eliminate the potential for mutually assured destruction, allowing both states to keep an anti-ballistic missile system that would launch a counter attack in the event of a hostile nuclear alert. However, the treaty restricted both states to two anti-ballistic missile systems that had to be at least 807 miles apart, with no more than 100 interceptor missiles and 100 launchers at each site.

To ensure that the treaty became part of a process, it was agreed that reviews would be conducted every five years in Geneva and amendments permitted. In 1974 the number of anti-ballistic missile sites allowed under the terms of the treaty was reduced to one. The U.S. site was at Grand Forks, North Dakota, and the Soviet site was in Moscow. In 1975 the U.S. dismantled its last anti-ballistic missile system, Safeguard.

In the years that followed, however, the trend began to be reversed. In the 1980s, President Ronald Reagan approved plans for a controversial missile defense system dubbed "Star Wars." His initiative prompted national and international protests. Then, in 1989, the Berlin Wall fell and the policies of the Soviet premier, Mikhail Gorbachev—*glasnost* (openness) and *perestroika* (restructuring)—helped to move the two long-term

WITHDRAWAL FROM THE ABM TREATY
On December 13, 2001, the White House announced: "Under the terms of the ABM Treaty, the United States is prohibited from defending its homeland against ballistic missile attack. We are also prohibited from co-operating in developing missile defenses against long-range threats with our friends and allies. Given the emergence of … new threats to our national security and the imperative of defending against them, the United States is today providing formal notification of its withdrawal from the ABM Treaty."

enemies toward a greater understanding. As the U.S.S.R. began to break up into smaller states, they all reaffirmed their support for the ABM Treaty. By 1991 it had been signed not just by the U.S., but by Russia, Kazakhstan, Ukraine, and Belarus.

In 1994, President Bill Clinton began to plan for a "theater missile defense system," abandoned when it was confirmed that it would contravene the ABM Treaty. However, under the administration of President George W. Bush, the treaty was reassessed. Former Secretary of Defense, Donald Rumsfeld, an earlier supporter of "Star Wars," described the treaty in 2001 as "ancient history." President Bush claimed that the treaty "does not recognize the present, or point us to the future. It enshrines the past … [It] hampers our ability to keep the peace, to develop defensive weapons necessary to defend America against the true threats of the twenty-first century."

Under Article 15, the ABM Treaty provided the right of either state to leave the treaty "if it decides that extraordinary events related to the subject matter of this treaty have jeopardized its supreme interests." The terrorist attacks on New York and Washington on September 11, 2001 were considered "extraordinary events" and the U.S. withdrew from the treaty on June 14, 2002. The treaty now binds neither of its original signatories.

ENCLOSURE 1

TREATY
BETWEEN THE UNITED STATES OF AMERICA
AND
THE UNION OF SOVIET SOCIALIST REPUBLICS
ON THE LIMITATION OF ANTI-BALLISTIC MISSILE SYSTEMS

The United States of America and the Union of Soviet Socialist Republics, hereinafter referred to as the Parties,

Proceeding from the premise that nuclear war would have devastating consequences for all mankind,

Considering that effective measures to limit anti-ballistic missile systems would be a substantial factor in curbing the race in strategic offensive arms and would lead to a decrease in the risk of outbreak of war involving nuclear weapons,

Proceeding from the premise that the limitation of anti-ballistic missile systems, as well as certain agreed measures with respect to the limitation of strategic offensive arms, would contribute to the creation of more favorable conditions for further negotiations on limiting strategic arms,

Mindful of their obligations under Article VI of the Treaty on the Non-Proliferation of Nuclear Weapons,

Declaring their intention to achieve at the earliest possible date the cessation of the nuclear arms race and to take effective measures toward reductions in strategic arms, nuclear disarmament, and general and complete disarmament,

Desiring to contribute to the relaxation of international tension and the strengthening of trust between States,

Have agreed as follows:

Article I

1. Each Party undertakes to limit anti-ballistic missile (ABM) systems and to adopt other measures in accordance with the provisions of this Treaty.

2. Each Party undertakes not to deploy ABM systems for a defense of the territory of its country and not to provide a base for such a defense, and not to deploy ABM systems for defense of an individual region except as provided for in Article III of this Treaty.

more

The Anti-Ballistic Missile Treaty was signed by President Richard M. Nixon and Soviet leader Leonid Brezhnev, in May 1972. Aimed at preventing an outbreak of mutually destructive nuclear war, it called for a restriction of the anti-ballistic missile sites in both countries. The treaty gave the first significant indication that the Cold War was becoming untenable.

Transcript of THE ANTI-BALLISTIC MISSILE TREATY

'TREATY BETWEEN THE UNITED STATES OF AMERICA AND THE UNION OF SOVIET SOCIALIST REPUBLICS ON THE LIMITATION OF ANTI-BALLISTIC MISSILE SYSTEMS

The United States of America and the Union of Soviet Socialist Republics, hereinafter referred to as the Parties,

Proceeding from the premise that nuclear war would have devastating consequences for all mankind,

Considering that effective measures to limit anti-ballistic missile systems would be a substantial factor in curbing the race in strategic offensive arms and would lead to a decrease in the risk of outbreak of war involving nuclear weapons,

Proceeding from the premise that the limitation of anti-ballistic missile systems, as well as certain agreed measures with respect to the limitation of strategic offensive arms, would contribute to the creation of more favorable conditions for further negotiations on limiting strategic arms,

Mindful of their obligations under Article VI of the Treaty on the Non-Proliferation of Nuclear Weapons,

Declaring their intention to achieve at the earliest possible date the cessation of the nuclear arms race and to take effective measures toward reductions in strategic arms, nuclear disarmament, and general and complete disarmament,

Desiring to contribute to the relaxation of international tension and the strengthening of trust between States,

Have agreed as follows:

Article I

1. Each Party undertakes to limit anti-ballistic missile (ABM) systems and to adopt other measures in accordance with the provisions of this Treaty.

2. Each Party undertakes not to deploy ABM systems for a defense of the territory of its country and not to provide a base for such a defense, and not to deploy ABM systems for defense of an individual region except as provided for in Article III of this Treaty.

Article II

1. For the purpose of this Treaty an ABM system is a system to counter strategic ballistic missiles or their elements in flight trajectory, currently consisting of:
   (a) ABM interceptor missiles, which are interceptor missiles constructed and deployed for an ABM role, or of a type tested in an ABM mode;
   (b) ABM launchers, which are launchers constructed and deployed for launching ABM interceptor missiles; and
   (c) ABM radars, which are radars constructed and deployed for an ABM role, or of a type tested in an ABM mode.

2. The ABM system components listed in paragraph 1 of this Article include those which are:
   (a) operational;
   (b) under construction;
   (c) undergoing testing;
   (d) undergoing overhaul, repair or conversion; or
   (e) mothballed.

Article III

Each Party undertakes not to deploy ABM systems or their components except that:

(a) within one ABM system deployment area having a radius of one hundred and fifty kilometers and centered on the Party's national capital, a Party may deploy: (1) no more than one hundred ABM launchers and no more than one hundred ABM interceptor missiles at launch sites, and (2) ABM radars within no more than six ABM radar complexes, the area of each complex being circular and having a diameter of no more than three kilometers; and

(b) within one ABM system deployment area having a radius of one hundred and fifty kilometers and containing ICBM silo launchers, a Party may deploy: (1) no more than one hundred ABM launchers and no more than one hundred ABM interceptor missiles at launch sites, (2) two large phased-array ABM radars comparable in potential to corresponding ABM radars operational or under construction on the date of signature of the Treaty in an ABM system deployment area containing ICBM silo launchers, and (3) no more than eighteen ABM radars each having a potential less than the potential of the smaller of the above-mentioned two large phased-array ABM radars.

. . .

claring their intention to ac

cessation of the nuclear

Article XIII

1. To promote the objectives and implementation of the provisions of this
    Treaty, the Parties shall establish promptly a Standing Consultative
    Commission, within the framework of which they will:
    (a) consider questions concerning compliance with the obligations
         assumed and related situations which may be considered
         ambiguous;
    (b) provide on a voluntary basis such information as either Party
         considers necessary to assure confidence in compliance with
         the obligations assumed;
    (c) consider questions involving unintended interference with
         national technical means of verification;
    (d) consider possible changes in the strategic situation which have a
         bearing on the provisions of this Treaty;
    (e) agree upon procedures and dates for destruction or dismantling
         of ABM systems or their components in cases provided for by
         the provisions of this Treaty;
    (f) consider, as appropriate, possible proposals for further
         increasing the viability of this Treaty; including proposals for
         amendments in accordance with the provisions of this Treaty;
    (g) consider, as appropriate, proposals for further measures aimed
         at limiting strategic arms.

2. The Parties through consultation shall establish, and may amend as
    appropriate, Regulations for the Standing Consultative Commission
    governing procedures, composition and other relevant matters.

Article XIV

1. Each Party may propose amendments to this Treaty. Agreed amendments
    shall enter into force in accordance with the procedures governing the entry
    into force of this Treaty.

2. Five years after entry into force of this Treaty, and at five-year intervals
    thereafter, the Parties shall together conduct a review of this Treaty.

> "Each party shall, in exercising its national sovereignty, have the right to withdraw from this treaty if it decides that extraordinary events related to the subject matter of this treaty have jeopardized its supreme interests."

Article XV

1. This Treaty shall be of unlimited duration.

2. Each Party shall, in exercising its national sovereignty, have the right to withdraw from this Treaty if it decides that extraordinary events related to the subject matter of this Treaty have jeopardized its supreme interests. It shall give notice of its decision to the other Party six months prior to withdrawal from the Treaty. Such notice shall include a statement of the extraordinary events the notifying Party regards as having jeopardized its supreme interests.

Article XVI

1. This Treaty shall be subject to ratification in accordance with the constitutional procedures of each Party. The Treaty shall enter into force on the day of the exchange of instruments of ratification.

2. This Treaty shall be registered pursuant to Article 102 of the Charter of the United Nations.

DONE at Moscow on May 26, 1972, in two copies, each in the English and Russian languages, both texts being equally authentic.

FOR THE UNITED STATES OF AMERICA:
RICHARD NIXON
President of the United States of America

FOR THE UNION OF SOVIET SOCIALIST REPUBLICS:
L. I. BREZHNEV
General Secretary of the Central Committee of the CPSU

North Vietnamese troops enter Saigon,
April 30, 1975

The

PARIS PEACE
ACCORDS

Agreement on ending the war and
restoring peace in Vietnam

January 27, 1973

In the early 1960s, the United States had offered military support to the government of South Vietnam. The South was fighting forces from Communist North Vietnam, led by Ho Chi Minh, and also Communist insurgents—the National Liberation Front, or Vietcong—within its own territory. As the decade progressed, the U.S. became more and more embroiled in the conflict, and the quick victory that had been anticipated when American troops first became involved did not come. When he took office in 1969, President Richard M. Nixon was determined to extricate the United States from the war and establish peace in the region.

The South Vietnamese had little stomach to resist the North after the U.S. withdrawal in 1973, and two years later North Vietnamese tanks rolled into Saigon, meeting no resistance.

Nixon's predecessor, President Lyndon B. Johnson, was already looking for a way out of the war in Vietnam in the late 1960s, and peace talks had begun in Paris in 1968. The last year of his administration had seen huge unrest, with riots and countless anti-war demonstrations. Hundreds of thousands of young men were dodging the draft. Rather than isolating the Communists in Vietnam, the war had prompted international outrage and solidarity with the Vietnamese people. Both the North Vietnamese and the Vietcong refused to surrender.

The U.S. knew that it could not stay in Vietnam much longer, but did not want to leave the country to Communist rule. The approach to the end of the war, however, was marked by an escalation in violence. To ensure that North Vietnam would agree to negotiate with the U.S., in late 1972 President Nixon launched a massive bombing raid, Operation Linebacker II, against targets in North Vietnam. That same year, Nixon and his National Security Adviser, Dr. Henry Kissinger, negotiated an agreement with China whereby China agreed to tolerate the bombing and encouraged the North Vietnamese to make peace with the U.S.

Meanwhile, Kissinger had been secretly working on terms for the resolution of the war with the chief North Vietnamese negotiator, Le Duc Tho, since 1970. When the various governments met in Paris in 1973, they found that they were not required to draw up a peace agreement. Kissinger and Le Duc Tho presented the Peace Accords to the other parties to sign on January 27.

The Peace Accords called for an immediate ceasefire and an end to "hatred and enmity." U.S. troops were to leave the country within 60 days, and prisoners of war would be released at the same time. The bodies of U.S. servicemen were to be repatriated. Negotiations would continue to enable the South Vietnamese to hold free elections to determine the future of their country, with the aim of accomplishing the eventual reunification of Vietnam.

PEACE PRIZES BUT NO PEACE
The secret negotiations conducted by Henry Kissinger, for the U.S., and Le Duc Tho, for North Vietnam, continued for three years before the Peace Accords were eventually signed in Paris. Kissinger and Le were jointly awarded the Nobel Peace Prize in 1973, but Le refused to accept his award, on the grounds that his country was still at war. Fighting continued in Vietnam until 1975.

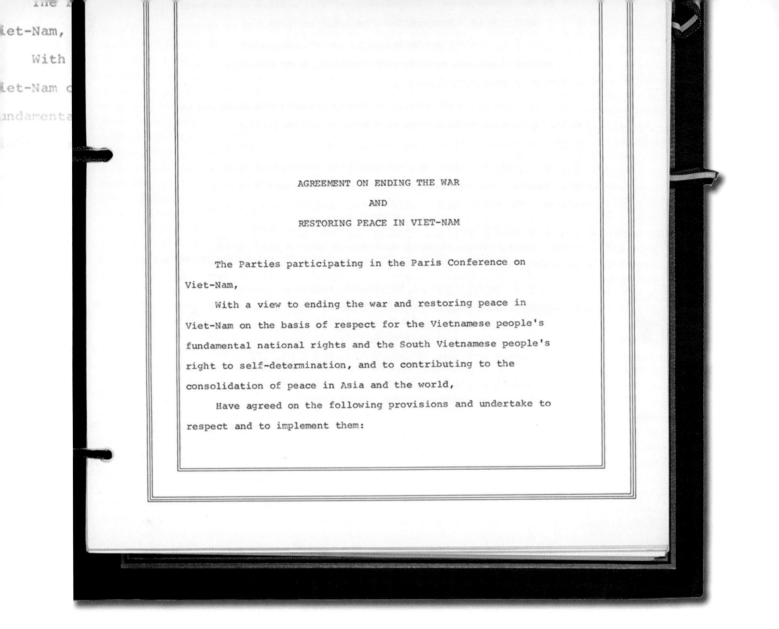

AGREEMENT ON ENDING THE WAR

AND

RESTORING PEACE IN VIET-NAM

The Parties participating in the Paris Conference on Viet-Nam,

With a view to ending the war and restoring peace in Viet-Nam on the basis of respect for the Vietnamese people's fundamental national rights and the South Vietnamese people's right to self-determination, and to contributing to the consolidation of peace in Asia and the world,

Have agreed on the following provisions and undertake to respect and to implement them:

The Peace Accords marked the end of the war in Vietnam, in which over a million Vietnamese and over 50,000 American servicemen died. The Accords were signed in Paris on January 27, 1973, by representatives of the governments of North Vietnam, South Vietnam, the Provisional Revolutionary Government (established by the Vietcong) and the United States.

However, although the Accords marked the end of U.S. military involvement in Vietnam, they did not end the war, or the "hatred and enmity" that had split the country. The day after he signed the Peace Accords, the South Vietnamese President, Nguyen Van Thieu, told his people, "If Communists come into your village, you should immediately shoot them in the head." Anyone could be considered a Communist, he said, by "talking in a Communist tone." But Thieu now had to rule without U.S. armed support, which proved impossible. When the North Vietnamese attacked the capital, Saigon, in March 1975, Thieu's army gave up the fight. Within 24 hours of its capture on April 30, Saigon had been renamed Ho Chi Minh City, after the North Vietnamese leader. The remaining U.S. intelligence servicemen and advisers fled the city by helicopter. The South Vietnamese were abandoned: there were desperate and chaotic scenes as those who had turned to the U.S. embassy for sanctuary clutched at the skids of helicopters lifting off from the embassy compound.

Transcript of THE PARIS PEACE ACCORDS

Article 1

. . . The United States and all other countries respect the independence, sovereignty, unity, and territorial integrity of Vietnam as recognized by the 1954 Geneva Agreements on Vietnam.

Article 2

A ceasefire shall be observed throughout South Vietnam as of 2400 hours GMT, on January 27, 1973. At the same hour, the United States will stop all its military activities against the territory of the Democratic Republic of Vietnam by ground, air and naval forces, wherever they may be based, and end the mining of the territorial waters, ports, harbors, and waterways of the Democratic Republic of Vietnam. The United States will remove, permanently deactivate or destroy all the mines in the territorial waters, ports, harbors, and waterways of North Vietnam as soon as this Agreement goes into effect. The complete cessation of hostilities mentioned in this Article shall be durable and without limit of time . . .

> "The United States will not continue its military involvement or intervene in the internal affairs of South Vietnam."

Article 4

The United States will not continue its military involvement or intervene in the internal affairs of South Vietnam.

Article 5

Within sixty days of the signing of this Agreement, there will be a total withdrawal from South Vietnam of troops, military advisers, and military personnel including technical military personnel and military personnel associated with the pacification program, armaments, munitions, and war material of the United States and those of the other foreign countries mentioned in Article 3(a). Advisers from the above-mentioned countries to all paramilitary organizations and the police force will also be withdrawn within the same period of time.

Article 6

The dismantlement of all military bases in South Vietnam of the United States and of the other foreign countries mentioned in Article 3(a) shall be completed within sixty days of the signing of this Agreement . . .

Article 8

(a)   The return of captured military personnel and foreign civilians of the parties shall be carried out simultaneously with and completed not later than the same day as the troop withdrawal mentioned in Article 5. The parties shall exchange complete lists of the above-mentioned captured military personnel and foreign civilians on the day of the signing of this Agreement.

(b)   The Parties shall help each other to get information about those military personnel and foreign civilians of the parties missing in action, to determine the location and take care of the graves of the dead so as to facilitate the exhumation and repatriation of the remains, and to take any such other measures as may be required to get information about those still considered missing in action.

(c)   The question of the return of Vietnamese civilian personnel captured and detained in South Vietnam will be resolved by the two South Vietnamese parties on the basis of the principles of Article 21(b) of the Agreement on the Cessation of Hostilities in Vietnam of July 20, 1954. The two South Vietnamese parties will do so in a spirit of national reconciliation and concord, with a view to ending hatred and enmity, in order to ease suffering and to reunite families. The two South Vietnamese parties will do their utmost to resolve this question within ninety days after the cease-fire comes into effect . . .

> "The return of captured military personnel and foreign civilians of the parties shall be carried out simultaneously with and completed not later than the same day as the troop withdrawal."

Article 11

Immediately after the ceasefire, the two South Vietnamese parties will: achieve national reconciliation and concord, end hatred and enmity, prohibit all acts of reprisal and discrimination against individuals or organizations that have collaborated with one side or the other; ensure the democratic liberties of the people: personal freedom, freedom of speech, freedom of the press, freedom of meeting, freedom of organization, freedom of political activities, freedom of belief, freedom of movement, freedom of residence, freedom of work, right to property ownership, and right to free enterprise . . .

Chapter V The Reunification of Vietnam and The Relationship Between North and South Vietnam

Article 15

The reunification of Vietnam shall be carried out step by step through peaceful means on the basis of discussions and agreements between North and South Vietnam, without coercion or annexation by either party, and without foreign interference. The time for reunification will be agreed upon by North and South Vietnam. Pending reunification:

> "The reunification of Vietnam shall be carried out step by step through peaceful means on the basis of discussions and agreements between North and South Vietnam, without coercion or annexation by either party, and without foreign interference."

(a) The military demarcation line between the two zones at the 17th parallel is only provisional and not a political or territorial boundary, as provided for in paragraph 6 of the Final Declaration of the 1954 Geneva Conference.

(b) North and South Vietnam shall respect the Demilitarized Zone on either side of the Provisional Military Demarcation Line.

(c) North and South Vietnam shall promptly start negotiations with a view to reestablishing normal relations in various fields. Among the questions to be negotiated are the modalities of civilian movement across the Provisional Military Demarcation Line.

(d) North and South Vietnam shall not join any military alliance or military bloc and shall not allow foreign powers to maintain military bases, troops, military advisers, and military personnel on their respective territories, as stipulated in the 1954 Geneva Agreements on Vietnam ...

Article 22

The ending of the war, the restoration of peace in Vietnam, and the strict implementation of this Agreement will create conditions for establishing a new, equal and mutually beneficial relationship between the United States and the Democratic Republic of Vietnam on the basis of respect of each other's independence and sovereignty, and non-interference in each other's internal affairs. At the same time this will ensure stable peace in Vietnam and contribute to the preservation of lasting peace in Indochina and Southeast Asia ...

*et-Nam,

With a view to ending the war and restor

*et-Nam on the basis of respect for the Vietn

*undamental national rights and the South V

The Return of Captured Military Personnel and Foreign Civilians

Article 1

The parties signatory to the Agreement shall return the captured military personnel of the parties mentioned in Article 8(a) of the Agreement as follows: - all captured military personnel of the United States and those of the other foreign countries mentioned in Article 3(a) of the Agreement shall be returned to United States authorities; - all captured Vietnamese military personnel, whether belonging to regular or irregular armed forces, shall be returned to the two South Vietnamese parties; they shall be returned to that South Vietnamese party under whose command they served.

Article 2

All captured civilians who are nationals of the United States or of any other foreign countries mentioned in Article 3(a) of the Agreement shall be returned to United States authorities. All other captured foreign civilians shall be returned to the authorities of their country of nationality by any one of the parties willing and able to do so.

Article 3

The parties shall today exchange complete lists of captured persons mentioned in Articles 1 and 2 of this Protocol.

Article 4

(a) The return of all captured persons mentioned in Articles 1 and 2 of this Protocol shall be completed within sixty days of the signing of the Agreement at a rate no slower than the rate of withdrawal from South Vietnam of United States forces and those of the other foreign countries mentioned in Article 5 of the Agreement.

(b) Persons who are seriously ill, wounded or maimed, old persons and women shall be returned first. The remainder shall be returned either by returning all from one detention place after another or in order of their dates of capture, beginning with those who have been held the longest . . .

President Richard M. Nixon and
Chief of Staff Bob Haldeman in the
White House

The

WATERGATE SCANDAL

The "Smoking Gun" tape
Recording made at the White House

June 23, 1974

On July 17, 1972, in the run-up to the 1972 Presidential election, five men were arrested for breaking into the headquarters of the Democratic National Committee at the Watergate Hotel complex in Washington D.C. In their possession they had wiretapping equipment. The trail from the break-in appeared to lead back to the White House. At first it seemed unthinkable that President Richard M. Nixon could be implicated. He had achieved a massive landslide in the 1968 election, carrying 49 of 50 states and over 60 percent of the popular vote. However, secret conversations, anonymous sources, and two years of investigation and cover-up revealed serious misdemeanors in Nixon's administration. The Watergate scandal exposed not only government espionage on political opponents, but also that the administration was involved in widespread surveillance of liberals, academics, artists, and others whom Nixon distrusted, and corruption at the highest levels of government.

■ *Richard Nixon had withheld recordings of his conversations in the Oval Office from the Watergate inquiry. After the Supreme Court ruled that he must release them, he complied and then resigned from office. Announcing his resignation on television on August 8, 1974, he claimed he "no longer had a strong enough political base." For the rest of his life he refused to acknowledge any personal wrongdoing in the Watergate scandal.*

DEEP THROAT, DEEP SECRET

The identity of the Washington Post's *source, "Deep Throat," was only revealed in 2005. At the time of the Watergate scandal, Mark Felt was the deputy director of the F.B.I. A tape from October 19, 1972 shows that Bob Haldeman suspected Felt was the leak but warned, "If we move on him, he'll go out and unload everything. He knows everything." When* Washington Post *journalist Bob Woodward wanted to talk to Deep Throat he would move a flowerpot with a red flag in it on his apartment balcony. Woodward knew the identity of Deep Throat, but never made the information public.*

The judge sentencing the men arrested for the Watergate break-in in the summer of 1972 suspected a cover-up, and announced that heavy sentences would be passed unless the defendants told him why the break-in had taken place. His tactic worked, and started an unstoppable chain of events. In March 1973, one of the defendants, James W. McCord Jr., wrote a letter to the court saying that there had been pressure on the defendants from the White House to plead guilty so that there would be no further investigation.

Meanwhile, Bob Woodward, a reporter on the *Washington Post* who was following the unfolding story, began to have meetings with a man known by the code name "Deep Throat," who revealed details of the cover-up. Woodward and Carl Bernstein, another *Post* reporter, published the information and forced further questions about who in the White House had been involved.

In May 1973 a Select Committee on Presidential Campaign Activities launched televised hearings in the Senate. At the hearings, Republican Senator Howard Baker from Tennessee asked a question that revealed the direction in which the investigation was turning: "What did the President know, and when did he know it?" The only way such a question could be answered would be to know what Nixon was saying to his most trusted advisers at the time. Then, on July 16, 1973, a former White House employee, Alexander P. Butterfield, announced that all Oval Office conversations were recorded. If the investigation into the Watergate scandal could hear the tapes, they would know what the President knew, and when.

On July 23, the Committee and the special Watergate prosecutor, Archibald Cox, subpoenaed the tapes of Nixon's conversations. Suspicions were further aroused when Nixon refused to give up the tapes, claiming the right of executive privilege and that there were national

```
                    TRANSCRIPT OF A RECORDING OF A
                    MEETING BETWEEN THE PRESIDENT
                    AND H.R. HALDEMAN IN THE OVAL
                    OFFICE ON JUNE 23, 1972 FROM
                          10:04 TO 11:39 AM
```

<u>June 23, 1972 FROM 10:04 TO 11:39 AM</u>   3

* * * * * * * * *

HALDEMAN: okay -that's fine. Now, on the investi-
                   gation, you know, the Democratic break-in
                   thing, we're back to the-in the, the problem
                   area because the FBI is not under control,
                   because Gray doesn't exactly know how to
                   control them, and they have, their
                   investigation is now leading into some
                   productive areas, because they've been able
                   to trace the money, not through the money
                   itself, but through the bank, you know,
                   sources - the banker himself. And, and it
                   goes in some directions we don't want it to
                   go. Ah, also there have been some things,
                   like an informant came in off the street to
                   the FBI in Miami, who was a photographer or
                   has a friend who is a photographer who
                   developed some films through this guy,
                   Barker, and the films had pictures of
                   Democratic National Committee letter head
                   documents and things. So I guess, so it's
                   things like that that are gonna, that are
                   filtering in. Mitchell came up with
                   yesterday, and John Dean analyzed very
                   carefully last night and concludes, concurs
                   now with Mitchell's recommendation that the
                   only way to solve this, and we're set up
                   beautifully to do it, ah, in that and
                   that...the only network that paid any
                   attention to it last night was NBC...they
                   did a massive story on the Cuban...

PRESIDENT: That's right.

HALDEMAN: thing.

PRESIDENT: Right.

HALDEMAN: That the way to handle this now is for us to

Tapes of conversations between President Richard M. Nixon and his Chief of Staff Bob Haldeman on June 23, 1972 revealed that Nixon wanted to stop the F.B.I. investigation into what had become known as the Watergate scandal. Nixon tried very hard to keep the tape from the investigation, and gave up only after three articles of impeachment were laid against him.

rea because the FBI is not under
ecause Gray doesn't exactly know
ontrol them, and they have, their
nvestigation is now leading into
roductive areas, because they've
o trace the money, not throu

GREAT AMERICAN DOCUMENTS

security issues at stake. In October the Court of Appeals upheld the order to release the tapes. Nixon's response was to order Elliot Richardson, the Attorney General, to fire Archibald Cox. He was fired, but only after Richardson and his deputy William Ruckelshaus had been forced to resign because they would not agree to do as the President asked. This episode became known as the "Saturday night massacre."

As public demand for publication of the tapes grew, the President was thrown on the defensive, declaring on November 17, "I am not a crook." When he eventually released the tapes on December 8, one of them had 18.5 minutes of silence, where recordings had been erased, and two of the nine requested were missing. The President maintained that they had never existed.

Meanwhile, the investigation into the government began to produce evidence of widespread corruption. In December 1973 Vice-President Spiro T. Agnew was found guilty of tax evasion. The following month, Herbert Porter, Nixon's campaign aide, pleaded guilty to lying to the F.B.I., and in February Nixon's personal lawyer pleaded guilty to charges of illegal election practices. Seven of Nixon's former aides were indicted on March 1, 1974 for conspiracy to hinder investigations. In April the Republican lieutenant governor of California and Nixon's previous appointments secretary were charged with lying.

Then, in July 1974, three articles of impeachment were directed at President Nixon for obstruction of justice, abuse of power, and contempt of Congress. Finally, on August 5, Nixon provided transcripts of the missing tapes he had previously denied existed. Conversations recorded in the Oval Office on June 23, 1972 proved that he had sanctioned a cover-up. The tapes recorded Bob Haldeman warning Nixon that the F.B.I. investigation might go "in some directions we don't want it to go." Nixon made it clear he wanted the F.B.I. to be misdirected and for the investigation to be halted: "This is a hunt that will uncover a lot of things. You open that scab there's a hell of a lot of things and . . . it would be very detrimental to have this thing go any further . . . Don't lie to them to the extent to say there is no involvement, but just say this is sort of a comedy of errors, bizarre, without getting into it . . . Don't go any further into this case, period." On hearing this tape, Congressman Barber Conable remarked that it "looked like a smoking gun," meaning that it proved Nixon's involvement, if not his guilt. Four days later, Nixon resigned, the only President to resign from office in U.S. history. Gerald Ford, who succeeded him as President, prevented a truck containing Nixon's papers and further Oval Office tapes from leaving the White House grounds: Congress allowed the material to be seized on behalf of the American people.

In all, 40 government officials were indicted in the Watergate investigation, and Bob Haldeman was imprisoned in 1977. Nixon was granted an unconditional pardon by Gerald Ford before he could be prosecuted. In a national broadcast, Ford announced: "Richard Nixon and his loved ones have suffered enough and will continue to suffer." Widely criticized at the time for his decision, Ford was later acknowledged to have put an end to the debilitating effect the Watergate scandal had on public morale.

Transcript of THE "SMOKING GUN" TAPE

Haldeman: Now, on the investigation, you know, the Democratic break-in thing, we're back to the—in the, the problem area because the FBI is not under control, because Gray doesn't exactly know how to control them, and they have, their investigation is now leading into some productive areas, because they've been able to trace the money, not through the money itself, but through the bank, you know, sources—the banker himself. And, and it goes in some directions we don't want it to go. Ah, also there have been some things, like an informant came in off the street to the FBI in Miami, who was a photographer or has a friend who is a photographer who developed some films through this guy, Barker, and the films had pictures of Democratic National Committee letterhead documents and things. So I guess, so it's things like that that are gonna, that are filtering in. Mitchell came up with yesterday, and John Dean analyzed very carefully last night and concludes, concurs now with Mitchell's recommendation that the only way to solve this, and we're set up beautifully to do it, ah, in that and that . . . the only network that paid any attention to it last night was NBC . . . they did a massive story on the Cuban . . .

Nixon: That's right.

Haldeman: . . . thing.

Nixon: Right.

Haldeman: That the way to handle this now is for us to have Walters call Pat Gray and just say, "Stay the hell out of this . . . this is ah, business here we don't want you to go any further on it." That's not an unusual development . . .

Nixon: Um huh.

Haldeman: . . . and, uh, that would take care of it.

Nixon: What about Pat Gray, ah, you mean he doesn't want to?

Haldeman: Pat does want to. He doesn't know how to, and he doesn't have, he doesn't have any basis for doing it. Given this, he will then have the basis. He'll call Mark Felt in, and the two of them . . . and Mark Felt wants to cooperate because . . .

Nixon: Yeah.

Haldeman: he's ambitious . . .

Nixon: Yeah.

Haldeman: Ah, he'll call him in and say, "We've got the signal from across the river to, to put the hold on this." And that will fit rather well because the FBI agents who are working the case, at this point, feel that's what it is. This is CIA.

Nixon: But they've traced the money to 'em.

Haldeman: Well they have, they've traced to a name, but they haven't gotten to the guy yet.

Nixon: Would it be somebody here?

rea because the FBI is not under
ecause Gray doesn't exactly know
ontrol them, and they have, the
nvestigation is now leading int
roductive areas, because they

Haldeman:	Ken Dahlberg.
Nixon:	Who the hell is Ken Dahlberg?
Haldeman:	He's ah, he gave $25,000 in Minnesota and ah, the check went directly in to this, to this guy Barker.
Nixon:	Maybe he's a . . . bum.
Nixon:	He didn't get this from the committee though, from Stans.
Haldeman:	Yeah. It is. It is. It's directly traceable and there's some more through some Texas people in—that went to the Mexican bank which they can also trace to the Mexican bank . . . they'll get their names today. And . . . [pause]
Nixon:	Well, I mean, ah, there's no way . . . I'm just thinking if they don't cooperate, what do they say? They they, they were approached by the Cubans. That's what Dahlberg has to say, the Texans too. Is that the idea?
Haldeman:	Well, if they will. But then we're relying on more and more people all the time. That's the problem. And ah, they'll stop if we could, if we take this other step . . .
Nixon:	Of course, this is a, this is a hunt, you will—that will uncover a lot of things. You open that scab there's a hell of a lot of things and that we just feel that it would be very detrimental to have this thing go any further. This involves these Cubans, Hunt, and a lot of hanky-panky that we have nothing to do with ourselves. Well what the hell, did Mitchell know about this thing to any much of a degree?
Haldeman:	I think so. I don't think he knew the details, but I think he knew.
Nixon:	He didn't know how it was going to be handled though, with Dahlberg and the Texans and so forth? Well, who was the asshole that did? [Unintelligible] Is it Liddy? Is that the fellow? He must be a little nuts.
Haldeman:	He is.
Nixon:	I mean he just isn't well screwed on is he? Isn't that the problem?
Haldeman:	No, but he was under pressure, apparently, to get more information, and as he got more pressure, he pushed the people harder to move harder on . . .
Nixon:	Pressure from Mitchell?
Haldeman:	Apparently.
Nixon:	Oh, Mitchell, Mitchell was at the point that you made on this, that exactly what I need from you is on the—
Haldeman:	Gemstone, yeah.
Nixon:	All right, fine, I understand it all. We won't second-guess Mitchell and the rest. Thank God it wasn't Colson.
Haldeman:	The FBI interviewed Colson yesterday. They determined that would be a good thing to do.
Nixon:	Um hum.

Haldeman: Ah, to have him take a . . .

Nixon: Um hum.

Haldeman: An interrogation, which he did, and that, the FBI guys working the case had concluded that there were one or two possibilities, one, that this was a White House—they don't think that there is anything at the Election Committee—they think it was either a White House operation and they had some obscure reasons for it, non-political . . .

Nixon: Uh huh.

Haldeman: or it was a . . .

Nixon: Cuban thing—

Haldeman: Cubans and the CIA. And after their interrogation of, of . . .

Nixon: Colson.

Haldeman: Colson, yesterday, they concluded it was not the White House, but are now convinced it is a CIA thing, so the CIA turn off would . . .

Nixon: Well, not sure of their analysis, I'm not going to get that involved.

Haldeman: No, sir. We don't want you to.

Nixon: You call them in . . . Play it tough. That's the way they play it and that's the way we are going to play it.

Haldeman: O.K. We'll do it.

 . . .

Nixon: When you get in these people when you . . . get these people in, say . . . —ah, without going into the details . . . don't, don't lie to them to the extent to say there is no involvement, but just say this is sort of a comedy of errors, bizarre, without getting into it—"the President believes that it is going to open the whole Bay of Pigs thing up again. And, ah, because these people are plugging for, for keeps and that they should call the FBI in and say that we wish for the country, don't go any further into this case, period!"

Haldeman: O.K.

Nixon: That's the way to put it, do it straight.

Haldeman: Get more done for our cause by the opposition than by us at this point.

Nixon: You think so?

Haldeman: I think so, yeah.

Egyptian President Anwar Sadat (left) shakes hands with
Israeli Prime Minister Menachem Begin in front of
President Jimmy Carter at Camp David

The
CAMP DAVID
ACCORDS

September 17, 1978

ALTHOUGH "ARAB INHABITANTS of the State of Israel" were accorded "full and equal citizenship and due representation in all its provisional and permanent institutions" as part of the Declaration of the Establishment of the State of Israel in 1948, few Palestinian Arabs stayed in the new Jewish state. In 1967 Israel defeated Jordan, Egypt, and Syria in the Six-Day War, capturing the West Bank from Jordan, the Golan Heights from Syria, and Gaza and the Sinai Peninsula from Egypt. There was fury across the Arab world. In 1973, Egypt and Syria struck against Israel on Yom Kippur, the holiest day in the Jewish calendar. Although taken by surprise, Israel beat them back. A period of uneasy peace ensued.

■ In 1978, the Israeli and Egyptian governments met at Camp David to draw up a peace treaty and agreement on the future of the Middle East. Mediation was conducted by President Jimmy Carter. Although peace in the Middle East proved elusive, Menachem Begin of Israel and Anwar Sadat of Egypt were both awarded the Nobel Peace Prize.

The U.S. Secretary of State at the time, Henry Kissinger, said of the 1973 war between Israel and its Arab neighbors: "What we wanted was the most massive Arab defeat possible . . . we sought to break up the Arab united front." It looked as though the U.S. and Israel had achieved their goal. In 1977, Anwar Sadat became the first Arab leader to visit Israel, where he addressed the Israeli parliament, the Knesset. It was a move toward establishing relations with Israel, following several stalled or unsuccessful international initiatives. The following year, Sadat agreed to meet Israel's Prime Minister Menachem Begin on neutral ground in order to draw up an agreement to end hostile relations. However, there was little amicable feeling between the two. In fact they loathed each other so much that most of the negotiating at Camp David was conducted by President Carter, who carried messages between the two and supplied feedback about the emerging accords to either side.

There were two agreements that came out of Camp David. One was the "Framework for Peace in the Middle East" and the other was the "Framework for the Conclusion of a Peace Treaty between Egypt and Israel."

The Peace Treaty was signed in March 1979. It ensured that economic boycotts of Israel would be lifted and that Israel would be allowed access to the Suez Canal. Ambassadors were exchanged, airline flights established, and, from 1980, Egypt began supplying crude oil to Israel. In return, Israeli forces withdrew from Sinai, and Egypt was rewarded with billions of dollars of U.S. subsidies, a practice that continues today.

The fact that the Peace Treaty accompanied a framework intended for the rest of the Middle East, with no commitment to Palestinian self-determination, infuriated people across the region. The framework allowed the Palestinians to have some form of government but stated, "Egypt, Israel, and Jordan will agree on the modalities for establishing an elected self-governing authority in the West Bank and Gaza. The delegations of Egypt

CAMP DAVID—THE PRESIDENT'S RETREAT

Camp David, set in a national park in Maryland, not far from Washington D.C., is the U.S. President's official country residence, a refuge, and a less formal area for entertaining than the White House. Nevertheless, it has been the venue for two series of Middle East peace negotiations (the latest in 2000) and numerous significant meetings between the President and other world leaders.

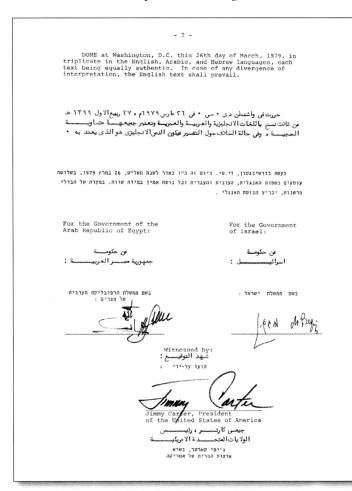

and Jordan may include Palestinians." This agreement would "define the powers and responsibilities" of the Palestinian authority. The police force "may include Jordanian citizens. In addition, Israeli and Jordanian forces will participate in joint patrols." Furthermore, the fate of Palestinian refugees was to be decided by a committee of "representatives of Egypt, Israel, Jordan, and the self-governing authority" of Palestine.

The Palestinians were offered the chance to join either the Egyptian or Jordanian delegation in determining their future, which would be decided by Israel and Israel's new ally, Egypt. The Palestine Liberation Organization, since 1974 the official Palestinian national authority, rejected the agreement and there was a feeling across the Arab world that the Egyptian government had betrayed the Palestinians in order to side with the United States, and benefit from U.S. aid. In 1981, President Sadat was assassinated, his killers later identified as Muslim radicals who opposed Sadat's landmark peace treaty with Israel, and Egypt was suspended from the Arab League until 1989. The anger has not gone away. Today the Kifaya—Arabic for "Enough"—movement, and the Muslim Brotherhood continue to protest against Egypt's relationship with Israel and America.

Despite the fact that the framework claimed that the Middle East "can become a model for coexistence and co-operation among nations," aggression, violence, and antagonism continue to characterize the region. Thousands of Lebanese and Palestinians were killed when Israel invaded Lebanon in 1982, and a Palestinian *intifada* (uprising) that began in September 2000 has caused the death of more than 1,000 Israelis in a series of terrorist attacks and suicide bombings. Since 2002, Israel has been constructing a 420-mile defensive barrier along the West Bank. The barrier has reduced terrorist attacks by 90 percent; however, it violates international law and restricts the movement and daily life of Palestinians in the area, who can no longer cross freely into Israel. In July 2006, conflict flared once more between Lebanon and Israel. Nearly 1,500 were killed, most of them civilians, and serious damage was done in both countries.

After difficult negotiations that frequently threatened to collapse, President Anwar Sadat of Egypt and the Israeli Prime Minister, Menachem Begin, drew up a "Framework for Peace in the Middle East" at Camp David in September 1978. The framework opened diplomatic channels between the two countries and proposed a solution to wider Middle East issues.

Transcript of THE CAMP DAVID ACCORDS

'Muhammad Anwar al-Sadat, President of the Arab Republic of Egypt, and Menachem Begin, Prime Minister of Israel, met with Jimmy Carter, President of the United States of America, at Camp David from September 5 to September 17, 1978, and have agreed on the following framework for peace in the Middle East. They invite other parties to the Arab-Israel conflict to adhere to it.

Preamble

The search for peace in the Middle East must be guided by the following:
• The agreed basis for a peaceful settlement of the conflict between Israel and its neighbors is United Nations Security Council Resolution 242, in all its parts.
• After four wars during 30 years, despite intensive human efforts, the Middle East, which is the cradle of civilization and the birthplace of three great religions, does not enjoy the blessings of peace. The people of the Middle East yearn for peace so that the vast human and natural resources of the region can be turned to the pursuits of peace and so that this area can become a model for coexistence and cooperation among nations.

"... the Middle East, which is the cradle of civilization and the birthplace of three great religions, does not enjoy the blessings of peace."

• The historic initiative of President Sadat in visiting Jerusalem and the reception accorded to him by the parliament, government and people of Israel, and the reciprocal visit of Prime Minister Begin to Ismailia, the peace proposals made by both leaders, as well as the warm reception of these missions by the peoples of both countries, have created an unprecedented opportunity for peace which must not be lost if this generation and future generations are to be spared the tragedies of war.
• The provisions of the Charter of the United Nations and the other accepted norms of international law and legitimacy now provide accepted standards for the conduct of relations among all states.
• To achieve a relationship of peace, in the spirit of Article 2 of the United Nations Charter, future negotiations between Israel and any neighbor prepared to negotiate peace and security with it are necessary for the purpose of carrying out all the provisions and principles of Resolutions 242 and 338.
• Peace requires respect for the sovereignty, territorial integrity and political independence of every state in the area and their right to live in peace within secure and recognized boundaries free from threats or acts of force. Progress toward that goal can accelerate movement toward a new era of reconciliation in the Middle East marked by cooperation in promoting economic development, in maintaining stability and in assuring security.

دى • سى • فى ٢٦ مارس ١٩٧٩م ، ٢٧ ربيع الأول ١٣٩٩ ه
ة العربية وتعتبر جميعهــا متساوي

• Security is enhanced by a relationship of peace and by cooperation between nations which enjoy normal relations. In addition, under the terms of peace treaties, the parties can, on the basis of reciprocity, agree to special security arrangements such as demilitarized zones, limited armaments areas, early warning stations, the presence of international forces, liaison, agreed measures for monitoring and other arrangements that they agree are useful.

> "This framework . . . is intended . . . to constitute a basis for peace not only between Egypt and Israel, but also between Israel and each of its other neighbors which is prepared to negotiate peace with Israel on this basis."

Framework

Taking these factors into account, the parties are determined to reach a just, comprehensive, and durable settlement of the Middle East conflict through the conclusion of peace treaties based on Security Council resolutions 242 and 338 in all their parts. Their purpose is to achieve peace and good neighborly relations. They recognize that for peace to endure, it must involve all those who have been most deeply affected by the conflict. They therefore agree that this framework, as appropriate, is intended by them to constitute a basis for peace not only between Egypt and Israel, but also between Israel and each of its other neighbors which is prepared to negotiate peace with Israel on this basis.

. . .

• **Egypt-Israel**

1. Egypt-Israel undertake not to resort to the threat or the use of force to settle disputes. Any disputes shall be settled by peaceful means in accordance with the provisions of Article 33 of the U.N. Charter.

2. In order to achieve peace between them, the parties agree to negotiate in good faith with a goal of concluding within three months from the signing of the Framework a peace treaty between them while inviting the other parties to the conflict to proceed simultaneously to negotiate and conclude similar peace treaties with a view to achieving a comprehensive peace in the area. The Framework for the Conclusion of a Peace Treaty between Egypt and Israel will govern the peace negotiations between them. The parties will agree on the modalities and the timetable for the implementation of their obligations under the treaty.

• **Associated Principles**

1. Egypt and Israel state that the principles and provisions described below should apply to peace treaties between Israel and each of its neighbors – Egypt, Jordan, Syria and Lebanon.

2. Signatories shall establish among themselves relationships normal to states at peace with one another. To this end, they should undertake to abide by all the provisions of the U.N. Charter. Steps to be taken in this respect include:
   1. full recognition;
   2. abolishing economic boycotts;
   3. guaranteeing that under their jurisdiction the citizens of the other parties shall enjoy the protection of the due process of law.

3. Signatories should explore possibilities for economic development in the context of final peace treaties, with the objective of contributing to the atmosphere of peace, cooperation and friendship which is their common goal.

4. Claims commissions may be established for the mutual settlement of all financial claims.

5. The United States shall be invited to participate in the talks on matters related to the modalities of the implementation of the agreements and working out the timetable for the carrying out of the obligations of the parties.

6. The United Nations Security Council shall be requested to endorse the peace treaties and ensure that their provisions shall not be violated. The permanent members of the Security Council shall be requested to underwrite the peace treaties and ensure respect or the provisions. They shall be requested to conform their policies and actions with the undertaking contained in this Framework.

For the Government of the
Arab Republic of Egypt:
MUHAMMED ANWAR AL-SADAT

For the Government of Israel:
MENACHEM BEGIN

Witnessed by:
JIMMY CARTER
President of the United States of America

The World Trade Center burns
following the September 11 terrorist
attack on New York City

MISSING PERSONS MESSAGE BOARD

Following the terrorist attacks on New York City and Washington D.C.

September 11, 2001

THE ENORMITY OF the September 11 terrorist attacks on New York City and Washington D.C. and their global consequences can sometimes obscure the human tragedies that took place. Faces remind us of each individual life that was lost. The original purpose of the message boards, and of the notices distributed in streets and hospital foyers, or posted on streetlights, walls, subways, and phone booths, was to find the missing, in the hope that they were wandering the city in a state of shock or waiting unidentified in hospital beds. Soon, however, the faces on the boards became records of the dead and, later, a memorial exhibition that toured the United States, finally forming part of a collective historical document at the Smithsonian Institute.

Until December 31, 2001, the New York Times published daily obituaries of the men and women who died in the World Trade Center attacks, and continued to publish additional profiles and tributes for some time after that. The profiles, under the title "Portraits of Grief," are part of the newspaper's permanent online archive.

On the morning of September 11, 2001, four commercial jet airliners were hijacked by 19 men affiliated to the international Islamic terrorist organization al-Qaeda. American Airlines flight 11 was flown into the North Tower of the World Trade Center in New York; United Airlines flight 175 was flown into the South Tower less than 20 minutes later. American Airlines flight 77 was flown into one of the ten sections of the Pentagon in Washington. The destination of United Airlines flight 93 is unclear—it crashed near Shanksville, Pennsylvania, after passengers learned about the earlier attacks and tried to overcome the hijackers. All 246 people on the four planes died, including the suicidal hijackers. The twin towers of the World Trade Center, once the world's tallest buildings, collapsed, and the other five World Trade Center buildings were either leveled or severely damaged. In New York, 2,602 people died, most of them in or above the floors of the twin towers where the planes struck the buildings. Of these, 343 were New York City firefighters, and 60 were police officers. The attack on the Pentagon killed 125. The average age of those who died in New York was 40.

Most of these events were recorded by chance in unforgettable images that were relayed almost instantly across the world. People using the cameras on their cell phones to record the aftermath of the first attack on the World Trade Center caught the moment when the second plane flew directly into the South Tower. A French film crew, in the city making a documentary about New York firefighters, recorded the attacks, the rescue operation, and the collapse of the towers as the events occurred. People were photographed falling or leaping from the towers, and fleeing the smoke and debris from the ruined buildings. Poignant rather than harrowing, perhaps because they were taken in happy times rather than in the last terrible moments, the faces on the missing persons boards became iconic images of the tragedy.

The enmity behind the attacks of 9/11 is rooted in opposing ideologies, in the United States' involvement in the Middle East, its support for Israel, and the West's dependence on oil from the region. In 1998, Osama bin Laden, the head of al-Qaeda, declared a holy war on the United States and issued a *fatwa* (a ruling on a point of Islamic law that is given by a recognized authority) calling for the killing of U.S. citizens. The coordinated 9/11 attacks, for which bin Laden later admitted

OPPOSITE:
A message board on a New York sidewalk with pictures of people missing in the attacks on the twin towers of the World Trade Center on September 11, 2001.

responsibility, were an attempt to inflict economic damage and show that the U.S. could be targeted in its homeland. They also aimed to destabilize regimes and international initiatives in the Middle East.

The response to the attacks matched the scale of the atrocity. President George W. Bush set up the Office of Homeland Security and the U.S.A. PATRIOT Act was passed, "Uniting and Strengthening America by Providing Appropriate Tools Required to Intercept and Obstruct Terrorism." Controversially circumventing civil liberties, it dramatically increased U.S. law-enforcement powers. Thousands of military reservists were called up, and President Bush declared "war against terrorism." The administration took a hard line, announced in the President's address to the nation on the evening of 9/11: "We will make no distinction between the terrorists who committed these acts and those who harbor them."

In the years since the 9/11 attacks, there have been further atrocities committed by groups affiliated with al-Qaeda, most notably in Bali in 2002 and 2005, in Madrid in 2004, and in London in July 2005. "War on terror" became an accepted phrase in political and journalistic rhetoric, and was used to justify military interventions and the introduction of emergency legislation around the world. The policy and its rhetoric have been much criticized in the U.S. While many supported the idea in the immediate aftermath of 9/11, it was increasingly seen to be an inappropriate strategy against ideological extremism, and radical Islamic militancy in particular. Although it remained a key issue of the Bush administration, by late 2006 other governments, including Britain, had stopped using the expression "war on terror," which was seen as a provocation of Muslim communities throughout the Islamic world.

AN AMERICAN TRAGEDY

On March 8, 2004, Debra Burlingame, sister of the pilot of the hijacked plane that was flown into the Pentagon, wrote in the Wall Street Journal: *"In the immediate aftermath of the September 11 terrorist attacks on our country, the families of those who perished on that day became forever linked through our shared anguish and grief. But the '9/11 families' are not a monolithic group that speaks in one voice . . . this was a tragedy that was experienced and felt not just by us, but by all Americans. The American people responded to the horrors of that day with unflinching courage and an outpouring of love, support, and empathy, the memory of which fills me with a gratitude that I can never repay."*

Index

Page numbers in **bold** refer to main entries. Page numbers in *italics* refer to picture captions.

Acknowledgments

Every effort has been made to contact the holders of copyright material. However, the publishers will be glad to rectify in future editions any inadvertent omissions brought to their attention.

The authors would like to thank the following people for their help in researching and supplying facsimile material for this book:

Pat Aske of Pembroke College, Cambridge; Jane Fitzgerald of the U.S. National Archives; Josh Horton; Ros Morley; Magdalena Söderqvist of SIPRI, Sweden; Yolanda Theunissen of the Osher Map Library and Smith Center for Cartographic Education, University of Southern Maine; Dr Simon Whitby, Director of the Bradford Disarmament Research Centre, University of Bradford.

The publisher would like to thank the following for permission to reproduce copyright material:

pp. 158–9 by kind permission of The Franklin D. Roosevelt Presidential Library; p. 135 by permission of The National Archives, Kew; p. 167 by kind permission of the Harry S. Truman Museum & Library; p. 66 Indiana Historical Bureau; p. 18 Collection of The New-York Historical Society; p. 237 by kind permission of The Nixon Presidential Library Project; p. 9 by kind permission of the Osher Map Library and Smith Center for Cartographic Education, University of Southern Maine; p. 216 by permission of the Master and Fellows of Pembroke College, Cambridge; p. 223 The Stockholm International Peace Research Institute (SIPRI); p. 131 Titanic Inquiry Project; pp. 26, 33, 36, 55, 60, 71, 83, 88, 93, 99, 105, 109, 113, 117, 121, 135, 143, 152, 162, 170, 174, 179, 183, 189, 195, 200, 205, 211, 230, 244 by kind permission of the U.S. National Archives.

Picture credits

The publisher would like to thank the following for permission to reproduce photographs:

akg images p. 133; Atwater Kent Museum of Philadelphia/The BAL p. 86; Bettmann/Corbis pp. 69, 75, 123, 126, 141, 147, 149, 156, 160, 165, 168, 181, 193, 198, 203, 209, 220, 242; Bolton Picture Library/The BAL p. 24; Brooklyn Museum/Corbis p. 53; Burstein Collection/Corbis p. 58; Geoffrey Clements/Corbis p. 115; The Collections of the Henry Ford p. 128; Corbis pp. 91, 177, 235; Corbis SYGMA p. 218; Tom Dillard/Dallas Morning News/Corbis p. 214; Hall of Representatives, Washington D.C., U.S.A./The BAL p. 40; Hulton-Deutsch Collection/Corbis p. 172; Library of Congress, Washington, D.C., U.S.A./The BAL p. 31; Mary Evans Picture Library pp. 119, 150; Wally McNamee/Corbis p. 221; Jacques Pavlovsky/SYGMA/Corbis p. 228; Pilgrim Hall Museum, Plymouth, Massachusetts/The BAL p. 12; Dick S. Ramsey Fund and Healy Purchase Fund B, Brooklyn Museum of Art/The BAL p. 7; Massachusetts Historical Society, Boston, Massachusetts, U.S.A./The BAL p. 16; Peabody Essex Museum, Salem, Massachusetts, U.S.A./The BAL p. 20; Peter Newark American Pictures pp. 97, 103, 107, 111, 129 and 187; Peter Newark American Pictures, Private Collection/The BAL p. 64; Collection of The New-York Historical Society, U.S.A./The BAL p. 81; Shlesinger Library, Radcliffe Institute, Harvard University/The BAL p. 137; Lee Snider/Photo Images/Corbis p. 248; Tom Stoddart/Getty p. 251; courtesy Winterthur Museum p. 34.

Quercus Publishing
21 Bloomsbury Square
London
WC1A 2NS

First published 2007

A catalogue record for this book is available from the British Library.

ISBN 1 84724 005 4
ISBN-13 978 1 84724 005 7

Printed in China

10 9 8 7 6 5 4 3 2 1

Researched, compiled and edited by Cambridge Editorial Partnership, Michael Young Centre, Purbeck Road, Cambridge CB2 2PF, with thanks to Martin Hall, Carol Schaessens, Kate Connelly and Ros Connelly. Designed by Paul Barrett Book Production.